Warriors of Anatolia

Also available from Bloomsbury

Alexander the Great: Themes and Issues by Edward M. Anson
Babylon: Legend, History and the Ancient City by Michael Seymour
Birth of the Persian Empire edited by Vesta Sarkhosh Curtis and
Sarah Stewart
Hammurabi of Babylon by Dominique Charpin
Imagining Xerxes: Ancient Perspectives on a Persian King
by Emma Bridges
The Age of the Parthians edited by Vesta Sarkhosh Curtis and
Sarah Stewart
The Cyrus Cylinder: The Great Persian Edict from Babylon
edited by Irving Finkel

Warriors of Anatolia

A Concise History of the Hittites

Trevor Bryce

BLOOMSBURY ACADEMIC
LONDON • NEW YORK • OXFORD • NEW DELHI • SYDNEY

BLOOMSBURY ACADEMIC
Bloomsbury Publishing Plc
50 Bedford Square, London, WC1B 3DP, UK
1385 Broadway, New York, NY 10018, USA
29 Earlsfort Terrace, Dublin 2, Ireland

BLOOMSBURY, BLOOMSBURY ACADEMIC and the Diana logo are
trademarks of Bloomsbury Publishing Plc

First published in Great Britain 2019 by I.B.Tauris & Co. Ltd.
Paperback edition published by Bloomsbury Academic 2023

Cover image: Late Hittite relief, early first millennium BC, depicting warrior
armed with spear and shield. It postdates the fall of the Bronze Age kingdom
by three or more centuries. From Carchemish, Turkey
(photo by DEA / M. SEEMULLER / De Agostini / Getty Images)

A catalogue record for this book is available from the British Library.

A catalog record for this book is available from the Library of Congress.

ISBN: HB: 978-1-3501-4078-3
       PB: 978-1-3503-4885-1
       ePDF: 978-1-7867-3528-7
       eBook: 978-1-7867-2528-8

Typeset by RefineCatch Ltd, Bungay, Suffolk

To find out more about our authors and books visit www.bloomsbury.com
and sign up for our newsletters.

I would like to dedicate this book to my wife Nan, in recognition of her unfailing support and patience for this and the many other projects in which I have engaged throughout my academic career.

CONTENTS

MAPS AND FIGURES

MAPS

FIGURES

*(All figures/photographs are by the author unless otherwise
acknowledged.)*

ACKNOWLEDGEMENTS

My thanks go firstly to I.B.Tauris editor Alex Wright for his invitation to write this book, his advice on what kind of book it should be, and for all his work in seeing the book through the initial stages of the publication process. My sincere thanks too to those other members of I.B.Tauris's editorial staff who have seen the book through to completion.

I am grateful also to the School of Historical and Philosophical Inquiry, University of Queensland, for the valuable infrastructure support it has provided throughout the various stages of the book's preparation.

I'd like to give specific acknowledgement here to the generosity of those persons who have contributed to the illustrations in this book. They are Paul Butler, Umut Çomak, Tolga Örnek, and Jonathan Tubb. Specific details of their contributions appear in the List of Maps and Figures.

INTRODUCTION

E verywhere you go in Ankara today, you'll find reminders of the Hittites. You can hail a Hittite Taxi Service cab to take you to an eating-place called the Hittite restaurant, or negotiate a price with the cabbie to drive you to the Hittite capital Hattusa, some 160 km to the east. There in the modern village called Boghazkale, you can stay overnight in a hostelry with a 'WELCOME TO HATTUSA' sign above it. And once back in Ankara, you can check into a hotel called the LUGAL. That word means 'King' in Hittite inscriptions. Alongside one of the thoroughfares into Ankara's central business district, you'll see a monumental image of a stag flanked by two bulls, all three

Figure I.1   Modern Hittite hospitality.

Figure I.2 The disc monument.

animals framed in a disk-like arch. The monument is a giant replica of an ancient Anatolian sculpture representing the supposed links between the Hittites and the people of the region today (though the original sculpture is actually pre-Hittite). Keep

Figure I.3 The stag container.

looking about you and you'll find Hittite symbols on a whole range of other modern-world stuff, from biscuits to buses.

No doubt you'll want to learn more about these Bronze Age forerunners of the Turks, and as a starting point it's worth checking out the local bookstores. On my recent visit to Ankara, a bookshop I explored in a suburban shopping-mall had stacks of publications on the Hittites, almost outnumbering nearby copies of Dan Brown, Clive Cussler and other airport bestsellers. The fact that I was at the time wearing a T-shirt with the word 'Hititleri' (Turkish for 'Hittites') stencilled on the front and a procession of 12 armed Hittite gods on the back earned me a discount on my purchases. And after returning to my hotel, I finished the last of my pieces of Turkish delight, a gift from a local host presented in an exquisite glass container, its surface embellished with an encircling row of golden Hittite stags.

In asking me to write about the Hittites, I.B.Tauris editor Alex Wright said he'd like a book that offers to students and general readers more than just core information on Hittite history and civilisation. Of course, such information is basic to an understanding of these 'warriors of Anatolia'. But Alex was also looking for 'something more daring, less formulaic', for 'fresh perspectives, new insights', something to make the book's readers think 'in novel and exciting and unexpected ways about the topics addressed'. I've kept this advice in mind while writing the book. At times, I've gone out on a bit of a limb with what I've proposed. And there are times when I've asked you, the reader, to join me. Scattered throughout the book are problems and questions I've invited you to consider. Are you prepared to take up the invitation? A fresh pair of eyes may just possibly see things that have escaped the scrutiny of professional scholars.

Anyhow, if you find my book a bit unconventional and quirky, I make no apologies. That has been my intention. But let me stress that I've been pretty careful about this. Above all, my book is intended to provide a reliable introduction to Hittite history and civilisation, one which touches on many features of the Hittite world, explores some of them in more depth and proposes a number of new ideas and approaches to longstanding problems – all, I hope, within the limits of historical credibility, if not provability (at least at present).

Let's look briefly at our time- and space-frames. The period covered by the Hittite civilisation spans half a millennium, from the seventeenth to the early twelfth century BC. In modern archaeological terminology, Hittite history starts towards the end of the Middle Bronze Age and lasts until the end of the Late Bronze Age. The chronological table in Appendix 2 gives you more details. Unfortunately, we don't have kinglists (as we do for several other ancient civilisations) to give us precise lengths of the reigns of Hittite kings. So we can only assign approximate dates to their reigns, linking these dates, on the few occasions where this is possible, with the reigns of Egyptian and Babylonian kings. But that too is not without its complications. I won't go into what these are, beyond simply noting that three chronologies have been proposed for Hittite history – a High, Middle and a Low Chronology. The Middle Chronology is the one I've used in this book.

What about the term 'Anatolia', which pops up frequently in the following pages? This term actually originates from a Greek word – *anatole*, 'rising'. It is used to refer to the region where, from a Greek perspective, the 'rising (of the sun)' takes place. First attested in the

Map I.1   Anatolia (NASA satellite image).

tenth century AD, 'Anatolia' is still often used for modern Turkey, particularly the western two-thirds of it (peninsular Turkey), and sometimes refers more specifically to Turkey's central highlands. 'Anadolu' is the Turkish form of the name. One of Anatolia's most distinctive features is its highland plateau which rises 1,000 m above sea level. The core territory of Hatti, kingdom of the Hittites, lay in the north-central part of the plateau. We now call it the Hittite homeland. On the north the plateau is bounded by the Pontic mountains, on the south by the Taurus ranges and in the east it merges into the Armenian mountains. These ranges sharply differentiate the plateau from the rest of the Anatolian region. In the west, the plateau slopes down more gently to the Aegean coast.

Syria will also figure prominently in our story of the Hittites, for it provided the key to international dominance in the Late Bronze Age Near Eastern world. This was because it spread over the crossroads of this world, between Anatolia to the northwest, Mesopotamia to the east, Arabia to the south and Egypt to the southwest. Many international routes of communication, used for both peaceful and military purposes, passed through it. In a Bronze Age context, we shall use the term 'Syria' to refer to the large expanse of territory lying between the Euphrates river and the eastern Mediterranean Sea. (Of course, the modern political state Syria extends well beyond the Euphrates.) In many periods of Near Eastern history, from the Bronze Age to the present day, the great powers of the age have sought control over the region, and often fought one another to achieve it. As you'll see, Syria was very closely connected with both the rise and the fall of the Hittite kingdom, and also with the gradual rediscovery of this kingdom in the modern era.

Wherever possible, we should allow the Hittites to speak for themselves as we seek to reconstruct the world in which they lived. Their most important texts are now fairly readily available in English translations. I've asterisked these in the general bibliography as well as in the Endnotes.

One of my most challenging tasks in writing this book has been to present as comprehensive an account as possible of the Hittites while sticking to the publisher's limit of 85,000 words. 'Concise' in the book's sub-title is the operative word! For readers wishing to study the Hittites in greater depth, I've given references in the endnotes to more detailed treatments of a number of topics dealt with only briefly here.

That's enough by way of introduction. I wish you an informative and enjoyable read.

An important update to p. 256

In 2019, after this book was published, an important new hieroglyphic inscription was discovered naming a Great King Hartapu, son of Mursili, in the same region as the other Hartapu-Mursili inscriptions referred to on p. 256. The scholars who have studied the inscription have dated it to the mid eighth century BC, in the so-called Iron Age Neo-Hittite period. There is no doubt about its late dating. The coincidence that there were two Hartapus, both sons of a Mursili, one dating to the Bronze Age, the other to the Iron Age, seems very unlikely, though not impossible. But much of what I say on pp. 256–7 should be reconsidered in light of the new inscription.

Publication details: Goedegebuure, Petra; van den Hout, Theo; Osborne, James; Massa, Michele; Bachhuber, Christoph; Şahin, Fatma: 'TÜRKMEN-KARAHÖYÜK 1: A new Hieroglyphic Luwian inscription from Great King Hartapu, son of Mursili, conqueror of Phrygia', *Anatolian Studies* 70 (2020), pp. 29–43.

CHAPTER 1

REDISCOVERING A LOST WORLD

I magine you have boarded a time machine that takes you 3,500 years into the past and deposits you in central Turkey, in a huge rock and mudbrick city surrounded by walls stretching as far as you can see. Everyone stares curiously at you. 'Water!' you say, as you feel your first blast of intense dry summer heat. You are immediately understood. Someone hurries off and returns with a bowl brimming with liquid. 'Watar,' he says as he hands it to you.

A STRANGE WORLD REVEALED

Let's move forward to the year 1834 AD, to the 28th day of the month of July to be precise. On the site of our time-travel visit, a Frenchman called Charles Texier now stands, staring uncompre-hendingly at the desolate ruin before him. For that is all the city now is. An ancient Celtic settlement called Tavium is supposed to lie thereabouts, and Texier has been sent by the French Ministry of Culture to find it. But Tavium dates to the period of Roman rule in Turkey. Texier has no idea what the city where he now stands is. But he realises that it is very much older and very much larger than Tavium could have been. The impressive buildings and immense walls of the city at the height of its glory have now completely disappeared. But the walls' stone foundations and those of the buildings within it still testify to the city's former grandeur. As do several of its still-surviving monumental gates. On one is carved a human figure over 2m tall. Wearing a helmet and short kilt, and armed with axe and sword, this figure obviously depicts a warrior. It will not be discovered until seventy years after Texier's visit, but there is much else about the city to mystify him.

He is even more mystified when he is shown by some locals to a large outcrop of rock that lies near the great city. It is called Yazılıkaya – a Turkish word meaning 'Inscribed Rock'. Here Texier sees two processions of carved figures, dressed in strange garb and approaching each other. There are symbols, worn but still visible, next to some of these figures, curious picture-like symbols. Maybe these represent a form of writing, their picture-like character recalling the hieroglyphic script of Egypt. But the signs are nothing like Egyptian hieroglyphs. There are other strange figures carved on the rock walls – a human-headed sword plunged into the ground, a group of 12 identical figures wearing short kilts, conical hats and footgear with upturned toes. Armed with scimitar-like swords, they are depicted in profile and appear to be running – or walking very fast. There are two other figures, wearing skullcaps and carrying staffs with curled-up ends. One of these figures is

Figure 1.1   Yazılıkaya today.

accompanied by a taller figure wearing a conical hat with horns attached; he has his arm around his companion in what appears to be a protective gesture. Again strange 'hieroglyphic' symbols are carved next to the figures. Texier is fascinated by his finds, and sketches many of them. But he has no idea what they are.

SOLVING THE MYSTERY

It would be decades before the mystery of the strange city and the nearby carved rock outcrop was solved. How this was done is in itself a fascinating story, made up of several different strands. Let's consider these strands one by one, and the ways in which they have been interwoven to produce the final solution.

Strand no. 1: Well known from the Bible are people and individual persons we call 'Hittites', after the biblical name *Hittîm*. Sometimes they are called 'the sons of Heth' – hence the German name 'Hethiter' for the Hittites. Several biblical Hittites are well known to us, like the ill-fated Uriah, sent by King David to his death on the battlefield so that David could have free access to his beautiful wife Bathsheba. Most of our biblical references imply that the Hittites were just one of a number of minor tribes living in the Judaean hill-country of southern Palestine. But there are a few Old Testament passages that suggest the existence of a 'Hittite nation' of considerably greater status and power. The most notable of these is from the Second Book of Kings, where the Aramaeans say to one another 'Look, the king of Israel has hired the Hittite and the Egyptian kings to attack us!' (2 Kings 7:6). This episode, dating to the time of the ninth-century prophet Elisha, speaks not only of Hittite kings, but gives these kings a status similar to that of the pharaohs of Egypt.

Strand no. 2: In 1822, the French scholar Jean-François Champollion successfully completed the decipherment of the Egyptian hieroglyphic script and the language for which it was used, a success closely associated with the famous Rosetta stone. It was the starting point for revealing to us the contents of thousands of Egyptian inscriptions. Some of these inscriptions contain references to a country called Ht (often vocalised as Kheta). This was clearly an important country. The pharaoh Ramesses II claimed victory over it (wrongly!) in the famous battle of Qadesh on the Orontes river in western Syria, and an earlier pharaoh Tuthmosis III had dealings with it during his campaigns in northern Syria.

Strand no. 3: In the 1830s, a cliff-face inscription in three languages, Old Persian, Babylonian and Elamite (the so-called Behistun/Bisitun monument, located in western Iran), provided the Orientalist Henry Rawlinson with the key to the decipherment of the most important ancient Near Eastern languages, including the (subsequently deciphered) Assyrian language. Passages from the Assyrian inscriptions, in particular those dating from the late second millennium through the early centuries of the first millennium BC, contain references to a land called Hatti, which seemed to be connected particularly with territories in northern Syria west of the Euphrates river.

Strand no. 4: Fifty years later, in 1887, a cache of clay tablets, now 382 in number, was discovered in Egypt, at a place called el-Amarna, on the site of the ancient city of Akhetaten. The city was newly built in the mid-fourteenth century as the royal capital of the pharaoh Akhenaten. Three hundred and fifty of these tablets record correspondence between the pharaoh and his subject-rulers and foreign peers. A number of the tablets, like the Assyrian records, refer to a land of Hatti, and in one case to a king of Hatti.

Strand no. 5: In the early years of the nineteenth century, an eccentric Swiss merchant called Johann Ludwig Burkhardt travelled widely in the Near East, dressed in oriental garb and calling himself Sheik Ibrahim. During a visit he made to the Syrian city Hama, he came upon a block of stone built into a house in the bazaar. Strange symbols on the stone were interpreted by him as a form of writing, a bit like hieroglyphic symbols, though quite different from those of Egypt. He wrote about his find in his book *Travels in Syria and the Holy Land*, published in 1822.

Fifty years later, another three similarly inscribed stones were found in buildings in the bazaar at Hama, and yet another stone with similar inscription was found built into the wall of a mosque in Aleppo. The following year (1872), an Irish missionary called William Wright received permission from the local Turkish pasha to prise out these stones (with strong protests from the local people who attributed magical healing powers to them) and ship them to Constantinople for closer study. It became clear that the symbols on the stones were like those found by Texier at Yazılıkaya and were part of the same ancient script. This script was now found in a number of other places as well – not only in Syria but also in the Anatolian peninsula, almost as far west as Anatolia's Aegean coast.

RIGHT FOR ALL THE WRONG REASONS

Now let us pull all these strands together. In a landmark lecture delivered in London in 1880 to the Society for Biblical Archaeology, a scholarly man of the cloth, the Rev. Archibald Henry Sayce, presented a bold and apparently new proposition: the Hittites of the Bible were the people of a vast empire which extended through Anatolia and a large part of Syria. This conclusion he based very largely on the widespread distribution of the 'hieroglyphic script' throughout these regions – a script which Sayce believed was the written language of the Hittites themselves – though no-one had the slightest idea then of what the inscriptions said. (Actually, William Wright had already published this conclusion a couple of years earlier in an obscure article, but it was Sayce who got the credit for it.)

Sayce's lecture might well be regarded as the very beginning of the rediscovery of a lost world. How on earth did it get lost in the first place, when we consider its size (Sayce was certainly right in his claim about the empire's vastness) and the fact that the great contemporary powers of Egypt, Assyria and Babylon were *never* lost to human knowledge? That's a matter to which we shall return. But at this point, let's make some important corrections to Sayce's conclusions:

(a) the 'Hittites' *never* called themselves Hittites;
(b) the 'hieroglyphic script' was *not* written in the Hittite language;
(c) the administrative centre of the empire was *not* in Syria (Carchemish on the Euphrates was a favoured location) but in north-central Anatolia;

(d) the Hittite empire dated *not* to the Iron Age (late second millennium onwards) but to the preceding Bronze Age, the Late Bronze Age in particular (from the seventeenth to the twelfth century).

How could Sayce have been so right and yet so wrong at the same time?

THE HITTITE LANGUAGE DECIPHERED

To answer this question, we need to move forward to the early years of the twentieth century. In 1906, a German Assyriologist called Hugo Winckler (a rather unpleasant man, to judge from accounts of the time) and his Turkish colleague Theodor Makridi, began the first major excavations in the city that had so mystified Charles Texier seven decades earlier. We should, however, acknowledge that the first official excavations of the site were conducted in the years 1893–4 by the archaeologist Ernest Chantre. The site's modern name was Boghazköy, today called Boghazkale. Right from the beginning, clay tablets in great quantities started coming to light. There was little doubt that this site was part of the great Hittite empire, as Chantre's excavations ten years earlier had already suggested. And Winckler could read quite a few of the tablets since they were written in the Akkadian language (Assyrian and Babylonian were its two main versions). This had been deciphered many decades earlier, and was widely used in its own time as an international lingua franca. But the majority of the tablets were written in a strange, unknown language. This must have been the language of the Hittites themselves.

From the texts that *could* be read it became clear, already in the first year of the excavations, that the ancient name of the site was Hattusa. There could be no doubt from these excavations that Hattusa was a very important city of the Hittite world. But it was to prove more than that! As Winckler perused the basketloads of tablets and tablet-fragments brought to him each day, he came across one in particular that caused him great excitement. It was a copy of an Akkadian version of a peace treaty drawn up between one of the most famous of all pharaohs, Ramesses II, sometimes called Ramesses the Great, and a Great King of Hatti, called Hattusili. Where else but in the Hittite royal capital would such a document be found? The site Winckler was excavating was the very heart of the Hittite empire! (In all fairness, we should point out that the actual credit for identifying this site as the Hittite capital belongs to Georges Perrot, an Oriental scholar who two decades earlier had written an article claiming that Boghazköy not Carchemish was the capital of the Hittite empire. But it was not until Winckler's excavations that hard evidence for this identification was found.)

The Akkadian tablets provided important information about the city and the empire it ruled. But this information was still very limited – and would remain so until the language used on the majority of the tablets, no doubt the language of the 'Hittites' themselves, could be read. That was a task finally achieved, during World War I, by a Czech scholar called Bedřich Hrozný, who had been released from war service to undertake it. Attempts by earlier scholars had failed. At least the *script* in which the language was written could be read since it was one commonly used in the Near Eastern world. Its invention is associated with an Early Bronze Age (third millennium) people of Mesopotamia called the Sumerians. They expressed their language in written form by pressing the triangular ends of reeds cut from the Tigris and Euphrates river-banks into soft clay. Modern scholars call this script 'cuneiform', after the Latin word *cuneus* for wedge, because of the wedge-like shapes produced by this process. And the script thus created was widely adopted by many civilisations, including the Hittite civilisation, throughout the Near Eastern world for several millennia to come.

So the unknown script on the Hattusa tablets could literally be read, or sounded out, even though the language they recorded was still unintelligible. Then the famous breakthrough! As he was perusing the texts, Hrozný came across a sentence which when transliterated into letters of our own alphabet read: *nu* NINDA-*an ēzzatteni wātar-ma ekutteni*. Now, NINDA was an old Sumerian

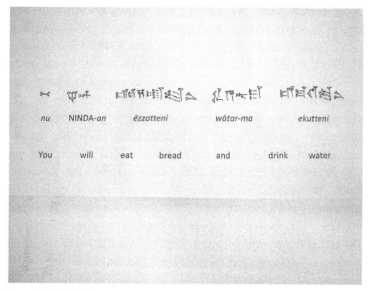

Figure 1.2   The key sentence.

logogram. This was a sign representing a single word which was adopted without change in other cuneiform scripts written in different languages. NINDA meant 'bread' – so it seemed that the sentence was about food. *ēzza-(tteni)* reminded Hrozný of the Latin word *edo* and the German *essen*, both of which mean 'eat'. *eku-(tteni)* recalled the Latin word *aqua*, suggesting that this word had something to do with water. And most interestingly, the word *wātar(-ma)* recalled the German word *Wasser*, and the English word 'water'. Hrozný concluded that *ēzzatteni* and *ekutteni* were second person plural verbs meaning 'eat' and 'drink' respectively. And thus he read the sentence as a whole as 'You will eat bread and drink water'.

But the real significance of his find was his conclusion from this sentence that Hittite was a member of a very large language family which we call Indo-European. Membership of the family covered a wide range of tongues, both ancient and modern, including Sanskrit, Greek, Latin, English, German and the modern romance languages. Hittite was now established as the very earliest of these languages preserved in written form. And Hrozný's sentence provided the key to reading and understanding the thousands of tablets and tablet-fragments inscribed in this language, found by the German excavators in the Hittite capital.

But we should not continue before giving credit to an earlier scholar who had identified the language as Indo-European a decade and a half earlier. Among the Amarna tablets, there were two pieces of corrrespondence exchanged between the pharaoh and a king of a country called Arzawa in Anatolia. Unlike the great majority of the Amarna tablets, they were written not in Akkadian, but in a then unknown language. In 1902, the Norwegian scholar J. A. Knudtzon, while not being able to translate the letters, declared that their language was an Indo-European one. Of course, he did not know then that it was the language of the Hittites. For at that time the Hittites were only just re-emerging from 3,000 years of almost total obscurity. Alas, Knudtzon failed to have the courage of his convictions. He gave way before sustained howls of protests from his scholarly contemporaries. The idea was ridiculous, they declared. After all, practically all the known languages of the age belonged to the Semitic language family – like Akkadian, and later languages like Aramaic, Hebrew and Arabic. It was absurdly far-fetched to suggest that a language related to Latin and Greek and English and French and so on could possibly have emerged in this part of the world so early in its history. So Knudtzon buckled under pressure and gave up his proposal, and Hrozný had to start all over again.

CHAPTER 2

HOW DO THE HITTITES TELL US ABOUT THEMSELVES?

READING THE ANCIENT SCRIPTS

With Hrozný the curtain began to be drawn aside to reveal the ancient Hittites, and what they tell us about themselves and the world they inhabited. Let's explore this world. But first we need to say something about the tablets, the cuneiform script written on them, the writers of the script and where the records they made were kept. By far the majority of these records were written on a readily available material – clay, the main writing material used in the Near Eastern world at least as far back as the fourth millennium.

With just one later main exception, the Sumerian script and all subsequent cuneiform scripts were syllabic. That is to say, each symbol, or group of symbols, represented a syllable. This could be a vowel on its own, a consonant + vowel, a vowel + consonant, a consonant + vowel + consonant, or occasionally a vowel + consonant + vowel. Sometimes a group of symbols could represent a whole word like 'god' or 'king' or 'land' or 'city'. In Sumerian, these words were pronounced DINGIR, LUGAL, KUR and URU respectively. Modern scholars call them logograms. Sometimes, logograms were used purely to identify the nature of the word they immediately preceded. In these cases, we call them 'determinatives'.

Thus if LUGAL immediately preceded a personal name, we'd know that the person in question was a king, and if a name was preceded by URU, we'd know it was the name of a city. When texts were read out, the determinatives were not said aloud.

From all this, it won't surprise you to learn that syllabic scripts could be made up of an enormous number of signs – when you think of all the possible combinations of vowels and consonants. Indeed the most developed cuneiform syllabic scripts contained over 700 sign groups! And if you look at Figure 1.2, you'll see that some sign groups, each representing a single syllable, consist of three or four or more separately impressed 'wedge' imprints. So acquiring even basic competency in the reading and writing of these scripts must have meant years of learning. How much simpler an alphabetic script would have been. I recall as a student taking just under an hour to learn the Greek alphabet – all 24 letters of it, many of them close to the letters of the Roman alphabet. By contrast, it took me a year to master even the basics of the Hittite script, which was mercifully much shorter than some syllabic cuneiform scripts, with just over 300 sign groups.

By the first millennium BC, several alphabetic scripts had developed in the Near East, most notably the Aramaic script, which was so much easier to learn and must help explain the widespread use of this script. Aramaic became the lingua franca of the age. And along the Syro-Palestinian coast the Phoenicians devised an alphabet from which the Greek alphabet and by extension the Roman one were derived. These alphabets were made up of linear signs; that is, signs produced by drawing them on writing surfaces suitable for this purpose, such as papyrus and leather. But already by the end of the fourteenth or early thirteenth century, the people of the kingdom of Ugarit in northwestern Syria had devised an alphabetic script, written on clay using cuneiform symbols impressed onto its surface.

THE SCRIBES AND THEIR TABLETS

The obvious question is, since an alphabet is much easier to learn and use than a syllabic script, why did the syllabic cuneiform scripts persist so long and why were they so widespread in the Near Eastern world? It may all have had to do with tradition, and a relatively 'closed shop' when it came to the acquisition of literacy skills. Scribes in all ancient Near Eastern cultures formed an elite professional class. Given that the great majority of the population were largely if not entirely illiterate, the scribe's services were indispensable at all levels of society – even to their royal masters. The more difficult it was to master literacy skills, the greater the importance of those who did, and the more privileged their position. The status scribes enjoyed, particularly those at the top of their profession, made well worthwhile their many years of training and the undoubted tedium associated with acquiring the skills demanded of the profession. Some of the most important scribes became close confidantes and advisers of the king. And those at the lowest levels of the profession, who served as clerks and copyists, might well have looked forward to career progression through ever higher levels of importance and responsibility.

So let's imagine what we might call the scriptoria of the Hittite world, the places where the scribes carried out most of their work. Figure 2.1 is a reconstruction of one of these. The scribal establishments were closely associated with the palace and the temples of the capital and regional centres of the Hittite world. Hatti's vassal states must also have had such establishments, where copies of the treaties imposed upon local rulers would have been kept, along with letters, or copies of them, that passed between the vassal and his overlord. Clay was the most common writing material used for these documents. But there was a special category of scribes who wrote on wood – as we know from references in the clay tablets to 'scribes of the wooden tablets'.

Unfortunately, no wooden tablets have survived from the archives, so we can only guess what their contents or functions may have been. Quite likely, they were used for ephemeral matters, such as memos or bulletins, or for making temporary records of accounts, grain distribution, inventories of goods and the like. To judge from the remains of a wooden tablet found in a Bronze Age shipwreck off the southwestern coast of Anatolia, the wooden tablets may have been diptychs – that is, two hinged tablets, with a

Figure 2.1   Scribes at work.

recessed surface filled with wax. Anything written on them could simply be erased and the tablets used again once a particular record had reached its use-by date.

Records intended to last for longer periods, or indefinitely, were inscribed on clay tablets. But since the tablets were unbaked, with very few exceptions in the Near Eastern world, their contents needed to be copied repeatedly on fresh tablets before the older ones crumbled away. Important documents were individually labelled, classified and stored by category on wooden shelves in the archive rooms of the temples and palaces. All these were by nature official documents, produced by the palace and temple bureaucracies. Very few archives of private individuals have come to light anywhere in the Hittite world; the most notable have been found in houses of prominent merchants and other citizens of Ugarit, capital of one of the Hittites' subject-states in northwestern Syria.

Yet none of the archives, official or private, would have survived for long after the fall of the Hittite kingdom were they not accidentally baked during the conflagrations which destroyed part of the capital and other centres of the Hittite world. When the buildings which housed the tablet-archives were destroyed by fire, the shelves on which the tablets were stored disintegrated and their contents were shattered and scattered on the floors. In the process, they were often baked and have thus survived to the present day. Even so, the vast majority of written records from the Hittite capital and from most other centres of the kingdom are lost to us for all time.

And we have almost zero chance of ever finding the originals of some of the most noteworthy documents of the Hittite world, like the famous treaty between the pharaoh Ramesses II and his Hittite counterpart Hattusili III. We know from copies of this treaty that it was originally inscribed on tablets of silver. Tablets made of gold and bronze, and perhaps also iron, a very precious metal in the Bronze Age, were also used for inscribing important documents. But all such tablets have disappeared – with one exception. Quite by chance, during excavations in 1986 of a ramp just outside one of Hattusa's gates (the 'Sphinx Gate'), an intact bronze tablet was discovered, fully preserved and in excellent condition. It records a treaty between a Hittite king, Tudhaliya IV, and one of his most important subject-rulers, a member of the Hittite royal family called Kurunta. As we shall see (Chapter 23), it contains some very significant historical information. We can hardly hope to be as lucky again. But who knows?

WHAT DO THE HITTITES TELL US ABOUT THEMSELVES?

So we have now come to the point where we can ask two basic questions: What information do the surviving tablets contain? How can we use this information to reconstruct a picture of the history and civilisation of the Hittite world? Fragmentary though the tablets often are, they are very wide-ranging in the topics they cover. Their contents include (a) sets of royal 'Annals', narrative accounts of a king's military achievements; (b) treaties drawn up between kings and their foreign peers and subject-rulers; (c) letters exchanged between kings (and sometimes other members of their families), foreign peers, subject-rulers and high officials; (d) royal edicts or proclamations in which a king makes pronouncements on such matters as the royal succession; (e) festival texts, setting out the procedures to be followed at the numerous annual ceremonies honouring various gods – and also telling us a great deal about feasting and entertainment in the Hittite world; (f) fragmentary copies of a collection of 200 Hittite laws, which tell us much about crime and punishment in the Hittite world, marriage provisions, including pre-nuptial agreements, sexual taboos, farming and business matters, and social hierarchies from the slave upwards; (g) legendary and mythological texts, some adopted from the pre-Hittite inhabitants of Anatolia and some from other Near Eastern civilisations.

CHAPTER 3

THE DAWN OF THE
HITTITE ERA

L et's now start building ourselves a picture of the Hittite world.[1] We've already noted that the official language of the Hittite kingdom was an Indo-European one. It's still not certain where the speakers of this language came from, or when. But most scholars believe they were one branch of a much larger Indo-European family originating from somewhere north of the Black Sea, maybe the steppes of Russia. Perhaps some time during the Early Bronze Age, they arrived in northern Anatolia, along with two other Indo-European groups whom, for reasons we'll come to soon, we call the Palaians and the Luwians. Some scholars believe that Indo-European speakers were always present in Anatolia, and would not have been a clearly identifiable group by the second millennium.

Be that as it may, early in the millennium, during the period we now call the Middle Bronze Age, personal names which we can identify as Indo-European make their first appearance in Anatolia. They do so in texts written by foreigners – Assyrian merchants who established a string of trading colonies between Assyria and the cities and kingdoms of north-central Anatolia. Their headquarters was a place called Kanesh or Nesa (modern Kültepe), sometimes written Nesha, just south of the Kızıl Irmak river ('Red River'). Known as the Marassantiya in Hittite texts, the ancient Greeks and Romans called it the Halys ('Salt') river.

At this time, the region within the river's confines was occupied predominantly by a people we call the Hattians, whose settlement there probably went back many hundreds if not thousands of years. One of their kingdoms was called Hatti, and its capital Hattus. Towards the end of the Assyrian colony period, conflicts broke out in the region. In one of these, a king called Anitta campaigned against and defeated the king of Hatti and destroyed Hattus. He ordered that the site be sown with weeds and never again resettled. Anitta's own base was at Nesa, where his father Pithana had shifted the seat of his kingdom from a place called Kussar, perhaps located in the anti-Taurus mountains. Increasingly turbulent conditions in the region where the Assyrian merchants traded were almost certainly responsible for the abrupt end of this trade around the middle of the eighteenth century. There followed a period, lasting several decades or more, of which we have very little knowledge, and no written records.

A KINGDOM EMERGES

That brings us to the dawn of the Hittite era. What do we know about the emergence and early development of the Hittite kingdom? Most of our information comes from later surviving copies of the oldest texts, copies written in what we have called 'Hittite', an Indo-European language. (Many if not all of the early texts were *originally* written in Akkadian, a Semitic language.) In fact, the Hittites themselves called their language 'the language of Nesa'. This designation goes back to the colony period when the language was presumably the predominant one spoken in Nesa. It was almost certainly spoken by Nesa's ruling class. So strictly speaking, we should call the Hittite language 'Nesite'. It's only by modern convention that we call it 'Hittite'.

From a fairly early period in Hittite history, the administrative elite of the kingdom used this Indo-European language as their official one. It's therefore generally assumed that at least the top layer of Hittite society was of Indo-European origin. But there's a bit of a problem here. The old assumption that an Indo-European people we call the Hittites swept through north-central Anatolia and imposed their rule upon the region's indigenous inhabitants, called Hattians, is no longer tenable. Indo-European and Hattian

speakers had begun intermingling centuries before the establish-
ment of the Hittite kingdom, and we can no longer talk in terms of
racially based conflicts leading to its genesis. The best we can say at
present is that a family group which maintained its Indo-European
heritage established a kingdom in north-central Anatolia during
the early seventeenth century, and founded a royal dynasty which
held sway over Hatti for the rest of the Bronze Age.

Initially at least, the population over which this dynasty ruled
may have been predominantly Hattian. Remnants of the Hattian
language survive in a number of passages embedded in Hittite
texts, generally of a ritual nature and labelled by the term *hattili*
('in the language of Hatti'). But the name 'Hatti' was perpetuated
throughout Hittite history on a much broader, more public level.
What we call the 'Hittite kingdom' was referred to as 'the Land of
Hatti' in Hittite and other Near Eastern texts. And the people we
call 'Hittites' were known simply as 'the people of the Land of
Hatti'. That is to say, the inhabitants of the kingdom defined
themselves not by the ethnic identity of their ruling class but by the
traditional name of the region in which they lived,[2] their numbers
swelled by an increasingly multi-ethnic population. Our own
persistence in using the terms 'Hittite kingdom' and 'Hittites' –
when we now know better – is simply a reflection of the old
assumption that the subjects of our book were linked to the biblical
people called *Hittîm*, rendered in English as 'Hittites'. If there's
any link between the Bronze Age and biblical 'Hittites' it's a very
tenuous one.[3]

We've also noted the presence of two other Indo-European
groups in Anatolia. Like the Nesite-speakers, they are already
attested in the texts of the Assyrian colonists – the Palaians and the
Luwians. Passages written in their languages, often of a ritual
nature, are incorporated into certain Hittite (Nesite) texts, where
the languages are identified by the terms *luwili* (i.e. 'in the language
of Luwiya') and *palaumnili* ('in the language of Pala'). Palaian-
speakers occupied part of the mountainous region south of the
Black Sea called Paphlagonia in Classical times. Luwians were very
much more widespread. Indeed by the end of the Hittite empire
Luwian-speakers were almost certainly the largest of all population

groups in the Hittite world, occupying extensive areas of central, southern and western Anatolia. During the succeeding Iron Age, they continued to be a major presence in Anatolia, especially in the south, and in northern Syria as well. They were a basic component of what we call the Neo-Hittite kingdoms.

It's time now to start reconstructing our history of the Hittite world, using texts found mainly in the Hittite capital's archives. We'll begin with one commonly referred to as the 'Proclamation of Telipinu'.[4] It was issued by a late sixteenth-century king called Telipinu, and I'll explain later what its main purpose was. Suffice it here to say that its long historical preamble is our most important source of information on the early history of the Hittite kingdom. It begins by telling us of the military exploits of a king called Labarna. Two or more members of this man's dynasty *may* have been kings before him, but he's the first one whose reign we know anything about.[5] In the first half of the seventeenth century (by my reckoning), he ruled over one of many small kingdoms in north-central Anatolia. These had emerged after the collapse of the earlier kingdoms in the region around the end of the colony period.

Conquer or be conquered. That was the rule of survival in the new era. The only way to ensure you would not be swallowed up by your neighbours was to beat them to it – by striking pre-emptively and swallowing *them* up. That's what Labarna did. According to the 'Proclamation', one country after another fell to his troops until he commanded a large swathe of territory extending south of the Kızıl Irmak river (we'll henceforth call it by its Hittite name – the Marassantiya) to the Mediterranean Sea. He probably expanded his kingdom by military force north of the river as well, into the region later to become core Hittite territory – the Hittite homeland. The unity of the land and the unconditional loyalty of its subjects to their king, from the troops to all members of the royal family, were the key ingredients of Labarna's successes – at least according to the Proclamation.

Telipinu had good reason to stress these qualities. For faction strife and rebellion seem to have plagued the last years of Labarna's reign. His son and likely designated successor, also called Labarna (according to my reconstruction of the royal dynasty), fell victim to a coup in the northern part of the kingdom. Here a breakaway regime established itself, in a city called Sanahuitta.[6] Was the kingdom built by Labarna already falling apart?

An emphatic 'No!' to that question was provided by a new successor to the throne. Perhaps the grandson of the first Labarna, the new king was proclaimed 'the Great King', 'the Tabarna', King of the Land of Hatti', 'Ruler of (the city of) Kussar'. (Tabarna is a variant of Labarna, which became a royal title in its own right, like 'Caesar', after Julius Caesar, in the titulature of Roman emperors.) The last of these titles seems to indicate that Kussar was his royal seat. You'll recall that several generations earlier this city was the original base of Pithana and his son Anitta, before Pithana shifted his capital to Nesa. Maybe the new king and his successors came from another branch of Pithana's and Anitta's family, this one remaining behind in Kussar. We have no actual evidence of any family connections. But Pithana's and Anitta's exploits nevertheless became an integral part of Hittite royal dynastic tradition.

The resurrection of a city accursed

Let's return to the new king. Almost certainly it was he who made the momentous decision to relocate the kingdom's capital. And he did so by resettling the weed-covered ruins of the city which was called Hattus in the colony period. Anitta had destroyed Hattus and declared its site accursed. Despite this, Labarna built the city afresh, and called it Hattusa. To commemorate his resettlement of it, he adopted the name Hattusili, 'man of Hattusa'.

What motivated him to set up a new royal capital on the old, abandoned site?

To begin with, Hattusa contained an ideal location for a royal citadel and palace. This is a large, flattish plateau, made almost impregnable to attack by natural barriers particularly on its eastern and northern sides. To the east of the citadel lies a deep gorge, through which runs a river valley which continues to the north, where the cliffs of a high ridge now called Büyükkaya ('Big Rock') rise steeply above it. You will understand how formidable these natural barriers were if you visit the site and clamber through the gorge or stand atop Büyükkaya. So too will you understand the name of the modern village Boghazkale – 'Gorge Castle' (formerly called Boghazköy, 'Gorge Village') which lies adjacent to the site. When combined with its impressive built fortifications, Hattusa's natural defences made at least its citadel area reasonably secure against enemy attack.

The city had other important natural features as well. In that period, the region within which it lay was thickly forested – essential in the provision of the large quantities of timber required both for the construction of Hattusa's defences and its palace, temples and residential buildings as well as for the manufacture of its tools, weapons and transport vehicles. A further feature was the seven springs that provided the city with an abundant all-year-round supply of water. Hattusili may also have believed he would be better placed to assert and maintain control over the volatile northern part of his kingdom by moving his capital to the region – though Kussar continued to hold a revered place in Hittite royal tradition as the ancestral home of the royal family.

But there were a number of negatives to locating the royal capital at Hattusa. Firstly, lying as it did on top of the Anatolian plateau, it was subject to extremely harsh environmental conditions – hot, dry summers and winters so cold that the capital was regularly isolated by heavy snow from the rest of Hatti's extensive territories and subject-lands through Anatolia and northern Syria. Given too the homeland's high degree of dependence on its farm produce, droughts and severe storms in the region could cause serious crop failures on the one hand or wipe out the season's food supplies on the other. Secondly, though a combination of natural and built fortifications gave the capital itself reasonable protection against its enemies, the whole region within the Marassantiya basin, the Hittite homeland, was highly vulnerable to enemy invasions. It did in fact suffer such invasions on a number of occasions, notably from a people called the Hurrians of northern Mesopotamia and northern Syria, but from other peoples as well.

The relocation of the capital may have helped Hattusili reassert his control over the northern part of his kingdom, which he finally achieved by routing the rebel forces there and destroying their stronghold Sanahuitta. But by moving his centre of power northwards, he potentially weakened his control over his southern territories, and greatly increased the distance between his base of operations and northern Syria, which was to play a major role in the history of the Hittite world. In addition to all this, we should note that the Hittite homeland was landlocked. It had no direct access to any sea, either for trade or military purposes, and on the rare occasions when it did engage in naval enterprises, these were carried out largely by proxy – by the ships of subject or allied states located in coastal regions, perhaps with Hittite marines on board.

Very likely this was *not* what Hattusili intended. In fact on one of his campaigns, he may have led his troops to the shores of the Black Sea – to what Classical sources call the Pontic region – with the intention of gaining permanent, direct control over part of the sea's southern seaboard. But if that was his ambition, neither he nor any of his successors ever realised it. In fact, the Pontic region came to be occupied by fierce mountain tribes called the Kaskans, who constantly invaded the homeland's northern territories across its ill-defined borders, and raided its cities and farmlands. Throughout Hittite history, the Kaskans remained a painful thorn in the Hittites' northern flank. Though a number of kings carried out successful invasions of their territories, they never subdued them completely or gained more than temporary control over any of them.

Let's also give some thought to the practical implications of shifting the capital from Kussar to Hattusa. The newly resettled city had not only to be built from scratch, but must have required the prompt erection of at least basic defences to supplement its natural fortifications (though one of the two later kings called Hantili claims to have been the first to build a city-wall). There were temples and a palace to be constructed. And of course there was the matter of putting people in the city and building accommodation and other facilities for them. Populating Hattusa and its peripheral territories must in itself have been a major operation, involving a large transfer of inhabitants, from Kussar and other cities and regions, with the range of skills and muscle-power necessary to sustain it. Grain crops and orchards needed to be established as quickly as possible, and grazing lands stocked with sheep and cattle, in order to keep the population alive while the city was in the process of becoming fully functional.

All in all, there were good reasons why Hattusa, a city which was highly vulnerable to the forces of nature and to attacks by its enemies, and which lay on the very fringe of the lands it came to rule, should never have become the royal capital. But the fact was that it did. And for a time, the kingdom over which it held sway became the greatest political and military power in the Near Eastern world.

THE HITTITES ON THE INTERNATIONAL STAGE

Hattusili took a major step towards elevating Hatti to Great Kingdom status by leading a number of campaigns across the Taurus range into Syria. Two of these are recorded in what survives of the king's Annals, which were first inscribed on or very close to a now lost golden statue.[7] The logistics alone of transporting a large army, from north-central Anatolia southeastwards across the Taurus into Syria must have been complex and daunting. (We'll talk about campaign logistics in Chapter 18.) And once his army had arrived in Syria, the military operations on which he embarked entailed enormous risks. For all the cities he attacked were subjects or allies of the powerful kingdom of Yamhad, the first Great Kingdom of Syria. (You mightn't have heard of Yamhad before, but you'll certainly know the name of its royal capital Aleppo.) An attack on any of Yamhad's subjects or allies was in effect an attack on Yamhad itself. Almost inevitably, such action would bring upon the invader the Great Kingdom's full military might.

But Hattusili pressed on regardless. Well aware that he was lighting a flame that could engulf himself and his entire army if the wind blew the wrong way, he besieged, sacked and destroyed one of Aleppo's most important allies, the city of Alalah (modern Tell Atchana) on the northern bend of the Orontes river, and then went on to ravage several more of Yamhad's protégés. Yet he got away with it! For reasons unknown to us, the king of Yamhad failed to take any retaliatory action (unless such action was recorded in a missing part of the text; see below), and Hattusili returned safely home, his wagons laden with the plunder of the conquered states.

After what the Annals tell us was Hattusili's 'first' campaign in Syria (we'll need to look more closely at this), the king apparently suspended operations there, and turned his attention in the opposite direction. Much of western Anatolia, as far as the Aegean coast, was occupied by a conglomerate of territories known collectively as the Arzawa lands. They were later to prove a troublesome bunch for a number of Hittite kings, even when they became Hittite vassal states. But these were early days in the relationship between Arzawa and the Hittite kingdom. Arzawa enters our story in a single sentence – Hattusili went there on what appears to have been little more than a raid, bringing back cattle and sheep as plunder. Did his western campaign (and we don't know how far west he went) have any purpose beyond a mere livestock-rustling expedition? We simply don't know. But the likelihood is that our text preserves only the very end of a campaign to Arzawa, which resulted in the capture and transportation to the homeland of large numbers of livestock. Cattle and sheep were a regular part of the booty brought back by later kings at the end of successful military campaigns.

But one important thing the text does tell us is that while Hattusili was off with his troops on his Arzawan venture, his absence prompted an attack on his core territory by a people from the east. They were the Hurrians, one of the Hittites' most formidable enemies. For the next two centuries Hitites and Hurrians would be locked in an almost constant state of war. On this occasion, the Hurrian invasion led to fresh uprisings among many of the king's subject-states. Only Hattusa remained intact. Hattusili's regime, let alone his kingdom, was in serious trouble. The action he took in response is recorded in only the briefest detail in the Annals. He *evidently* drove the Hurrians from his land (though the text does not tell us this), and set about restoring his authority over the rebellious states by launching brutal punitive attacks against them. Then in the 'following' year, he reasserted his control over the rest of the defecting states that had escaped his wrath earlier. Included among them was Sanahuitta, which was finally captured and destroyed.

This whole episode of invasion, attack and counter-attack provides our first instance of what was to be a recurring theme throughout Hittite history: Major military expeditions far from the base of Hittite power left the homeland dangerously exposed to incursions by its enemies, from almost anywhere across its porous frontiers. Which highlights an ongoing problem Hittite kings faced – a chronic shortage of manpower. For much of its history, Hatti simply did not have enough forces to mount major military campaigns against distant enemies without seriously compromising its homeland defences. And successful attacks on the homeland by enemy forces often had a domino-effect, prompting the defection of many of the kingdom's own subject-states. How the various kings dealt with this problem is something we'll look at in more detail later.

But let's return to Hattusili's Annals. In the 'fifth' and last recorded year of the Annals, the king returned to Syria. This campaign was a much more ambitious, far-reaching one than his earlier foray across the Taurus. Declaring himself to be like a lion on the rampage, Hattusili led his troops through Syria in an orgy of destruction and plunder as one city after another fell before his arms. Wagon after wagon was laden with the plunder of the cities and lands he destroyed, their palaces and temples and other places stripped of their statues and furniture and items of gold and silver and other precious materials, for transport back to Hattusa. The king was merciless in victory, repaying the courage of two of the local rulers who had defended their cities to the bitter end by harnessing them to one of the wagons laden with their cities' spoils. Like beasts of burden, they were made to haul the wagon back to their conqueror's capital. Hattusili gloated over their fate.

There was one achievement of which Hattusili was particularly proud. His rampage through Syria took him across the Euphrates to the western fringes of Mesopotamia. Only one other king had managed this crossing, he claimed: the legendary Mesopotamian ruler Sargon, king of Akkad, who had crossed the river in the other direction seven centuries earlier.

All this we learn from Hattusili's Annals. It's one of our most important sources for the early history of the Hittite kingdom, but there are some very problematic aspects of it. Firstly, Hattusili may have ruled for 30 or more years. If so, then taken at face value, his Annals cover only a small chunk of his reign, perhaps an early part of it. But we must remember that the surviving version of the Annals is not the original one, just the last in a line of copies made by successive generations of scribes. This one is probably to be dated to the thirteenth century, three or four centuries after the original was composed.

So how closely does this final version represent the *original* one? Let me make a suggestion. We know that early in the fourteenth century the Hittite kingdom was almost wiped out by enemy forces and Hattusa itself was razed to the ground. (I'll come to this.) Many of the city's existing records must have been lost during the disaster. But perhaps through being accidentally baked during the fires which destroyed the tablet-archive rooms, some tablets survived, either intact, or in fragments. This is exactly the situation we have today with the retrieval of many accidentally baked tablets and tablet-fragments. I suggest that fragmentary chunks of clay copies of the Annals did survive, even if the greater part of the document was lost. From these chunks, the later scribes tried to piece together a sequence of events recorded in the Annals in their efforts to recreate the document. What they did was to make a reasonably coherent compilation of the surviving pieces, compressing the episodes these pieces recorded into a period of five years. But in so doing, they lumped together events that may in fact have taken place many years apart – if Hattusili did have a long reign. He may well have conducted a number of campaigns into Syria throughout this reign. But one thing clear is that he never succeeded in capturing what must have been his prime objective in Syria – the city of Aleppo, capital of the kingdom of Yamhad. By the end of his reign, Aleppo was still intact.

Hattusili's military achievements in Syria and other lands were impressive, even if from our perspective his campaigns in foreign regions look like sheer naked adventurism, with few lasting benefits, political, strategic, or material, for his kingdom. There was absolutely no prospect that the Syrian lands and cities which fell to his armies would ever be incorporated into his own kingdom. Early

Hittite kings had neither the organisational capacity nor the manpower to contemplate an expansion of their sovereignty over these or any other conquered lands that lay far from their centre of power. Hattusili's campaigns were little more than smash and grab raids – conquest for conquest's sake.

That said, the king's exploits had won him a reputation as a great warrior, one of the most important attributes of kingship in Near Eastern royal ideology. His achievements on the battlefield, far surpassing in their range those of the first Labarna, were amply demonstrated by the cartloads of plunder brought back from the sacked cities, plunder that would swell the treasuries of Hittite palaces and temples, with a portion set aside for the king's officers and other loyal adherents as a reward for their services. Beyond that, Hattusili's battlefield successes served to demonstrate to his enemies the already formidable military capabilities of his fledgling kingdom. Hatti was now a force to be reckoned with.

Before leaving this part of our story, we should mention one important side-effect of Hattusili's Syrian campaigns. Indirectly, these campaigns were responsible for the introduction, or reintroduction, of writing into Anatolia, following the end of the Assyrian colony period. This was because scribes from the conquered cities were almost certainly among the prisoners brought to Hattusa as part of the king's war-booty. Employed in the capital's palace and temple bureaucracies, the imported scribes became the first producers of written documents in the Hittite world. They did so using a cuneiform script – but it was the script used to record the Babylonian version of the Akkadian language, not the Assyrian version used by the merchant colonists. Perhaps soon after their arrival, a local scribal class began to develop. And though the Babylonian language probably remained for a time the official language of the Hittite bureaucracy, Hittite scribes eventually began using their own language for the written documents, probably from the middle of the sixteenth century. In a kind of transitional stage, documents were written in both languages – what we call bilinguals.

CHAPTER 4

THE LEGACY OF AN AILING KING

We come now to what *may* be the end of Hattusili's reign – or least to a period when the king lay seriously ill. Information about this comes from one of the most extraordinary documents to emerge from the Hittite archives. Commonly known as the Testament of Hattusili and preserved in a thirteenth-century Hittite–Akkadian bilingual copy,[1] it records a scene set in Kussar, ancestral home of the Hittite royal family. We learn from the text that King Hattusili was in the city at the time and fell ill there.

Let's recreate the scene, and the context in which it occurs, from what the Testament tells us.

AN AILING KING'S BEQUEST

Hattusili's illness is a serious and perhaps terminal one. If he dies, his kingdom, already in crisis, will be plunged into chaos. Bitter divisions within the royal household make it essential that the succession to the throne be firmly secured before his death. His high-ranking military officers and other dignitaries have been summoned to his bedside – for he has something of vital importance to say to them.

The VIPs, representatives of the most powerful elements in the realm, gather in silence as the king prepares to address them. A scribe has been summoned to record his every word – perhaps the last words he will ever speak. They may prove crucial to the kingdom's survival. Already the land of Hatti has suffered turmoil. The king blames it largely on the treachery of his own children, a son and a daughter. He reminds the gathering of their 'offences'. The son Huzziya, appointed as regional governor in the city Tappassanda (otherwise unknown), had been persuaded to join in a local uprising against his father. Huzziya was apparently a popular figure in the kingdom, and may well have been next in line for the throne. Now, he was under arrest for treason. Yet his fall from grace merely served to widen and intensify discontent among the king's subjects. There were fresh uprisings throughout the kingdom, apparently led by the prince's sister. The king finally reasserted his authority over the land and banished his daughter, but only after many of his subjects had been slaughtered.

Once more, the question of the succession arose. With his own son ruled out of contention, the king had turned to his nephew, and announced his appointment as the new Labarna, the heir designate. But that appointment too ended disastrously. The nephew proved unfit to assume the responsibilities of kingship – so Hattusili informs the gathering: 'He was an abomination to the sight! He shed no tears, he was without compassion, he was cold and pitiless!' Repeatedly ignoring the king's advice, the assembly is told, he listened only to his cold-hearted siblings and his evil mother. In a bizarre mix of animal metaphors, the king refers to his sister as a 'serpent', who 'bellowed like an ox' when she heard that her son had been sacked. But the king had no choice. The nephew had to go. His rule would have led only to more bloodshed and chaos in the kingdom. That could not be allowed to happen. He had to be stripped of all his powers and, like the king's daughter (and probably his son), banished from the capital. 'Until now nobody [in my family] has obeyed my will,' the king sighs.

And then we come to the main purpose of the meeting. With Hattusili's repudiation of his nephew, there is only one other possible successor to the throne – the king's grandson Mursili. And that is what the king announces to his gathering. The problem is that Mursili is still a child, too young to assume the responsibilities of kingship. But there is no-one else. We can now fully understand how critical the king's meeting is with the chief dignitaries of his land. For they are called upon not only to endorse (yet another) successor to the throne, but one who could not effectively rule what is still a highly unstable kingdom for some years to come – if his grandfather is in fact close to death.

As yet there are no established rules of royal succession. To be sure, there seems to have been no question that the next king would come from the same family group as his predecessors. But within this family, the job was up for grabs, depending on which family member succeeded in building sufficient factional support for himself and disposing of his rivals and enemies. And the kingdom itself would suffer severe damage in the process. This is why the hastily convened assembly's support for the ailing king's choice can be seen as vital to the kingdom's stability and security. But it is not only their agreement that Hattusili seeks. Although a regent may have been appointed during the new king's minority, the chief responsibility for protecting the youth and training him to assume the full powers of kingship, both as an administrator and as a warrior, is to lie with those now assembled around Hattusili's bedside – *if* they consent to do their king's bidding.

Apart from a few explanatory notes inserted by the scribe, the Testament is almost certainly *a verbatim record of what the king actually said* – not a later tidied-up and edited version of it, like most official documents of the kingdom. Let's not miss the significance of this. These are the very first preserved spoken words in an Indo-European language. A king talks directly to us across a time-gap of more than three-and-a-half millennia.

As it stands, the speech is something of a mish-mash. Parts of it are quite formal, rational and directly to the point when the king addresses the assembly on the matter of the succession, and gives his child-successor advice on how he should behave as he prepares for the onerous duties of kingship. But other parts of the speech are laden with bitter personal accusations against those who have allegedly betrayed the king – particularly his sister, 'the serpent who bellowed like an ox'. She above all is responsible for what her son has become.

Yet despite their grievous offences, the king has shown exemplary mercy to those who have betrayed him. The rebellious daughter (and probably also the son) and rejected nephew have not been executed. Their punishment is simply banishment from the capital to places where they will live in comfort and safety. And there will be no further recriminations for past acts of disloyalty and treachery committed by any of the king's subjects. Mercy and clemency will be comprehensive and unconditional. This in accordance with the new spirit of peace and harmony which is to be the king's legacy to his heirs and subjects.

We come now to the Testament's final words. The king gives instructions that a record of all he has said is to be read out to Mursili every month. And then with a last piece of advice to his new heir, his speech is finished. Or so it seems. The king sinks back upon his couch, silent, and the scribe puts down his stylus. But then the king rallies, briefly. He turns to a woman close to his bedside. She's called Hastayar. We do not know her relationship to the king. She is almost certainly a close female relative – maybe his wife, maybe a favourite concubine. After some words of advice to her, he says, finally, 'Wash me well, hold me to your breast, protect me from the earth (lying against) your breast' (transl. P. Goedegebuure). These are private words, not intended for the record. But faithful to his instructions, the scribe on hearing the king speak again hastily picks up his stylus, records what he says, and ensures that they are forever preserved. The great Hittite warlord, suddenly fearful at the prospect of his own death, bids Hastayar hold him close, keeping him from death's clutches.

THE TRUTH OF THESE MATTERS?

Fascinating though this document is, it leaves many questions unanswered. Let's remember that everything we are told comes directly from the king's own mouth, without any corroboration. Should we accept at face value the accusations of treachery and conspiracy he makes against his own family? Doth the king protest too much? Reading between the lines, I have the impression that he was deeply unpopular with many of his subjects, at least at this stage of his reign, and that the uprisings against him were not entirely without good cause. What's more, it seems that hostility towards the king did not extend to all members of his family. Hattusili's own children appear to have enjoyed considerable popular support. And even the rejected nephew may have been unfairly maligned. He had been dumped by the king after a number of confrontations between the two, for which the nephew was perhaps not altogether to blame. The fact that though he has been banished from the capital, the king assures the assembly that he will be granted a generous severance package may well indicate that he was not without influential supporters. The promise Hattusili gives may have been a tacit admission of this, to dampen down any resentment at his sacking. What emerges clearly from the Testament is that the kingdom's subjects were not challenging the right of the current royal dynasty to rule their land. Quite the opposite. Much of the discontent seems to have arisen from a fear that the kingship would pass out of its hands. It was the king, not his dynasty, who was the object of such apparent hostility in the land.

Then there is the question of the setting for the Testament – the city of Kussar, ancestral home of the royal family. What was the king doing there? Kussar may well have continued to occupy an important place in the kingdom, and perhaps Hattusili was visiting it on a tour of inspection of all his major cities when he fell ill. Another possibility is that if there were continuing instability in the kingdom at this time, Hattusili may have decided it was safer for him to leave Hattusa and return to Kussar – at least until the problems relating to the succession had been fully resolved.

We should question too whether the Testament really belongs to the end of Hattusili's life. Was it a deathbed speech, as often assumed? It may well be that the king recovered from his illness, perhaps a fever of some kind. On the basis of a brief but puzzling reference in a later document (to which we shall come), it's possible that he not only recovered his health, but continued his campaigns in Syria and was killed there. Indeed, we cannot be sure that he had even begun his Syrian campaigns by this time. It would be reasonable to assume that he ventured so far from home, taking with him the substantial resources required for military enterprises in the Syrian region, only after he felt confident that his hold over his kingdom was fully secure.

A WORTHY SUCCESSOR

In any case, his last wishes for the succession were fulfilled, and his grandson (and adopted son) Mursili did succeed to the throne. But Hattusili may well have continued to reign for some years to come before then. In terms of his military responsibilities, Mursili followed in his grandfather's footsteps, quite literally, as he conducted further campaigns in Syria. The culmination of these was his final capture of the prize that had eluded Hattusili – the city of Aleppo. And with its capture and destruction, he delivered the final *coup de grâce* to the kingdom of Yamhad. From a fragment of text which tells us this, we learn that in capturing Aleppo, Mursili 'avenged his father's (i.e. his grandfather's/predecessor's) blood'. This *may* mean that Hattusili had been killed in his ongoing contest with Aleppo, leaving his final mission unaccomplished. Hence the suggestion that Hattusili did not die in Kussar, but later on, perhaps much later on, in Syria.

And now his successor, flushed with his victory over Aleppo, sought another world to conquer. Leading his troops to the Euphrates river, he marched them downstream to Babylon. Laying siege to the city, he captured, looted and destroyed it. Thus in the reign of the Babylonian king Samsu-ditana, the dynasty that had ruled Old Kingdom Babylonia for almost 300 years came to an abrupt and violent end. (See the BBC documentary *The Dark Lords of Hattusa* for a graphic and bloodthirsty re-enactment of Babylon's fall to the Hittites.) Mursili's sack of Babylon 'made the gods sick', according to the king's brother-in-law Hantili. But as we shall see, Hantili was grinding his own personal axe – almost literally – when he made this statement.

Laden with the spoils of his conquest of Aleppo and Babylonia, Mursili began his homeward march. Like his predecessor, he made no attempt to annex or establish sovereignty over any of his conquered territories. In fact, his conquests paved the way for other powers to fill the vacuum left by the fall of the Babylonian dynasty.

In the years to come, peoples from the east called the Kassites set up a ruling dynasty that would hold sway over the whole of Babylonia for the rest of the Bronze Age. Of more direct concern, the Hittite conquests in Syria facilitated the growth and spread through the region of one of the Hittites' most dangerous enemies. We have already briefly met them. They were the Hurrians.

CHAPTER 5

'NOW BLOODSHED HAS BECOME COMMON'

D espite ensuring his place in the Hittites' roll of honour for the rest of the kingdom's history, Mursili fell victim to a conspiracy within his own family just a few years after his eastern triumphs. He was assassinated by his brother-in-law Hantili. 'Now bloodshed (in the royal family) has become common,' laments Telipinu in his Proclamation. One might expect that the assassin himself would soon be for the chop. But not so. Hantili managed to live to a ripe old age. And to give credit where credit is due, he followed his murdered predecessor and *his* predecessor in fulfilling his warrior responsibilities by continuing Hittite campaigns in Syria all the way to Carchemish on the Euphrates. Yet the kingdom suffered grave setbacks during his reign. There were further invasions by the dreaded Hurrians who apparently roamed the Hittite homeland and plundered it at will, failing only to capture Hattusa itself before they were driven out of the land.

NEW RULES OF ROYAL SUCCESSION

Hantili's death led to renewed struggles within the extended royal family for the throne, and his first three successors, Zidanta, Ammuna, and Huzziya, secured the kingship by conspiracy and bloodshed. All the while the kingdom suffered – its subject-states in rebellion, its land ravaged by drought. The gods had a hand in this, claims Telipinu, disgusted by the continuing feuds in the royal family which now seemed in self-destruct mode. By the end of Huzziya's reign, Hatti was on the verge of disintegration. Time now for Telipinu, Huzziya's brother-in-law, to make his grand entrance. After ending Huzziya's reign by usurping the throne for himself, he issued a statement of reassurance. There would be no more bloodshed, no more reprisals. Huzziya and his five brothers had their lives spared, but just to be on the safe side, the usurper banished them to a place where he felt sure they'd be unable to attempt a counter-coup or any other form of retaliation.

Did his reign, beginning around 1525, mark the dawn of a new era? On the military front, he established his credentials as a war leader by winning back many of the subject-territories lost to Hatti during his predecessors' reigns. But most important was his attempt to bring stability to the topmost levels of Hittite society – above all the kingship. And this brings us to the chief purpose of his Proclamation: to lay down fixed rules for the royal succession. The long historical preamble leading up to this, while useful to us for the historical information it provides, is designed primarily to highlight one axiomatic principle: a kingdom united is strong and will achieve great things against its enemies; a kingdom divided will become prey to its enemies and risk annihilation. And a kingdom cannot be united unless there is a smooth, formal process of succession from one king to the next. Here is the Proclamation's key clause:

> Let a prince, a son of the first rank, become king. If there is no prince of the first rank, let him who is a son of the second rank become king. But if there is no prince, no heir, let them take an *antiyant*-husband for her who is a daughter of the first rank, and let him become king.

In the first instance, a king should be succeeded by a son from his chief wife. If he has no sons by his chief wife, a son of one of his concubines becomes eligible. But if he has no sons by either a wife or a concubine, then the husband of one of his daughters becomes eligible. An *antiyant*-husband is a son-in-law who formally 'enters into' his wife's family and is adopted by her father as his son. In this way, the possibilities for a 'son of the king' becoming the next king are extended. Indeed, there were several occasions in the kingdom's history when a king's son-in-law, or adoptive son, did become the next king.

DID THE NEW RULES WORK?

Of course, all this raises an important question. Who is going to ensure that these mere words will end the succession struggles that had been so destructive in the past? Responsibility must lie firstly with the king's own family and the kingdom's most powerful officials. But *quis custodiet ipsos custodes?* 'Who will guard the guardians themselves?' (to borrow a phrase from the Roman poet Juvenal). Telipinu had thought of that. Enforcement of the rules of succession is be assigned to an assembly called the *panku*. Basically a Hittite adjective meaning 'all, entire', *panku* crops up occasionally in early Hittite history as a term for some sort of assembly with supervisory and judicial powers. Its precise composition is unclear. Indeed it may have varied, depending on what functions it was required to perform. In this case, Telipinu calls upon a specific group of officials and palace functionaries to supervise the new succession rules and take action if they are breached. This action includes a process of trying those charged with plotting against a reigning king. If found guilty they are to be executed – even if they are members of the royal family! The king's person is thus made sacrosanct.

How successful were the new rules? The results were mixed. Telipinu, like Hantili, probably died of natural causes. But he was followed by a series of generally weak and ineffective rulers, often via the familiar path of intrigue, assassination and usurpation. Even though these kings seemed to maintain control over most of the kingdom's subject-territories, they could no longer claim the status and power their kingdom had enjoyed during the reigns of Hattusili and Mursili. Indeed the kingdom's very existence was under constant threat from its traditional enemy the Hurrians.

They had already invaded the Hittite homeland during Hattusili's reign and did so again, almost without hindrance during the reign of Mursili's assassin and successor Hantili.

ENTER THE KINGDOMS OF MITTANI AND EGYPT

What made the Hurrian menace all the greater was that a group of states with a predominantly Hurrian population had formed a powerful political and military confederation called the kingdom of Mittani. From their homeland in northern Mesopotamia, with its capital at Washshuganni (precise location uncertain) Mittanian armies had marched across northern Syria into the easternmost parts of the Anatolian peninsula, establishing Mittanian sovereignty over much of this region. Sooner or later the very heartland of the kingdom of Hatti would be overwhelmed, so it must have seemed, by the relentless advance of Mittani's forces, at whose core lay a fearsome elite chariot group called the *maryannu*. There was little that any of the first successors of Telipinu could do to stop them.

But the news from the east was not all bad. For another major player had entered the international arena – the kingdom of Egypt. In the middle decades of the fifteenth century, the pharaoh Tuthmosis III followed in the footsteps of his earlier namesake Tuthmosis I by conducting renewed campaigns in Syria and laying the foundations for Egyptian authority over a large part of southern Syria and Palestine. The good news for Hatti was that the Egyptian ventures kept Mittanian imperialist ambitions in check – which were a more immediate threat to Hittite territory. And there was no likelihood that the pharaoh had any ambition to extend his conquests further afield into Anatolia, even if he had had the military resources to do so. Thus while the Egyptians were active in Syria, Hatti could breathe a huge sigh of relief, and one of its kings (we're not certain who) showed his gratitude to Tuthmosis, and ensured his goodwill, by sending him tributary gifts. Mittani's other neighbours, the kings of Babylon and Assyria did likewise – no doubt believing that Egypt had effectively put an end to Mittani's militaristic ambitions against them as well.

It was all too good to be true. Successful though they were in military terms, Tuthmosis' campaigns failed to establish permanent Egyptian authority in either Syria or Palestine. Towards the end of his reign there were local uprisings against Egyptian rule, and after his death Egypt withdrew from all further involvement in the region – for the time being. That provided the current Mittanian king Saushtatar with a fresh opportunity to restake his kingdom's claim over a large part of Syria, spearheaded by the formidable might of the *maryannu*. First he invaded Assyria in northern Mesopotamia, and sacked its capital Ashur, reducing the former great kingdom to vassal status. Then he crossed the Euphrates and led his forces on a trail of conquest and devastation through northern Syria to the Mediterranean coast. And just beyond lay the southern territories of the kingdom of Hatti. Once more, the kingdom, still suffering from a long period of internal instability, faced a crisis of major proportions from its most dangerous enemy.

All this leads us up to the early fourteenth century, and the beginning of a new era in Hittite history. Sometimes called the Hittite New Kingdom, it started with yet another assassination. The current king Muwattalli was bloodily despatched by the supporters of a man called Tudhaliya who now assumed the throne in his place. It was an inauspicious start to his reign. But Tudhaliya consolidated his position on the throne, and launched his armies on a series of new military enterprises which paved the way for Hatti's re-emergence as a great international power – one of the four Great Kingdoms of the Late Bronze Age Near Eastern world.

CHAPTER 6

THE SETTING FOR AN EMPIRE

I n Chapter 7, we shall see how Tudhaliya went about laying the foundations of the Hittite empire. Later, we shall watch the empire's progress through triumph, setback, disaster and resurgence until its final collapse in the early twelfth century. But first of all let's try to reconstruct the physical setting in which these developments took place.

The satellite image of Anatolia and northern Syria in Map I.1 highlights the main physical features of the regions covered by our story. Now have a look at Map 6.1, 'The Hittite world'.[1] This provides a reconstructed layout of the cities, towns, kingdoms and countries which made up the Hittite world, based mainly on information provided by our written sources. Archaeological remains, topographical features and other data often supplement this information. But much remains conjectural. Therein lies the problem of what the archaeologist James Mellaart once described as 'the guessing game known as Hittite geography'. We need no longer be quite so cynical. Since Mellaart made that statement 40 years ago, scholars have made significant progress in their research on the political geography of the Hittite world.

RECONSTRUCTING A MAP OF THE HITTITE WORLD

In any case, locating the Syrian territories which came under Hittite control always involved less guesswork than finding places for most

Map 6.1 The Hittite world.

of Hatti's Anatolian cities and states. This is because we can match up many Syrian city-names known from written records with actual sites – like Carchemish on the Euphrates, Aleppo (called Halab/p by the Hittites), Alalah (modern Tell Atchana on the northern bend of the Orontes). So too we can identify the Bronze Age royal city of Ugarit in western Syria, from its extensive surviving tablet-archives and building remains, and we have a fairly clear idea of the extent and boundaries of the kingdom (also called Ugarit) of which it was the capital. Similarly, a number of cities and territories controlled by Egypt in southern Syria and Palestine can be precisely located, for their descendants exist today, like Beirut, Byblos, Sidon and Tyre, along the Levantine coast. Using these cities as markers, we can reconstruct with a fairly high degree of accuracy the network of city-states and larger kingdoms in Syria and Palestine, even if their precise boundaries remain uncertain.

Late Bronze Age Anatolia is a rather different proposition. But let's start with a positive. The Hittite capital Hattusa was identified almost as soon as excavations began on the site in the early twentieth century. And in fairly recent years a number of other Hittite cities have been discovered, within or near the 'homeland' region. They've long been known to us from the capital's written records, but we did not know precisely where they were – until their sites were excavated and tablet archives found there established their identification. Most notable among them was the important Hittite city called Sapinuwa (modern Ortaköy), which lay 60 km northeast of Hattusa. Archaeological and written evidence now combine to indicate that this was a major administrative centre of the kingdom, probably a base for Hittite armies, and the site of an important royal palace (where the king resided during his visits to the region). Some 3,000 clay tablets were found in the palace complex. Not yet fully published, they provide us with important information about the daily affairs of the region. Many are letters exchanged between the Hittite king and his regional officials, and between the officials themselves. We'll come back to this.

Sites like Sapinuwa are fairly exceptional. More often, we have ones that are clearly Hittite, or have a Hittite phase, but no texts that identify them. A classic case is the site now known as Alaca Höyük, about 40 km northeast of Hattusa. Alaca was already an impressive site in the Early Bronze Age, illustrated by 13 'royal' shaft graves from this phase of its existence. The graves contained rich funerary goods, most notably ritual disk and arc standards, each of which incorporated a stylised bull or stag or both, usually made of bronze inlaid with gold or silver. As I've noted in the Introduction, a giant replica of one of them has been erected in Ankara to remind us of Turkey's ancient heritage. In the Hittite period, Alaca was very likely an important cult centre – perhaps the city called Arinna in the texts, city of the Sun-Goddess. Its well-preserved monumental entrance-way, flanked by sphinxes, is embellished by lively entertainment and festival scenes, plus a depiction of the king and queen standing before the altar of the Storm God – all perhaps scenes taken from a festival celebration. The city also contains the remains of what is probably a palace, some residential quarters and several temples – but alas, no texts that confirm what it was called in Hittite times.

When we move further west in Anatolia, our attempts to reconstruct a map of the Hittite world become even more problematical. We know from our texts the names of many countries and cities located somewhere in the western half of the Anatolian peninsula, but no precise information, either archaeological or written, as to where the great majority of them actually lay. What we do know is that a large part of the region was occupied by a territorial conglomerate called the Arzawa lands in Hittite texts. It probably covered much of the region between the Salt Lake and the Aegean Sea. We've already met Arzawa as the object of a plundering expedition by the Hittite king Hattusili I. The focus of this conglomerate seems to have been a specific kingdom called Arzawa. (We often refer to it as Arzawa Proper or Arzawa Minor to distinguish it from the rest of the lands to which the Arzawan label is applied.)

We can be pretty sure that it extended inland from Anatolia's Aegean coast. And its chief city Apasa, known from the texts, *may* have been located close to the site of Classical Ephesus (which presumably derived its name from the Hittite city). Fairly recently, Late Bronze Age pottery and what is probably part of a Late Bronze Age fortification wall were discovered on a hill near Ephesus. Just possibly these are remnants of the Arzawan city of Apasa. Perhaps more substantial Bronze Age remains lie beneath Classical Ephesus. If so, or even if not, this exemplifies one of the main problems with attempting to find Bronze Age material in the west. There has been so much reoccupation of the region in later times, beginning with Greek settlements in many parts of it from the late second millennium onwards, that any remnants of the Bronze Age may have been destroyed for all time by later settlements or buried irretrievably beneath them. As one frustrated Bronze Age archaeologist commented: 'We can't get at the really interesting stuff because of all this Classical junk sitting on top of it!'

Even if more Bronze Age remains of the Hittite period do come to light, the chances of written records being found among them is extremely slight. Unbaked clay tablets would have long since crumbled to dust. It's purely a matter of good fortune that such large quantities of clay tablets *have* survived in other parts of the Bronze Age world, by being accidentally baked in the conflagrations which destroyed the cities where they were located. We know that a number of western Anatolian countries, especially the

Arzawa lands, must have had scribal establishments, because of their rulers' frequent written communications with the Hittite king – letters, treaties and the like. But these communications have survived only in the archives of the Hittite capital. The sad fact is that in western Anatolia none of the remaining Bronze Age sites, like the one now called Beycesultan near the source of the Maeander river, have produced any written records. In its Late Bronze Age phase, Beycesultan may have been an important city of the Arzawan complex, mentioned many times in the texts. But without written information we cannot identify it.

In the far northwest, the site called Troy (Homer's Ilios) has been identified by many scholars as the centre of a kingdom called Wilusa in Hittite texts. Probably a part of the Arzawa complex, it must have had its own chancery, for we know that the Hittite and Wilusan kings were in written diplomatic contact. But extensive excavations at Troy have failed to reveal the slightest trace of writing there in the Bronze Age. The very first evidence of writing at Troy, a bronze convex seal inscribed with its owner's name and his profession (he was a scribe), dates some time between 1050 and 1000. This is well after the Bronze Age ended. But despite lack of hard evidence, most scholars accept the identification of Homeric Troy with Hittite Wilusa – and the plaque at the entrance to the site today, which reads ILIOS WILUSA, seeks to put the matter beyond doubt.

As it happens, we do have one surviving though fragmentary Bronze Age inscription in the west which could be very helpful in piecing together some of the political geography of the region. This is a rock-cut inscription accompanying a relief sculpture in a mountain pass (called Karabel) some 28 km east of Izmir. The sculpture depicts a male human figure armed with bow, spear and sword. When the Greek historian Herodotus visited the site in the fifth century BC, he claimed that the figure was an Egyptian king called Sesostris, and that the Egyptian inscription (sic) read thus: 'With my own shoulders I won this land.' Herodotus got it completely wrong. The script is in fact the hieroglyphic script I mentioned earlier, and which we still have to discuss. For the moment, let us simply say that the Anatolian epigraphist David

Hawkins has correctly deciphered the inscription, which identifies the sculpted figure as a man called Tarkasnawa, king of the land of Mira.[2] Now we know that Mira was one of the Arzawa lands, and the likelihood is that this monument lay on its northern boundary. Beyond it, the Hittite texts tell us, was another Arzawan kingdom, called Seha River Land, which had a land called Lazpa as its dependency. Most scholars agree that Lazpa is the island called Lesbos by the Greeks. And Wilusa seems to have lain close to this country – which increases the likelihood of its identification with the region of Troy, called the Troad in Classical texts.

There is one other promising-looking identification. A number of Hittite texts refer to a land called Milawata or Millawanda, which lay alongside or extended to the Aegean sea. It seems very likely that Milawata was the Bronze Age forerunner of the Classical city Miletos, built at the mouth of the Maeander river. Excavations have revealed an extensive Bronze Age settlement on the site which came under strong Greek influence during the last part of the fourteenth and the first decades of the thirteenth century. As we shall see, there is good reason to believe that a Greek king was overlord of this

Figure 6.1   Classical Miletos, Lion Harbour.

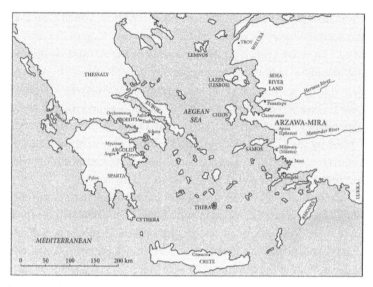

Map 6.2 Late Bronze Age Greece and western Anatolia.

region at this time. But although both archaeological and written sources seem to support an identification of Milawata as the Bronze Age forerunner of Miletos, they don't actually prove it. Once again, hard evidence, in the form of tablets from the site itself identifying it, has yet to be found.

GREEKS IN HITTITE TEXTS?

Speaking of the Greeks – in the 1920s, a Swiss scholar called Emil Forrer who made a study of the recently deciphered Hittite texts became particularly interested in ones that indicated direct Hittite contacts with a number of countries in western Anatolia, all the way to the Aegean Sea. Now, archaeological excavations had pointed to evidence of a *Greek* presence, particularly in the form of artefacts, at various places along the Aegean coast and its hinterland. The Greeks of this era are commonly known as Mycenaeans. This is a modern name for them, arising from the fact that the citadel of Mycenae in southern Greece is today considered the most important of the Late Bronze Age Greek sites; and indeed, Mycenae in Greek tradition was the city of Agamemnon, immortalised in legend as the leader of the Greek forces in the Trojan War.

Forrer reasoned that the Hittites must have come into contact with, or at least known about, the Bronze Age Greeks who had inspired Homer's epics the *Iliad* and the *Odyssey*, composed four or more centuries after the Bronze Age. This prompted his search for Greeks in the Hittite texts. And he found them! Or so he claimed in an announcement he made in 1924. The basis of his claim was that Homer referred to his Greek warriors at Troy as Achaians (he also called them Danaans and Argives). And Hittite texts referred to a land somewhere in the west as Ahhiyawa, and on occasions to a king of Ahhiyawa. From all this Forrer concluded that Achaia was the, or at least *a*, name of Bronze Age Greece, and that Ahhiyawa was the Hittite way of writing this name. So, he declared, Homer's Greeks had been found in the Hittite texts. What was even more exciting was his statement that he had also found references in these texts to the Trojan War and to some of its chief participants.

Forrer's claims aroused great popular interest, and even some scholarly support. For the first time there was now evidence, from independent contemporary written sources unearthed in the Hittite capital, that Homer's great epic of the Trojan War *was based on historical fact*. It all seemed too good to be true. And scholarly scepticism quickly set in. A large part of Forrer's case was based on his identification of Homeric names with names found in the Hittite texts – like Attarissiya, equated with the name of Agamemnon's father Atreus, and Alaksandu, equated with the name of the Trojan prince (Paris) Alexander. These equations provoked much hostile criticism from other scholars who regarded Forrer's equations as scientifically unsound, dismissing the similarity in names as being purely coincidental – what we might call 'kling-klang etymology'. At the forefront of the critics was a German scholar called Ferdinand Sommer, who in 1932 published a full edition with commentaries of all the 'Ahhiyawa texts' (there are fewer than 30 of them). In the process, he utterly ruled out any possibility they had anything to do with Mycenaean Greece.

That was in 1932. The debate between Forrer and his critics became bitter and acrimonious and deeply personal – without any resolution. Since then, discussion has continued in a more restrained way, about the identity and location of Ahhiyawa, and whether or not it had anything to do with the Greek world. Over the years, Cyprus, Rhodes, mainland Greece, and somewhere on the western coast of Anatolia have all been suggested as candidates for the land of Ahhiyawa. At present, most scholars support the Ahhiyawan-Mycenaean Greek identification, but purely on the basis of circumstantial evidence. This is their line of reasoning: If a western land called Ahhiyawa, whose kings appear to have had peer status with contemporary Hittite kings, and which, as we know from Hittite texts, was closely involved in western Anatolian affairs, was *not* a Late Bronze Age Greek land, what else could it be? There is no other feasible candidate that fits the requirements. But we have not yet found one piece of hard evidence – in the form, say, of some Hittite tablets at Mycenae or any other Late Bronze Age Greek site – to verify it.

In the absence of any other plausible possibility, I believe we have to go with Forrer's identification, though we may reject all or many of his specific name-equations. If so, then 'Ahhiyawa' in Hittite texts seems to refer on some occasions to Bronze Age Greece in a very broad sense, as a kind of ethno-geographical term. But on other occasions, it refers quite specifically to a land ruled by a king who had at least political dealings, and perhaps also commercial and military dealings, with the Hittites and the lands of western Anatolia. Indeed, one thing that strongly favours the identification is the Bronze Age city of Miletos, if this is Hittite Milawata. As I've noted, we have clear evidence from archaeological excavations of a substantial Mycenaean presence in the city in the late fourteenth century and part of the following century – at precisely the same time Hittite records indicate that an Ahhiyawan king was in control of the city and its peripheral territories.

But within the broad context of the world of Ahhiyawa, what precisely was the Ahhiyawan kingdom whose ruler was accorded peer status in Hittite texts with the Great King of Hatti? Mycenaean Greece consisted of a number of kingdoms, which might have joined together from time to time for military or commercial operations, but probably retained their political independence from one another. The kingdom whose ruler established a base in Anatolia and had dealings with the king of Hatti must have been one of these. Mycenae itself is a favoured candidate. But there are other possibilities, including Thebes further to the north, or even Pylos on the western side of the Peloponnese (southern Greece).

We'll have more to say about Ahhiyawa later. But for now let's just add one further detail which is actually of considerable importance in the history of writing. One of the Ahhiyawa texts found in Hattusa is a letter which appears to have been written by a king of Ahhiyawa to his counterpart in Hatti.[3] Dating to the early–mid thirteenth century, it refers to an earlier dispute between the Ahhiyawan and Hittite kings over possession of some islands which probably lay just off Anatolia's western coast. The copy we have is in Hittite, but if the letter is of Greek origin, it is profoundly significant. For it would be the very earliest written document we have in the history of European literature, even though it survives only in a Hittite translation. Indeed, the original letter may also have been written in Hittite, dictated by the Greek king or his representative to a bilingual scribe.

THE HITTITE WORLD IN REVIEW

My map of the Hittite world is based partly on (a) established fact, (b) fairly strong circumstantial evidence and (c) guesswork – though *informed* guesswork. We can but hope that with ongoing investigations items in the (c) category can be pushed into (b) and that some if not all (b) items can be promoted to the (a) category. That may be wishful thinking. Indeed, we cannot rule out the possibility that future research will force us to downgrade some of our items into a (d) category – i.e. 'completely wrong'.

But provided you bear all these qualifications in mind, my map will give you an overall idea of the general layout of the Hittite empire and its neighbours at the height of its power. Administratively, the empire consisted of (i) core territory, the land within the Marassantiya basin which we have called the Hittite homeland; here was located the capital Hattusa and many of the empire's major cult and administrative centres; (ii) a number of vassal states spread over many parts of Anatolia and northern Syria and (iii) from the second half of the fourteenth century, two viceregal kingdoms in northern Syria, one at Carchemish, the other at Aleppo; these were ruled by close members of the king's family, generally his sons, who between them shared most of the Great King's responsibilities for the administration of Hatti's Syrian territories. In the mid thirteenth century, a third viceregal kingdom ruled by another member of the royal family was established in southeastern Anatolia, in the city of Tarhuntassa. The vassal states were administered by local rulers, bound by treaties to the Great King. Most of these components of empire are marked on the map, along with the regions where Hittite influence fluctuated over the centuries.

Let's turn our attention now to the historical developments that led to Hatti's becoming one of the greatest of all the ancient Near Eastern kingdoms, with subject-territories spread across the Anatolian peninsula to the Euphrates in the east, and southwards through Syria to the frontiers of Damascus. We'll take up our story where we left it in Chapter 5, with the accession of a king called Tudhaliya, and the beginning of what I have called the New Kingdom.

CHAPTER 7

BUILDING AN EMPIRE

We've noted that in the fifteenth century, the warrior-pharaoh Tuthmosis III had sought to establish permanent Egyptian control over large parts of Syria and Palestine. But ultimately his campaigns failed to achieve this. Egypt's withdrawal from the region after his death led to the resurgence of Mittanian power there, under the Mittanian king Saushtatar, and the imminent threat of further Mittanian expansion into the territories of the kingdom of Hatti. This was one of the major challenges facing the Hittite king Tudhaliya when he mounted the Hittite throne around 1400 (or a bit earlier). Mustering the forces at his disposal for an invasion of Syria and the conquest of Mittani's territories in the region would be one of the new Hittite king's top priorities.

DIPLOMACY INSTEAD OF BRUTE FORCE

Before attempting such a massive undertaking, Tudhaliya had first to sort out another problem closer to home. Some time during the upheavals which preceded Telipinu's reign, a new independent state emerged in Anatolia's southeastern corner. The territory it covered probably once subject to the kingdom of Hatti, the new state was called Kizzuwatna. Because it lay astride the routes through the Taurus mountains from Anatolia into Syria, its location was clearly of great strategic importance to the Hittites. But Telipinu had to tread warily. Other territories lost to Hatti during his predecessors' reigns he had regained by military action.

With Kizzuwatna he adopted a different tactic. Instead of attempting to subdue it by force, he made a treaty of alliance with its king Isputahsu. Diplomacy rather than military action was used to win Kizzuwatna to his side, and Telipinu's treaty-partner retained his independence.

The relationship which Telipinu initiated with the southern state was a carefully calculated one. The kingdom of Kizzuwatna had very likely been created under Hurrian influence, and we know that in later years at least it contained a substantial Hurrian population. It may already have had a strong Hurrian alignment when Telipinu ascended the Hittite throne, and Hittite aggression against it would very likely have brought forces of the Hurrian kingdom of Mittani directly into the conflict. To avoid this, Telipinu persuaded the Kizzuwatnan king to form an alliance with him, and at least remain benevolently neutral in any forthcoming conflict between Hatti and Mittani. Let me emphasise here that the conclusion of the treaty marks a major new development in the history of the Hittite kingdom – the use of diplomacy instead of force to secure the kingdom's safety and to spread and maintain its influence. We'll see more examples in later periods.

On this occasion, however, the Hittite–Kizzuwatnan accord failed to provide a permanent solution to the problems of securing Hatti's southeastern frontier. Despite Telipinu's treaty, Kizzuwatna's later kings fluctuated in their loyalties between Hatti and Mittani, using their bargaining power to play off one kingdom against the other. In this way, they secured their state against an aggressive takeover by either of its powerful neighbours: an attack by one upon it would almost certainly bring the other into the conflict in support of it. Even so, by the time Tudhaliya became king, Kizzuwatna was firmly in the Mittanian camp. That was a serious problem, for a Mittanian-aligned Kizzuwatna deprived the Hittites of their main routes into Syria, and gave the Mittanian king a 'soft underbelly' for launching an invasion of Hittite territory. Tudhaliya's response to this problem was to follow Telipinu's example – he persuaded the current Kizzuwatnan king Sunashshura to shift his allegiance to Hatti. How he managed to do it – by threats or by more positive inducements – we simply do

Figure 7.1   Aleppo citadel.

not know. All we can say is that with Kizzuwatna on his side, the way to Syria now lay open before him.

A NEW SYRIAN VENTURE

In the footsteps of his great predecessors Hattusili and Mursili, the Great King Tudhaliya led his troops across the Taurus. Once there, the city and kingdom of Aleppo became a prime focus of his attention. Aleppo had long since risen from the ashes of its destruction by Mursili, and was now once more a thriving royal capital ruled by a succession of kings who extended their sway over the neighbouring territories. But it was no longer the great power it had been in earlier days, and already in the century preceding Tudhaliya's Syrian campaign it had become subject to Mittani. That's why Tudhaliya had his sights set so firmly on it. Almost certainly, the ultimate aim of his Syrian campaign was to weaken if not eliminate Mittanian power on the western ('Syrian') side of the Euphrates, and thus greatly reduce the threat of Mittanian campaigns further west. Aleppo was an important bulwark of Mittanian power in Syria. By one means or another, its allegiance to

Mittani had to be broken. Far better to do this through diplomatic negotiation than by force of arms. A Hittite alliance with Aleppo, if not actual control of it, was a crucial step towards ridding Syria of its Mittanian overlord.

Like many of the rulers of Syrian states throughout history, Aleppo's king faced the threat of being crushed between two major players in their contests for supremacy over the region – in this case, Hatti and Mittani. Neutrality was impossible. The Aleppan had to decide which of the two powers posed the greater threat to his kingdom if he opposed it and supported the other. Initially, it seems, he chose to support Hatti. That meant abandoning his Mittanian allegiance and bringing down upon himself the wrath of the Mittanian king. But he calculated that the best chance for his kingdom's survival lay with Hatti, and so he made peace with Tudhaliya. The Mittanian king would have none of this, and persuaded, or intimidated, him into switching back to his former allegiance. Infuriated, Tudhaliya unleashed his troops on the city and destroyed it. Allegedly both the Aleppan and the Mittanian kings perished during Tudhaliya's onslaughts.

Now I should say that much of this information comes from the preamble to a treaty concluded a century or more after the events recorded here. The treaty was drawn up in the first decades of the thirteenth century by the Hittite king Muwattalli II with Aleppo's current king Talmi-Sharrumma.[1] Aleppo was now a vassal state of the Hittite empire, and Talmi-Sharrumma was warned of the dire consequences to his kingdom if he violated his obligations to his overlord. Muwattalli reinforced this warning by recounting what allegedly happened when Aleppo broke its peace accord with Hatti in earlier days.

How much of this information is reliable – given that the preambles to Hittite treaties are often biased and selective in their accounts of the past? We can probably accept the basic truth of a Hittite campaign conducted into Syria by Tudhaliya, the setback this may have caused to Mittanian imperialist enterprises, and the re-emergence of Hatti under Tudhaliya's leadership as an international power. But we should be highly sceptical about the extent of the damage this inflicted on the Mittanian empire (alternatively called Hanigalbat in the text). The Mittanian king certainly survived any confrontations he may have had with Tudhaliya. And Tudhaliya's campaign across the Taurus provoked just one of a series of conflicts between Mittani and Hatti. Many more decades would pass before one of the contestants finally emerged triumphant.

As yet, there is no indication that Tudhaliya or indeed his immediate successors sought to establish permanent control over the Syrian territories where the Hittites had campaigned successfully. But it became increasingly clear that some form of lasting authority or influence over the crossroads of the ancient Near East was important if not vital to Hatti's development as an imperial power. And not just for military or political reasons. Many of the routes that passed through Syria, either eastwards through Mesopotamia and the lands beyond, or southwards to Egypt, or northwestwards to Anatolia, carried trade items important for the maintenance of a kingdom unable to produce these items itself. They included commodity metals like tin, which was alloyed with copper to produce bronze. So far, we have no evidence that tin was mined in Anatolia in this period, or at least in sufficient quantities to sustain bronze-making industries, though there were many sources of copper in the region. Since tin had probably to be imported into Hatti from sources as far distant as Afghanistan, it was essential that the supply-routes which brought it, along with other trade items, into the Hittite kingdom were kept secure against enemy attacks and raids by local brigands.

THE KING HEADS WEST

It might seem extraordinary, then, that with their external interests so firmly oriented to the lands lying to their southeast, the Hittites should also commit their resources to campaigns in the west, perhaps all the way to the Aegean Sea. These campaigns are reported in what remains of the so-called Annals of a King Tudhaliya. We can't be absolutely sure that he was the same Tudhaliya who campaigned in Syria, or another king so called (and if he was the same king whether his western enterprises preceded or followed those he conducted in Syria). But in the interests of simplicity, I'll attribute all military campaigns conducted by a Tudhaliya in this period to just one king.

In his Annals,[2] Tudhaliya tells of his extensive military operations in western Anatolia, including the region called Arzawa. We've noted that 'Arzawa' was a term applied in Hittite sources to a group of western lands, among which a kingdom we now refer to as 'Arzawa Proper' or 'Arzawa Minor' (simply called 'Arzawa' in our texts) seems to have been prominent. Four other countries are listed as members of the Arzawa group. All are shown on Map 6.1. Beginning with northwestern Anatolia, they are Wilusa, Seha River Land, Mira and Hapalla. It's possible that the Arzawa lands were originally components of a single kingdom, which later split into separate states. But they may have developed independently of one another from the beginning of their existence.

In any case, the region where they were located was inhabited by the most populous of the Indo-European groups in Anatolia – the Luwians. Almost certainly Luwians became the largest population group of the Arzawa lands. Through central and southern Anatolia too, Luwian-speakers had spread themselves widely during the early centuries of the second millennium. And in Anatolia's southeastern corner, particularly in the land called Kizzuwatna, they became one of the two major population groups of the region. (Hurrians made up the other group.) Right along the southern Anatolian coast, Luwian elements survived for centuries after the collapse of the Bronze Age civilisations.

In the surviving fragments of his Annals, we learn of two campaigns conducted by Tudhaliya in the west. During the first of these, he allegedly conquered Arzawa and a number of other lands, and brought home with him captured infantry and teams of horse as booty. But far from intimidating the western countries, his campaign merely fuelled their hostility against him. A military confederacy of 22 states and cities along the Aegean coast declared war. Tudhaliya returned promptly to the west to deal with this new threat, and claimed a decisive victory over the confederacy. He refers to it as his conquest of Assuwa, from which we assume that Assuwa was the general name for the region where the alliance members were located. (Some scholars believe that the Graeco-Roman name Asia was derived from Assuwa.) In an attempt to reduce, if not prevent absolutely, further threats from the conquered regions, he took from them for resettlement in the Hittite homeland some 10,000 infantry and 600 teams of horse along with the confederacy's elite charioteers – the so-called 'lords of the bridle'.

A rebellion by the deported enemy militia was crushed and the ringleader killed. So overall – and taking Tudhaliya's account at face value – the king's western campaigns were resoundingly successful. But his victories came at a cost. As in the reign of Hattusili I, the commitment of Hittite military forces to campaigns in the far west left the homeland vulnerable to attack by enemy forces from other directions. Particularly the Kaska people, tribal groups who inhabited the mountainous Pontic region on the southern shores of the Black Sea. While Tudhaliya and the bulk of his army were fighting in the west, Kaskan tribesmen invaded and devastated parts of their homeland. When the king got back home, he drove the invaders from his lands, and followed this up in the next campaigning season with a retaliatory invasion of Kaskan territory.

But it was not only the Kaska people he had to worry about. The eastern frontiers of his kingdom were also dangerously vulnerable, most critically at times when the kingdom lacked sufficient defences to protect them while the bulk of the army was elsewhere. They were susceptible particularly to renewed attacks by Mittani, with the support of allies located in the frontier zone between the two kingdoms. One of these, Isuwa, fluctuated in its backing for Hatti and Mittani, and could certainly not be counted on by Tudhaliya at times when his eastern frontiers were under threat of a Mittanian invasion.

All this raises for us a major question.

WHY DID THE HITTITES GO WEST?

When Hittite core territory was left so exposed to enemy attacks while the bulk of the kingdom's forces were fighting elsewhere, when the Hittites' interests lay primarily in protecting their northern and eastern frontiers, and extending their power and influence southeastwards into Syria, and when they faced the constant threat of destruction by the powerful Mittanian army, why did they bother with the west at all?

Before answering this question, I'd like to relate a personal anecdote. When I was a young student, one of my favourite pieces of art from the ancient world was the bull-jumping fresco discovered at Knossos in Minoan Crete. A reproduction of it hung for many years on the wall of my study. But when I finally realised my dream of visiting Crete and seeing the original of this 'masterpiece' of ancient art, my initial response was one of deep disappointment. With the exception of a few small faded fragments, what I saw was almost entirely reconstruction, pure guesswork – though of course the intelligent, informed guesswork of experts in the field. And as my disappointment receded, I accepted that it was better to make what we could of the few scraps that were left to us and to try to recreate the composition to which these scraps belonged than to do nothing. At least the reconstruction gives us a partial glimpse into the world of the original, inaccurate though its details may be.

The same applies to our attempts to reconstruct the history of the Hittites. More often than not, we have to try to recreate this history from fragmentary texts which often represent only a small fraction of the documents of which they were a part. It's rather like attempting to do a thousand-piece jigsaw when only a few pieces of the original are left and we have to use our imagination and powers of deduction to supply the missing pieces – fully aware that we'll often get it only partly right, or almost completely wrong.

The remains of Tudhaliya's 'Annals' are a case in point. We have a number of isolated scraps of information from them – our 'jigsaw pieces' – which we use in our attempts to reconstruct the history of the king's reign. What makes this reconstruction more difficult is that we cannot unreservedly accept at face value the information that it, and texts like it, contain. There may be a significant difference between the true facts of an episode and what the author who records it wants us to believe. All the documents that provide us with a basis for reconstructing Hittite history are slanted to present their composers in the most favourable light.

We have no objective, independent contemporary historians to chronicle from an impartial viewpoint the episodes that make up the kingdom's history. This is not to deny that there may often be much truth among the spin. Most scholars accept that the bald, matter-of-fact nature of the majority of Hittite records gives the information they supply a greater ring of authenticity than the flamboyant rhetoric which is so marked a feature of the records of Egypt's pharaohs or the rulers of the Neo-Assyrian world.

Bearing all this in mind, let's return to our question. Why did the Hittites make substantial commitments of their military resources to far-distant campaigns in the west, with all the risks this entailed of attacks on their homeland during their absence, and in view of their clear interest in establishing and maintaining their influence in Syria – which lay in precisely the opposite direction to their western enterprises?

My view is that the Hittites believed they had no choice. It is clear from both Tudhaliya's Annals and what's left of those of his successor Arnuwanda, that the western Anatolian states had the capacity to form powerful alliances among themselves. While individually these states posed no serious risk to Hatti, in combination they could become a distinct danger to it. So much so that western forces led by Arzawa invaded Hatti's southern lands, and along with other forces around its periphery threatened to obliterate the entire kingdom. Indeed the pharaoh Amenhotep III, whose reign covered much of the first half of the fourteenth century, believed that the Hittite kingdom was finished. He wrote to the king of Arzawa about a proposed marriage-alliance, no doubt as the prelude to a diplomatic alliance, in recognition of the Arzawan king's potential status as the new overlord of Anatolia.[3]

CHAPTER 8

LION OR PUSSYCAT?

B uilding a large kingdom or empire involves a catch-22 situation. If your kingdom remains small, you will almost certainly be absorbed by a more powerful neighbour. But the more you grow your kingdom, the larger its boundaries become, and the more you expose your territories to attacks by external forces. Hittite kings simply could not leave the west to its own resources. If they did, an alliance of states from the region could pose as serious a threat to the security of Hatti's lands as an eastern alliance under Mittanian leadership. Reluctant as they were to commit to campaigns in the west, the Hittites undertook them essentially for defensive purposes – sometimes only after the failure of repeated attempts to resolve contentious issues with problematic western countries by peaceful means. The lion of ancient Anatolia often sought to play the role of a pussycat.

THE CONSTANT FUGITIVE

This becomes evident in a fascinating document composed by Tudhaliya's successor Arnuwanda, initially his co-regent and probably his adopted son. The document is commonly called the Indictment of Madduwatta.[1] It's in the form of a long letter of complaint written by King Arnuwanda to someone called Madduwatta. Tudhaliya had appointed Madduwatta subject-ruler of a rugged land called Zippasla which probably lay somewhere on the southwestern or western fringe of Hittite subject-territory, not far from the eastern edge of the Arzawa lands. He had fled as a refugee to Tudhaliya after a dispute with 'a man of Ahhiya' called Attarissiya. 'Ahhiya' is a rare, early shorter form of 'Ahhiyawa'. And so we assume that Attarissiya (whom Forrer identified with the legendary Greek king Atreus, or at least his namesake) was a Mycenaean Greek.

As the designation 'man' (LÚ) indicates, Attarissiya was not a king, for which the term LUGAL would have been used. He may have been a Greek of noble origin who had established himself on the Anatolian mainland, either as an agent of a Greek mainland king, or as an independent operator. He had the backing of a small army of infantry and at least 100 chariots, which he no doubt intended to use to extend his influence and power in Anatolia. Madduwatta may originally have been one of Attarissiya's subjects, or the ruler of a neighbouring land, forced to flee after falling foul of him. He took with him a substantial body of followers, including not only family members and retainers, but also troops and chariots.

Initially, Tudhaliya welcomed the refugee and set him up with a small principality of his own on the periphery of Hittite subject-territory. He probably reinforced his already existing nucleus of an army with additional infantry and chariotry. Terms and conditions were imposed upon him, very similar to those imposed by later Hittite kings on vassal rulers. Tudhaliya's expectation must have been that the refugee-turned-subject-ruler would provide a useful bulwark against Arzawan encroachment on Hittite territory. This would lessen the need for further costly campaigns in the west by the Hittite king himself. For despite his alleged string of decisive conquests of the Arzawan lands and other western states, all these states retained their independence of Hittite authority – and could at any time re-form their coalitions and once more threaten the security of the Hittite kingdom. Setting up a trusted subject-ruler in command of a small army on the edge of Hittite territory in this region might help reduce the threat without the need for direct Hittite intervention.

Of course all this depended on the subject-ruler remaining both loyal to and an effective agent of Hittite interests in the region. Madduwatta proved to be neither. He had plans of his own. Through both the remainder of Tudhaliya's reign and at least the first years of Arnuwanda's, Madduwatta repeatedly violated his obligations to his Hittite overlord – so we may conclude from

Arnuwanda's litany of complaints against him. Seeking to carve out a mini-empire for himself in southwestern Anatolia, he invaded Arzawa, in defiance of the express instruction of his overlord. But he achieved nothing except a massive retaliatory attack from the Arzawan king Kupanta-Kurunta, who invaded and occupied his land. Madduwatta was forced to flee for his life. Tudhaliya sent Hittite troops to the rescue, who drove the enemy from his land and restored it to him.

THE FUGITIVE TURNS TREACHEROUS

Then Attarissiya reappeared on the scene with his army, intent on killing Madduwatta and seizing his land. Once again, Madduwatta fled before the invaders, and once again Tudhaliya despatched an expeditionary force to expel the enemy. The mission successfully completed, Madduwatta was once more reinstated in his land. But Tudhaliya was now having serious doubts about his subject's trustworthiness – and his ultimate intentions. So he ordered the Hittite expeditionary force to remain with Madduwatta for the time being, no doubt to keep an eye on the serial fugitive's conduct, and ensure that he remained under control. But His Majesty was outwitted. Madduwatta contrived to rid himself of his unwelcome guests by secretly plotting with other nearby forces, who lured the Hittites into an ambush and then set about destroying them and killing their commander.

Surprisingly, there seems to have been no retaliatory action from Tudhaliya. At least none that we hear of. This emboldened Madduwatta to go one step further by appearing to conclude an alliance with the Hittites' arch-enemy, Kupanta-Kurunta, king of Arzawa. The alliance was to be cemented by a marriage between K-K and Madduwatta's daughter in Madduwatta's territory. K-K would be the honoured guest. But it was all a put-up job, or so Madduwatta wrote to his overlord,[2] to enable him to get K-K into his clutches and then assassinate him.

The text becomes fragmentary at this point, but it seems that K-K became suspicious of what his son-in-law-to-be was up to and called the whole thing off. The Hittite king too seems to have been suspicious of Madduwatta's ultimate intentions. Even so, when the text becomes clearer we find him increasing the territory governed by his treacherous vassal. This enabled Madduwatta to extend his own power further into western Anatolia, adding large slices of Arzawan territory to his now rapidly expanding kingdom. All the time he claimed he was merely acting as the agent of Hittite interests in the region.

The Madduwatta problem continued to plague Tudhaliya's successor Arnuwanda through his co-regency down into his sole rule. Madduwatta added more and more territory to his de facto kingdom in the southwest, including the land of Hapalla (which Arnuwanda protested was now Hittite territory) and probably the region called the Lukka Lands, which would have extended their conqueror's sway to Anatolia's southwestern coast. Pirates operating from Lukka later attacked coastal cities of the land Alasiya (Cyprus) as well as cities lying on the coast of Egypt. Very likely Lukka ships formed the fleet with which Madduwatta now attacked Alasiya. Again Arnuwanda protested. The people of Alasiya were Hittite tributaries! But what made Madduwatta's attack on their land intolerable above all else was that he carried it out in collaboration with his former enemy Attarissiya – the man from whom he had fled to Arnuwanda's father!

Here endeth the first tablet of the tale of Madduwatta. The story must have continued on a second tablet, now lost to us, and maybe the treacherous refugee-ruler got his come-uppance in the end. But that's mere speculation. The part of the story we do have presents us with an intriguing game of brinkmanship by Madduwatta. The Hittite lion who had rampaged through the cities and kingdoms of Syria in Hattusili's and Mursili's reigns seems now to have become a mere pussycat toyed with by a cunning rat. Madduwatta is portrayed as a treacherous, unscrupulous villain who consistently abused the trust placed in him both by the king who had granted him asylum in the first place and his successor who allowed him to build his own 'mini-empire', with virtually no retaliation beyond a few slaps on the wrist.

AN EXAMPLE OF DIPLOMATIC SPIN?

At least that is the way it appears to us. We must keep in mind when reading this document that it presents a purely Hittite viewpoint of the whole matter, which may be far from a balanced one. What would Madduwatta's own response have been to the string of accusations made against him? The words put in his mouth by the document's author may well provide a distorted and incomplete version of what the accused may actually have argued in defence of his actions. In any case, we don't know what the main purpose of the 'Indictment' was. On the surface, it seems to portray the first kings of what I have called the New Kingdom as weak and gullible, particularly in their dealings with the west. James Mellaart was prompted to comment that at this time Hittite power in the west counted for nothing.

Yet what emerges most strongly from the Indictment is the Hittites' extreme reluctance to get themselves directly and permanently involved in western Anatolian affairs. Let me stress again that Hatti's political and military interests lay primarily in asserting its influence in the southeast, and keeping at bay its enemies to the north, east and southeast of the homeland. Threats from the western lands were an annoying but unavoidable and dangerous distraction. If a few military campaigns in the region were sufficient to deter these threats, then so much the better. At this stage in their history, the Hittites were not interested in establishing permanent control over the lands they conquered in the west. With the exception of Hapalla, the western lands retained their independence after Tudhaliya's campaigns. And despite what the Indictment says, Madduwatta may have been given considerable leeway by his overlords in fulfilling his own territorial ambitions in the west when he extended his military enterprises into western lands like Arzawa and probably Lukka.

But there were times when he risked taking his ambitions too far. He did so when he invaded Hapalla and Alasiya, lands claimed by Arnuwanda as Hittite possessions or tributaries. In these cases, he had the good sense to pull back, after testing the limits of Hittite tolerance. His skill lay in keeping open the communications with his overlords and continuing to acknowledge or pay lip service to their supremacy – convincingly enough to enable him to pursue his own goals. And his overlords let him do so, as long as he helped buffer the Hittite frontiers against threats from the west, by taking over some of the western lands for himself, while he still remained, at least officially, a Hittite subject.

So what was the actual purpose of the Madduwatta document? What we have in the Hittite archives must be a copy of an original sent to Madduwatta himself – otherwise, there would be no point in the document at all. I think it most likely that the so-called Indictment is intended as a prelude to a new set of agreements between Madduwatta and his current Hittite overlord Arnu-wanda. The subject-ruler is called upon to acknowledge his past misdemeanours as a means of clearing the space for a new pact with the Great King, involving concessions on both sides: Madduwatta would still continue to hold sway over the territories he had won in the west, while acknowledging overall Hittite sovereignty, and keeping out of the territories the Hittites already claimed as their own. Arnuwanda may well have hoped that this would be enough to keep western lands like those of the Arzawa group out of the Hittites' hair – a least for the time being.

All this is my take on the Madduwatta document and my attempt to read between its lines. Can you provide a more plausible interpretation?

PROBLEMS ELSEWHERE

We don't know what eventually became of Madduwatta, but his current boss Arnuwanda had to turn his attention urgently to threats to his kingdom's security from other regions. A serious crisis had emerged in the homeland's northern territories when Kaska tribal groups crossed the Hittite frontier and sacked many cult-centres in the region. The devastation inflicted by the invaders is described in a prayer to the Sun-Goddess by Arnuwanda and his queen Asmunikal:

> The Kaska-men destroyed your temples and smashed your images, O gods. They plundered silver and gold, libation vessels and cups of silver, gold and copper, your objects of bronze and your garments, and they shared them among themselves. They divided up the priests, the holy priests, the priestesses, the anointed ones, the musicians, the singers, the

cooks, the bakers, the ploughmen, and the gardeners, and made them their servants [. . .][3]

Arnuwanda simply did not have the resources to mount effective armed resistance to the invaders. All he could do was try to keep them from advancing further into the homeland by drawing up a series of pacts or treaties with them, no doubt conceding to them much Hittite territory they had already won. Similarly, he sought to secure his lands south of the homeland by treaties he concluded with the peoples and cities there, like the important port-city of Ura on the southeastern coast. And he sought to renew Hittite influence over Kizzuwatna by settling in the kingdom military colonists from a region called Ismerika binding them in allegiance to him. The treaty in which he did so still survives.[4]

Yet all this was little more than band-aid diplomacy, and in any case was overshadowed by alarming news from the east. Mittani was on the rise again! It had a new king, Artatama, probably the son and successor of Saushtatar. What made this news worse still was that Egypt had once more cast an aggressive eye on the Syrian region, under two successive pharaohs, Amenhotep II and Tuthmosis IV. Worst of all, the second of these pharaohs made an alliance with the Mittanian king, cemented by a marriage between the two royal houses. No longer would the two Great Kings fight over Syrian territory. They reached an amicable agreement to divide it between them. Egypt won control of Qadesh on the Orontes river, along with the Syrian coastal states of Amurru and Ugarit. All territory beyond in northern Syria was conceded to Mittani. This agreement left no room for any form of Hittite influence in the region where Arnuwanda's father appears to have effectively campaigned just a short time before. But the loss of this influence was soon to prove the least of the Hittites' problems.

CHAPTER 9

FROM NEAR EXTINCTION TO THE THRESHOLD OF SUPREMACY

A rnuwanda may have been a conscientious ruler who did his best with the limited resources at his disposal to stabilise his kingdom and keep its enemies at bay. But his kingdom remained a fragile one, and on his death a crisis of catastrophic proportions was rapidly approaching. That was the situation facing the new king Tudhaliya, whom we'll call the third of that name. Once more, Kaska tribes were at the forefront of the problems. Arnuwanda's probably naive efforts to pacify them by diplomatic means achieved at best a temporary respite before these aggressive mountain people were on the move again, crossing the Hittite frontiers, now pushed further south, in hundreds-strong raiding parties which looted Hittite towns and cities, and plundered Hittite grainlands.

URGENT BULLETINS TO REGIONAL OFFICIALS

Thanks to major finds made in fairly recent years, we have some up-to-date accounts of these raids. From the 1970s onwards, excavations have uncovered several important cities within the Hittite homeland, already known from references to them in texts from Hattusa. These cities served as administrative centres of the kingdom, and all have provided us with tablet archives. They are Sapinuwa, the largest (modern Ortaköy), Sarissa (modern Kuşaklı) and Tapikka (modern Maşat). We'll focus on the third of these. Tapikka, where excavations began in 1973, served as both an administrative centre and a military outpost in the homeland's northern frontier region. It lay 100 km northeast of Hattusa. Within the remains of the city's chief building (the so-called 'palace'), 116 tablets dating to the first half of the fourteenth century were found, 96 of them containing the texts of letters.[1] Many came from the Great King himself and were addressed to his local officials in Tapikka. They provide an excellent example of the hands-on approach, or micro-management style of His Majesty. This was particularly important at that time in Hittite history, when the kingdom was under severe threat from the Kaskan forces, not least because of their plundering of what was probably one of the richest grain-producing areas of the homeland. It was not only the Hittites' territory that was at risk but also, quite literally, Hatti's bread of life!

The letters exchanged between the king and local officials, who were often summoned to Hattusa for face-to-face briefings with His Majesty, could best be described as bulletins, hastily written and reflecting the king's concerns of the moment. There are none of the niceties of more formal communications. This is what the king writes to an official in Tapikka: 'Thus His Majesty: Say to Kassu: "Re what you have written to me about the chariots, note this: I have now sent forth the chariots. Look out for them."' The bulletins contain demands by the king for up-to-date reports of enemy movements in the region; there are also responses to officials' requests for auxiliary troops to reinforce a region's existing defences, instructions from the king regarding the relocation of populations in areas most directly threatened by the enemy, and instructions about the treatment of defectors and enemy prisoners.

The urgent tone of many of the bulletins provides a kind of microcosm of how grave the situation was confronting the kingdom in Tudhaliya III's years. Yet the mood of doom and gloom that pervades many of the communications is occasionally lightened by pieces of trivia. These are due to the scribes who actually wrote the documents. Sometimes they appended short notes to the official communications, personal postscripts for their scribal colleagues at the other end. Thus after writing down His Majesty's instructions to a Tapikka official about action to be taken over enemy troop movements in his region, the scribe adds a note of his own:

> To Uzzu, my beloved brother(-scribe), from your beloved brother Surihinili: I hope all is well with you. May the gods keep you safe! Just to say that everything is fine with your house (in Hattusa). And everything is fine with your wife. There's nothing for you to worry about. My beloved brother, do send back your greetings to me.

Sometimes the tone of these notes is not so cordial. It seems that one of Uzzu's brother-scribes in Hattusa had sent him a maid-servant on loan. Problems arose when the maid started pinching the family silver (or the Hittite equivalent). Uzzu complained repeatedly until his correspondent wearily replied 'You keep writing to me about my maid. I don't want to hear anything more!' This prompted Uzzu to take the matter into his own hands by threatening to punish her himself, probably with a good beating. Her owner had no desire to receive back damaged goods, so he wrote to Uzzu: 'See that you hand her over to the messenger in good condition and he will bring her back to me. And whatever the girl has stolen you can take threefold compensation for it.' I rather like these little appendages. Ephemeral and trivial though they may be, they bring us very closely in touch, for a moment, with ordinary people in the Hittite world, as well as providing some light relief in an otherwise very grim period in the kingdom's history.

HATTI UNDER EXISTENTIAL THREAT

It is almost certainly to Tudhaliya's reign, some time during the first half of the fourteenth century, that we can assign the events referred to in a document by a later king, Hattusili III. We are presented with a scenario of apocalyptic proportions:

In earlier days the Hatti lands were sacked by its enemies. The Kaskan enemy came and sacked the Hatti lands and he made Nenassa his frontier. From the Lower Land came the Arzawan enemy, and he too sacked the Hatti lands, and he made Tuwanuwa and Uda his frontier. From afar, the Arawannan enemy came and sacked the whole of the Land of Gassiya. From afar, the Azzian enemy came and sacked all the Upper Lands and he made Samuha his frontier. The Isuwan enemy came and sacked the Land of Tegarama. From afar, the Armatanan enemy came, and he too sacked the Hatti lands. And he made Kizzuwatna, the city, his frontier. And Hattusa, the city, was burned down.[2]

This text gives the impression of a massive simultaneous attack on Hittite territories from many directions. Hence the term 'Concentric Invasions' commonly used to describe the events narrated. That would imply close co-ordination among the invaders. But such a high level of planning seems unlikely among such widely diverse enemies. The attacks recounted in the passage may well have occurred, though possibly over an extended period of time. And while their impact on Hittite territory may indeed have been devastating, they could hardly have left the entire land of Hatti in ruins and under enemy occupation as the text's author would have us believe. Otherwise, the Hittite kingdom would simply have been wiped off the map. Tudhaliya did eventually regain his lost territories – which means he must have had a reasonably large base from which he organised his fight back. And, contrary to the impression given by the text, it is possible that there was some ebbing and flowing in Hatti's fortunes during this period, with some of the lost territories being recovered before other parts of the kingdom were invaded.

It may well be that the Hittite capital was captured and destroyed in this period. But before then, the king had time to shift his royal court to an alternative secure location. This would in fact have been the first of probably three occasions when the royal seat of the kingdom was shifted elsewhere – for different reasons in each case. Where did the king go, and whom did he take with him?

The most likely answer to the first question is that he shifted his court to a city called Samuha. We have yet to identify the remains of this city, but it probably lay in the east of the kingdom, perhaps on the upper course of the Marassantiya river or even further east on the Euphrates. We conclude that Samuha became the new royal seat from the fact that it served as the base for Tudhaliya's campaigns to drive out the invaders and regain his kingdom.

This we learn from the biography of the king's partner in the fight-back programme and his successor on the throne – a man called Suppiluliuma, the first of two Hittite kings of this name. The biography called in the Hittite text 'The Manly Deeds of Suppiluliuma' (DS for short) was composed by Suppiluliuma's son and second successor Mursili (II).[3] It's our main evidence for the remarkable comeback in which Tudhaliya and Suppiluliuma not only succeeded in regaining all their lost territories, but laid the foundations for the greatest phase in the history of the Hittite kingdom.

Before moving to this, let's give a bit more thought to what was undoubtedly one of the most significant achievements of Tudhaliya's reign – the shift of the seat of the kingdom to the east. Consider what this entailed. The evacuation of Hattusa with all its important possessions, the statues of its gods, its priests, its palace functionaries, its militia and a large part of its population as well, must have been a highly planned and carefully executed operation – with all the risks of moving to a new location an entire city through many miles of territory infested with enemy forces. This new location must have been prepared some time in advance, and already sufficiently fortified to protect the newcomers while they consolidated their position there. The obvious success of the operation was in its own way equal to any of the achievements of Hittite kings on the field of battle. It becomes all the more noteworthy when we think of other such ventures which ended, as this one easily could have, in disaster. I have in mind the biblical account of the attempt by the Jewish king Zedekiah to abandon Jerusalem secretly when it was under siege by the Babylonian Nebuchadnezzar's forces, only to be caught with his army in open territory. His forces were routed, and he himself was captured and suffered a terrible punishment. Read about it in 2 Kings 25.

THE TIDE TURNS

Surviving fragments of DS provide us with scraps of information about Tudhaliya's campaigns of reconquest. Most of these campaigns were conducted in partnership with his comrade-in-arms Suppiluliuma. As far as we can tell, the overall plan of recovery was to concentrate firstly on the enemies nearest the Hittites' operating base at Samuha, in particular the Kaska people in the north and the warriors of the land of Azzi-Hayasa in the northeast. Their forces were flushed from the homeland, and the Hittites followed up their counterattacks against them by invading and plundering their own lands. The Kaska region in particular was subjected to repeated onslaughts. These inflicted heavy casualties and ended with large numbers of prisoners-of-war, booty-people, being brought back to the Hittites' base territory. Suppiluliuma was later to take away Azzi-Hayasa's independence and make it a Hittite subject-state. Then, as the homeland was slowly won back, Tudhaliya and Suppiluliuma turned their attention further westwards. Here, they liberated former Hittite subject-territories like the Hulana River Land and then went on to attack and ravage the countries that had occupied them.

But the most dangerous of all the Hittites' Anatolian enemies had yet to be confronted. Arzawa formed the largest and most powerful enemy bloc, and the territories it covered in the west were vast. Conquests of them would take Hittite armies far from their homeland. Unfortunately at this time, Tudhaliya seems to have suffered repeated bouts of illness (perhaps as a result of war wounds?) and was increasingly confined to his bed in Samuha. But resolution of the Arzawa problem could not be delayed indefinitely, and Suppiluliuma sought from the king permission to take over his forces as sole commander-in-chief for operations against the western invaders: 'O my lord! Send me against the enemy from Arzawa!' The king gave his consent, and thus Suppiluliuma's Arzawan campaigns began.

His undertaking was no easy one, and its ultimate success long remained elusive. To be sure, he claimed great victories against his foe, but he suffered major setbacks as well. As one group was defeated, others rose up and joined forces with fellow enemy-groups against the Hittite counter-offensive. Even when Suppiluliuma finally managed to expel all the Arzawan troops from Hatti's peripheral territories, Arzawan military might continued to pose a major threat to the kingdom's security. Hittite campaigns into Arzawan territory were undertaken to eliminate this threat, and sometimes ended in humiliating defeats. It allegedly took Suppiluliuma 20 years to re-establish Hittite control in Anatolia, or at least in the regions which were subject to Hittite authority. His Anatolian campaigns may have begun while Tudhaliya occupied the throne, but they must have continued well down into his own reign. And we cannot be sure that Tudhaliya ever again saw Hattusa. He may have died in Samuha before the ravaged city was once more able to serve as the kingdom's royal seat.

ANOTHER ROYAL COUP

Despite the close relationship between Tudhaliya and Suppiluliuma, especially as partners on the battlefield, Suppiluliuma was not the designated heir to the throne. Another Tudhaliya, called in the texts 'Tudhaliya the Younger', had been given the nod. Why not Suppiluliuma? Both he and 'the younger' Tudhaliya were apparently sons of the elder Tudhaliya. And by his military exploits Suppiluliuma had certainly proved himself worthy of the throne, especially in those troubled times. But the other man had been clearly marked out for the job – perhaps because he was the older of the two (despite his epithet), or, it has been suggested, Suppiluliuma may have been an adopted son of the former king who preferred the succession to pass to his natural son. In any case, Tudhaliya the Younger was clearly the legitimate appointee to the throne, and initially Suppiluliuma and all the dignitaries of the land and all the armed forces swore allegiance to him.

We don't know whether the new Tudhaliya ever occupied his throne. But despite his oath of allegiance, Suppiluliuma's ambition to become king could not be restrained. As tensions increased between the two 'brothers', many of the land's powerful elements swung their support behind Suppiluliuma, and the hapless Tudhaliya was assassinated. To be completely fair to Suppiluliuma, the text which tells us this (one of the prayers of Suppiluliuma's son Mursili II) doesn't explicitly say that Suppiluliuma actually took part in the murder. Of course he may well have dropped hints to this effect in the hearing of his supporters. But he may have had in mind a less drastic fate for Tudhaliya, like exile, where a number of out-of-favour members of the royal family ended up at various times in Hittite history. Even so, the usurper had obviously 'sinned' by violating his oath of allegiance to Tudhaliya, and was at least indirectly responsible for his death. Finally, according to Mursili, the gods by whom oaths of allegiance were sworn took vengeance on Suppiluliuma and his supporters for their treacherous behaviour by wiping them all out in a plague.

But that was many years in the future. In the intervening period, Suppiluliuma mounted the throne and proved himself the greatest of Hittite kings – at least the greatest of the warrior-kings. He did so by making his kingdom, which had recently teetered on the brink of extinction, the supreme military power of the Near Eastern world. The kingdom of Hatti could now truly be called an empire.

CHAPTER 10

THE GREATEST
KINGDOM OF THEM
ALL

D espite its military might, the Hittite empire could never
be secure while Hatti's most powerful rival continued to
flourish and dominate much of the eastern part of the
Near Eastern world – the kingdom of Mittani. The total destruction
of Mittani would soon become, if it not already was, Suppiluliuma's
major objective for much of the rest of his career. This would mean
taking the war to the enemy, leading his troops across the Euphrates,
deep into the heartland of Mittanian territory, occupying and
sacking the Mittanian capital Washshuganni and then conquering all
Mittani's subject-territories in Syria.

DIPLOMATIC PREPARATIONS FOR BRUTE FORCE

To begin with, Suppiluliuma needed to tread carefully. Above all,
he had to avoid upsetting Egypt. As he was aware, Egypt and
Mittani were bound in a treaty-alliance, and the last thing he
could have wanted was to bring Egypt into a Hittite war with
Mittani, on Mittani's side. The risk of doing so would be
intensified if the Hittite started picking off Mittani's Syrian allies
and subjects, without giving some sort of reassurance to the
current pharaoh, doubtless Akhenaten. Egypt had subject-
territories in southern Syria and Palestine, and the pharaoh

Figure 10.1 Suppiluliuma I.

might reasonably be concerned that a Hittite conquest of Mittani's Syrian subjects would pave the way for Suppiluliuma's seizure of Egypt's territories to the south.

Hence Suppiluliuma made a point of maintaining friendly relations with the pharaoh, as he recalled in a letter he wrote to one of his first successors:

> Neither my messengers whom I had sent to your father, nor the request which your father had made in these terms: 'Let us establish between ourselves nothing but the friendliest of relations' – I have not refused these. All that your father said to me, I did absolutely everything. And my own request, that I made to your father, he never refused it; he gave me absolutely everything.[1]

Whatever diplomatic overtures Suppiluliuma made to the pharaoh were apparently successful. Relations between the two kingdoms remained peaceful throughout the period of Suppiluliuma's Mittanian and Syrian campaigns. This was despite complaints from some of the pharaoh's Syro-Palestinian vassals about alleged

Hittite subversive activities and military intervention in their territories. The pharaoh's clear intention to avoid getting caught up in a conflict between Hatti and Mittani was a good outcome for Suppiluliuma.

While preparing for a final showdown with Mittani, Suppiluliuma received further good news. The Mittanian king Shuttarna II had recently died, and on his death conflict had broken out between factions within the royal family over the succession. As Suppiluliuma well knew from his country's own history, conflicts of this kind could weaken and divide a kingdom, making it vulnerable to outside attack. The Mittanian throne was seized by a man called Tushratta, but his occupation of it was challenged by a second claimant, Artatama. This may have been the time Suppiluliuma chose to launch an attack across the Euphrates on the land of Isuwa, one of the countries whose forces had invaded and occupied Hittite territory during the dark days of Tudhaliya III's reign. Now at last Suppiluliuma was ready to take retaliatory action against it. But Isuwa was an ally of Mittani, and it's very likely that Suppiluliuma's campaign brought the new Mittanian king Tushratta into the field. Tushratta won a resounding victory against the Hittites – at least that's what he told the pharaoh in a letter he wrote to him.[2]

Tushratta may have exaggerated the magnitude of his victory, but a Mittanian victory it almost certainly was. And as Suppiluliuma retired to lick his wounds, he could reflect that he had learned an important lesson from the encounter. Tushratta had proved himself a formidable foe. Mere military might would not be enough to beat him. Force would need to be combined with effective diplomatic action if the Hittite warlord was to achieve ultimate success. And so before launching an all-out assault on Tushratta's kingdom, Suppiluliuma made overtures to his Mittanian rival Artatama, and concluded a treaty with him. The treaty hasn't survived, so we don't know what its terms were. But at the very least it probably helped ensure that Artatama and the forces that backed him would not stand in the way of a Hittite campaign against the Tushratta regime. This was presumably on the understanding that if the campaign were successful and

Tushratta was killed or at least driven from power, Suppiluliuma would support Artatama's accession, followed up by friendship between the two kingdoms. Of course if Suppiluliuma did make such an agreement, he must have done so with his fingers firmly crossed behind his back, as later events were to prove.

In the lead-up to war, he also made attempts by diplomatic means to win away from the Mittanian side some of its allies and subject-states in Syria – with mixed results. His great prize was Ugarit, a wealthy Syrian coastal state. Ugarit was a valuable timber-producing region, and had rich, fertile steppes excellent for grazing purposes and the production of abundant quantitities of grain and other agricultural products. It was the centre of thriving manufacturing industries, and contained four or more seaports, including its capital city, also called Ugarit. But other Syrian states refused to have anything to do with Suppiluliuma, and in fact carried out reprisal attacks on Ugarit for joining him. But Suppiluliuma honoured the terms of alliance he had made with the Ugaritic king Niqmaddu II by sending an expeditionary force to his rescue, driving the invaders from his land and adding substantial slices of their territory to his ally's kingdom. Later Ugarit was to become a Hittite vassal state, rather than just an allied one. It became the Hittites' Syrian 'jewel in the crown'.

Suppiluliuma won over at least one other Syrian state to his side, the kingdom of Nuhashshi, and may well have sought to extend his influence into, if not his authority over, a number of Egyptian vassal states, if we are to believe the complaints of some of their rulers to Akhenaten. But the majority of Syrian states remained firm in their Mittanian allegiance. They would have to be won over by force of arms, for Suppiluliuma was now ready to embark on his final showdown with Mittani.

OPEN WAR WITH MITTANI

Once more, he crossed the Euphrates, conquered the land of Isuwa, then struck into the heartland of Tushratta's kingdom, capturing and plundering its capital Washshuganni. He had moved with such speed and ferocity that Tushratta was caught completely offguard, and could do no more than take to his heels, abandoning his capital and taking with him as many of his troops as he could extract from it. Then Suppiluliuma swung back across the Euphrates, and in what appears to have been a series of lightning attacks conquered Mittani's subject-states and allies between the Euphrates and the Mediterranean coast, all the way down to the borders of Damascus. He stopped there because Damascus lay within Egyptian subject-territory – which for the Hittites was a no-go area.

The kings of the conquered states and cities were deposed and deported together with their families to Hattusa. This included the ruler and leading citizens of the city of Qadesh on the Orontes. Suppiluliuma had actually intended to bypass the city, acknowledging that it was then under Egyptian sovereignty. But when its ruler launched an unprovoked attack on his troops, he seized the city and added it to his list of conquests. All this Suppiluliuma claimed to have achieved in a single year. There has been much scholarly debate about the actual length and the specific details of this so-called 'One-year Syrian War'. But whatever its length and however sweeping Suppiluliuma's victories, Tushratta remained beyond the Hittites' grasp. The final conquest of Mittani had yet to be achieved.

It would be some years before that happened. Before his Syrian conquests were firmly bedded down, Suppiluliuma suspended his eastern operations and returned to his homeland. Almost certainly this was because of renewed threats to the core territory of his kingdom by the Kaska people, and renewed anti-Hittite uprisings throughout the Anatolian region. The king's preoccupation with his Mittanian and Syrian enterprises no doubt provided one of the main incentives for these. Suppiluliuma may now have spent a number of years back in Anatolia to reassert his authority there. And while doing so, he assigned operations in Syria to deputies, notably his son Telipinu. Matters came to a head when Tushratta, sensing a weakening in the Hittite momentum against his kingdom, made one final attempt to restore his authority west of the Euphrates by launching an attack on the region around Carchemish, which was itself a Mittanian stronghold. Telipinu responded by leading a Hittite army against his forces, taking control of much of the territory outside Carchemish and establishing there a winter camp, a fortified settlement called Murmuriga. From here he could renew his operations the following spring. But the city of Carchemish itself remained unsubdued, and the Hittite camp was placed under siege by Tushratta's forces.

Alarmed at the dire consequences that could follow from a Mittanian victory and the capture of his army, Telipinu sought an urgent meeting with his father who was in southern Anatolia at the time. The briefing from his son left Suppiluliuma in no doubt that he had to return to Syria at the earliest possible opportunity, and with all the forces he could muster. It was a make or break situation for the Hittites. Decisive and prompt action from the king was essential. As soon as the winter had passed, he prepared for his return to a Syrian theatre of war. Pausing briefly on the way at a place called Tegarama, he carried out a full review of all his troops and chariotry. And from them, he formed an expeditionary force under the command of his son, the crown prince Arnuwanda. The expeditionary force was sent ahead of the main army to carry out preliminary operations in the Syrian region and pave the way for the arrival of the main military force, under the command of the king himself.

Capturing Carchemish, Mittani's last major stronghold, became Suppiluliuma's prime military objective. Its conquest would strike his enemy a lethal blow and virtually rule out all possibility that the Syrian states would ever again have a Mittanian overlord. Carchemish was placed under siege by Hittite forces under the king's personal command.

Appeal from an Egyptian royal widow

It was during preparations for the siege that a letter was brought to the king from the queen of Egypt.[3] When its contents were read out to him, Suppiluliuma stared in amazement at the messenger. 'Such a thing has never happened to me in all my life,' he declared. The letter announced the sudden death of the queen's husband, pharaoh of Egypt. But the cause of Suppiluliuma's amazement was the request the royal widow had made of him: that he provide one of his sons to become her next husband, and consequentially Egypt's next ruler. This was because the royal dynasty of Egypt had come to an end, the queen said, and she refused to marry anyone of lesser status among her own countrymen.

Suspicious of her request, Suppiluliuma despatched his vizier to Egypt to check out the truth of the matter. The main reason for his suspicion was that the now deceased pharaoh had recently ordered an attack upon the city of Qadesh, formerly an Egyptian subject but now under Hittite sovereignty. The Hittites had repelled the attack and carried out a retaliatory one on Egyptian subject-territory further south. But Suppiluliuma's fury at this act of treachery, all the greater because of his own alleged scrupulousness in keeping out of Egyptian territory in his war with Mittani, remained unabated. He now suspected that the queen's letter was merely a front for further Egyptian treachery.

While his vizier was on his way to Egypt, Suppiluliuma completed his conquest of Carchemish and returned to Hattusa before the winter snows set in. But before doing so, he took a momentous step in the history of the Hittite empire. In the wake of his capture of Carchemish, he appointed his son Sharri-Kushuh as Hittite viceroy there. Around the same time, or perhaps earlier, he appointed another of his sons Telipinu, whom we have already met, as viceroy in Aleppo. He set up Telipinu as ruler there after taking prisoner the previous local king and despatching him and his family as deportees to Hattusa. Thus for the first time in Hittite history direct Hittite rule was established over parts of the kingdom outside the homeland. In Suppiluliuma's newly acquired Syrian territories, his appointed viceroys in Carchemish and Aleppo had bestowed upon them all the chief functions of the Great King of Hatti – military, administrative, judicial and religious. All other Syrian territories conquered by the Hittites became Hittite vassal states, their rulers bound by treaty to their Hittite overlord.

The following spring the king's vizier returned from Egypt, along with Egypt's leading envoy Hani. Both bore assurances that the queen's appeal to Suppiluliuma was sincere. There was no-one left of the royal line to succeed the dead pharaoh, and the request for a Hittite prince to mount the throne of Egypt could be taken at face value. A furious letter from the pharaoh's widow accompanied the diplomats. In it the young queen took Suppiluliuma to task for doubting the truth of her request. After some self-righteous grumbling in response to the letter, Suppiluliuma was won over, no doubt highly attracted by the prospect that his son would be the new pharaoh, and that all future pharaohs would have Hittite blood in their veins. So he despatched one of his five offspring to Egypt for the royal wedding, a young man called Zannanza.

Shortly afterwards, news came that Zannanza had been killed on the journey. And despite protestations of innocence from the new pharaoh Ay, now hastily installed on his kingdom's throne, Suppiluliuma held the Egyptians responsible for his son's death. A punitive expedition was sent to raid and plunder Egyptian vassal territory by way of revenge.

Ironically, the thousands of prisoners-of-war which the Hittites deported to the homeland in the wake of this expedition brought with them a plague which allegedly ravaged the homeland for 20 years, decimating the population. Suppiluliuma himself, and his son and first successor Arnuwanda, were among the plague's victims.

So who was the dead pharaoh? In the *Deeds*, he is called Niphururiya. This the Hittite form of his name corresponds precisely to Egyptian Nebkheperure, the throne-name of the pharaoh Tutankhamun. And we know that Tutankhamun's death did in fact bring to an end the famous Egyptian Eighteenth Dynasty. His wife in the *Deeds* is simply referred to as *dahamunzu*, a Hittite rendering of an Egyptian term meaning 'wife of the king'. If Tutankhamun was the pharaoh in question, then the queen who wrote to Suppiluliuma must have been his wife Ankhesenamun. These identifications, I believe, are the correct ones. But other scholars identify the pharaoh as Akhenaten, and in that case *dahamunzu* would have been his wife Nefertiti. If they're right, then we would have to make a number of alterations to our reconstruction of the history of this period. But I don't believe that is necessary.

What we can be sure about is that the whole episode put an end to all possibility of a peace between Hatti and Egypt. In fact, tensions between the two kingdoms continued to mount from this time onwards, finally culminating in the famous battle of Qadesh in 1274. We'll get to this later.

THE END OF MITTANI AND THE RISE OF ASSYRIA

With the fall of Carchemish to the Hittites, Tushratta's days were clearly numbered. He still eluded capture by the Hittites, and his whereabouts remained unknown. If he had in fact gone into hiding, he was finally tracked down by his own countrymen and assassinated. Among the assassins was one of his sons, probably a man called Shattiwaza.

But his death did not mark the end of Hittite campaigns in the region. For another six years or so, the Hittites continued military operations on both sides of the Euphrates. The throne of what remained of the former Mittanian empire, now commonly known by a traditional name Hanigalbat, was occupied by Artatama. By then an old man, he appointed his son Shuttarna as regent. We recall that Suppiluliuma had made a treaty with Artatama many years earlier which probably promised Hittite support for his succession, and presumably for that of his rightful heirs. But the fall of Tushratta, and his empire with him, had created, for the Hittites, another problem in its wake – the rise of Mittani's former vassal Assyria.

Already in Akhenaten's reign, the Assyrian king Ashur-uballit had made clear his aspirations of joining the 'Club of Great Kings'. Worryingly for the Hittites, Shuttarna began establishing close ties with Assyria, which could in the future pose just as great a threat to the security of Hatti as Mittani had done. Suppiluliuma dealt with the problem by establishing close ties of his own, with Shattiwaza, son and probably co-murderer of his father Tushratta. Marrying off one of his daughters to Shattiwaza to strengthen further his bonds with him, he then instructed his son Sharri-Kushuh, viceroy of Carchemish, to conduct with Shattiwaza a series of military campaigns through former Mittanian territory. These resulted in the capture of the region's most important cities, the demolition of the current regime and the installation of Shattiwaza as the new

Great King of Mittani. It was a title in name only. Shattiwaza was
no more than a puppet ruler subject to the Hittite Great King.

SUPPILULIUMA'S LEGACY

An account of Suppiluliuma's operations against Mittani must have
been the highlight of his biography, written by his son Mursili. But
unfortunately, this part of the biography is almost entirely lost to
us. Our knowledge of what happened is based largely on a small
number of other texts. Notable among these are two treaties
(particularly their historical preambles) concluded between
Suppiluliuma and Shattiwaza.[4] Though they constitute a single
diplomatic agreement, the treaties are presented as if Suppiluliuma
was the author of one and Shattiwaza the other – to preserve for
Shattiwaza the fiction of diplomatic independence.[5] It hardly needs
saying that we must allow for some degree of exaggeration and
'selective reporting' in what these Hittite-biased documents tell us.
They are not objective historical accounts, but purpose-designed to
present Suppiluliuma's conflict with Mittani in the light most
favourable to the Hittite cause.

So what really was Suppiluliuma's legacy, to his successors
in particular and to the Hittite world in general? Undoubtedly he
was a brilliant military commander who was largely responsible
for bringing his kingdom from the brink of extinction to its peak as
the most powerful Great Kingdom in the Near Eastern world.
In the process, he had destroyed the Hittites' long-standing
and most formidable enemy, the kingdom of Mittani. He had also
firmly consolidated the foundations of empire by his development
of the vassal state system whereby the rulers of local kingdoms
were bound to him as their overlord by formal agreements called
treaties. And he had established, for the first time, direct rule over
important parts of the Hittite world far removed from the
homeland – by installing viceregal seats at Carchemish and Aleppo.
Henceforth, these remained centres of direct Hittite power in Syria
until the end of the Hittite empire.

On the downside of things, Suppiluliuma's elimination of the
Mittanian empire had paved the way for the resurgence of Assyria,

which would quickly take over all Mittani's former territories east of the Euphrates and pose a serious threat to Hittite territories on the other side of the river. He had left relations between Egypt and Hatti in a precarious state, and it was only a matter of time before a strong new Egyptian dynasty would emerge to challenge Hittite authority in Syria. In Anatolia, Hatti's authority had yet to be fully established, and almost immediately after the king's death there were widespread uprisings in many parts of the region. The severe plague which devastated the homeland for many years was an unintended consequence of the Hittite expedition despatched by Suppiluliuma against Egypt's Syro-Palestinian states to avenge the death of his son. And within the palace he left his first two successors with a major problem – the serious abuse of power by his current chief wife, a Babylonian princess who used the royal title Tawananna as a personal name.

CHAPTER 11

INTERMEDIARIES OF THE GODS: THE GREAT KINGS OF HATTI

B efore we see how Hittite history unfolded after Suppiluliuma's death, let's focus for a while on the Great Kings of Hatti as a group. They were the most powerful men in the Hittite world, and indeed in the whole of the Near Eastern world for much of the last half of the Late Bronze Age. I've already spoken of the kings' role as the military leaders of their people and the warrior culture they embodied, and I'll have more to say about this below. But equally important were the kings' other major roles and responsibilities. What were these? And who ensured they were carried out?

First, let's briefly recapitulate something we talked about earlier. One of the remarkable features of the Hittite kingdom is that through the 500 years of its existence, supreme power in the land was exercised, almost without interruption, by a single royal dynasty, founded some time in the early seventeenth century. Even after the collapse of the kingdom in the early twelfth century, members of this dynasty continued to hold sway in the Euphrates region, notably at Carchemish, for at least several more generations. What makes the dynasty's longevity all the more remarkable is that it came from a minority ethnic group within the kingdom, speakers of the Indo-European language called Nesite. Indo-European speakers had been in Anatolia for many generations, probably many centuries before

Figure 11.1   Hittite double-headed eagle, symbol of imperial power, Alaca Höyük.

the beginning of the Hittite era. And while they mingled with the indigenous and much larger Hattian population, a number of them had retained their ethnic identity and managed to establish their supremacy over the land that became the nucleus of the Hittite kingdom. Of course we've already seen that the history of the Hittite monarchy was sometimes stained with the blood of coups and attempted coups as rival branches of the royal family sought to install one of their own on the seat of power by seizing it from its incumbent or his designated successor. But it all stayed within the family, and apart from an occasional interloper, the same royal blood flowed through the veins of all occupants of the Hittite throne, even though this blood was regularly diluted by marriage links with distinguished foreign families.

THE GODS' DEPUTY

Strictly speaking, the king's person was sacrosanct. He held power by divine right, for he was the gods' chief representative on earth, the intermediary in all things between them and their mortal worshippers. His role as chief priest of the Hittite realm is sometimes depicted in relief sculptures where he wears the skullcap and ankle-length robe of priestly office, and carries a staff with curved end, another of his insignia of office. In royal propaganda, he claims divine endorsement for his authority by stating that he was 'favoured by (all) the gods', who collectively extended their protection over their approved deputy-on-earth. But each king also had a special patron deity (for example, Mursili II's patron was the Sun Goddess of Arinna, Muwattalli II's the Storm God of Lightning, Hattusili III's the goddess Ishtar) who kept their protégé safe from harm both in war and in peace. In this respect at least, the divine protectors seem to have been pretty good at their job, because out of a total list of 29 rulers of the Hittite kingdom only a few were driven from the throne or assassinated, and (with one *possible* exception) none were killed or fatally wounded in battle, despite the numerous, often yearly, campaigns in which they engaged.

The downside of being the gods' deputy-on-earth was that you had also to bear responsibility for offences committed by your subjects, offences which provoked the wrath of the gods and could only be appeased by an appropriate punishment. Sometimes your life could be threatened by divine wrath. You might be forewarned of this in a dream, or through examination of the entrails of a sacrificed animal. If the news was bad, you could try to avoid punishment yourself by appointing a substitute – human or animal or life-sized wooden image – to take your place during the period you were deemed most at risk. In the case of an animal substitute, the victim was taken to a high place, where it was clearly visible to the offended deity, then sacrificed and burnt, representing the death and cremation of the king. A human substitute if used was generally a prisoner-of-war who would quite literally become king for a time – dressed in the king's regalia, and 'anointed with the fine oil of kingship'. The real king was dismissed from the palace, his replacement was wined and dined and he slept in the royal bedroom. This was during the period when it had been ascertained from divine consultation that the real king was most vulnerable. But if the danger-period passed with the substitute none the worse for it, he was sent back to his own land unharmed and the real king resumed his position. (All this recalls an Old Babylonian substitution rital, the difference being that in the Babylonian one, the substitute *was* actually executed at the end of his brief period on the throne.)

If you yourself as king had committed some egregious offence which provoked divine wrath, then your entire kingdom could be made to suffer for it. Foreshadowing Old Testament belief, the sins of the fathers could be visited on their sons, just as the sins of the kings could be visited on their subjects. Thus Suppiluliuma's son King Mursili II finally ascertained through oracular enquiry that the plague which ravaged the Hittite land allegedly for 20 years was due to divine wrath caused by several offences, including the violation of an oath and the neglect of sacrifices, which his father had committed years before. Once these offences were identified, appropriate expiation could be made and the affliction brought to an end.

The king's religious obligations included constant tours through his land to attend and participate in the kingdom's most important religious festivals. These often lasted many days and were regular annual events in the religious calendar. If a king failed to turn up, the consequences of divine displeasure could be severe. But he had other pressing duties to attend to as well, and sometimes of necessity he had to appoint high-ranking deputies, notably members of his own family, to stand in for him when the celebration of a particular festival normally required his personal presence.

THE KING'S SECULAR RESPONSIBILITIES

Two other responsibilities of kingship stand out conspicuously. The first we've already referred to. Royal ideology required the king to be a great warrior, and to demonstrate regularly his abilities on the field of battle. As preparation for kingship, he was trained in the arts of war from an early age and often gained experience on the battlefield itself when he was barely more than a child. After assuming kingship, he could expect to spend most years of his reign leading his army against enemy or rebellious vassal states. Success on the battlefield, demonstrated by large processions of booty-people – prisoners-of-war – through the streets of his cities, along with cartloads of treasure taken from his victims, provided the king's subjects with tangible evidence of his prowess as a great warrior. This was an essential attribute of kingship. Interestingly, though the king's military campaigns and triumphs were recorded in great detail in the texts, relief sculptures of the king as a warrior are rare. And in striking contrast to Egyptian iconography and Assyrian reliefs of a later age, surviving Hittite reliefs never portray the king in battle. In the few cases where he is depicted as a warrior, he is kitted out for battle in armour and with weapons, but in a static position, sometimes in isolation and sometimes in the presence of a god. War iconography plays little part in Hittite royal propaganda.

The king's other chief responsibility was to oversee the administration of justice in his land. We can probably see a visual symbol of this in the curved staff, often referred to by the Latin word *lituus* (from the similarly shaped staff carried by Roman augurs), which the king sometimes holds in relief carvings where he is depicted as a priest. The staff has been interpreted as a stylised shepherd's crook. In a broad sense, it might have symbolised the king's role as shepherd of his people, particularly as guardian of those most in need of his protection. The symbol is used by the Babylonian king Hammurabi in his Laws, where he portrays himself as the arbiter of justice in his land, and particularly as the protector of the weakest and most vulnerable of his subjects. In a Hittite context too the 'shepherd's crook' may reflect the king's role as the protector of his people in his role as Chief Justice. But unlike Hammurabi and other Mesopotamian rulers, Hittite kings never include the epithet 'Shepherd' among their titles; in a Hittite context, only the Sun God is called 'the Shepherd of Mankind'.

Many of the king's judicial responsibilities could be and were delegated to local officials within his administration, including regional governors whose duties required them to act as circuit judges, touring their provinces to preside over local assizes where various civil and criminal cases were to be tried. But all the king's subjects had the right of appeal to His Majesty himself against a verdict handed down to them at a lower court. Thus a priest in the city of Emar on the Euphrates who was involved in a dispute with a

Figure 11.2   Suppiluliuma II as warrior, Hattusa.

local garrison commander over property and taxes successfully appealed to the king against a lower court ruling which had found in favour of his opponent. Also, certain major offences, including sorcery, bestiality, various forms of moral pollution and a range of other offences which attracted the death penalty were judged in the king's court, and in many cases by the king himself in his capacity as Chief Justice of the land. Of course, the king's numerous other

responsibilities and commitments must have led to frequent
delegation of this role to another member of his family or to
someone else high in authority in the kingdom's elite ruling class.
The important point is that even the lowliest of the king's subjects
had recourse to the highest authorities to settle their grievances by
judicial process.

The 'Great Family'

When he was not off travelling on military campaigns or religious
pilgrimages, the king lived in heavily fortified and isolated
splendour in his palace on Hattusa's acropolis, today known as
Büyükkale ('Big Castle'). But mere bricks and mortar, even when
coupled with assurances of divine protection, were not in
themselves sufficient to ensure the safety of His Majesty's person,
from conspiracies and coups at home, and against his enemies
abroad. A lot of human backup was needed as well. This no doubt
came in many layers. But the innermost core of it was an elite,
highly trained spear-bearing bodyguard called the *MESHEDI*.
Comparable in some respects to Rome's praetorian guard (though
their numbers were much smaller), the *MESHEDI* provided an
immediate first-line barrier between the king and his subjects and
enemies, whether he was on tour (he had royal residences along his
tour routes), on campaign, or at home. Their commander, the
GAL.*MESHEDI*, was one of the most powerful and influential men
in the kingdom. Generally, if not always, he was a close relative of
the king, often his brother or son. Thus the future king Hattusili III
held this post while his brother Muwattalli occupied the throne,
and when Hattusili himself was king, he appointed his son and heir
Tudhaliya to it.

Among other members of the 'Great Family', and arguably at
times the most powerful of them all, was the king's chief wife,
traditionally called the Tawananna. We shall deal with her
separately in Chapter 20. The king also acquired one or more
concubines (no doubt to ensure a suitably large pool of royal
offspring for marriage alliances, diplomatic posts, potential heirs to
the throne etc.), arranged in a kind of pecking order. As we know

from Telipinu's Proclamation, sons from concubines were eligible to succeed to the throne in the event that the king's chief wife failed to provide him with an heir. A special status was accorded to whichever son the king designated as his successor. Called the *tuhkanti*, he was often trained from an early age in the various responsibilities of kingship, religious, administrative and military, to ensure a smooth succession after his father's death.

BECOMING A GOD

So what happened to a king after his death? Let's begin with his funerary rites. While the multitude of surviving festival and ritual texts provide almost no information about a king's coronation ceremonies (which must have been elaborate and lasted quite a few days), we do have a quite detailed description of the burial ceremonies prescribed for a king, and also his queen. As with all ritual texts, the rites associated with a royal burial had to be performed with scrupulous attention to detail, ensuring that the whole process was error-free, and that the deceased had a smooth transition from this world to the next. Fourteen days of ritualistic procedures are prescribed. They begin on Day 1 with a solemn intonation: 'When a great sin befalls Hattusa and the king or queen becomes a god, [...]'. An ox is sacrificed and placed at the feet of the corpse. As its throat is cut, the sacrificer addresses the corpse: 'What you have become let this become! May your soul descend into this ox!' A libation of wine is poured. Drained of its contents, the wine vessel is smashed. It is not for use again, at least not in this world. A male goat is swung to and fro over the corpse, for purificatory purposes.[1]

On Day 2, food offerings and libations are made, and in the evening the body is placed on a pyre and consumed. At dawn on Day 3, the burnt pyre is sifted for the king's bones which are cleaned and placed on a chair at the head of a banqueting table laden with food and drink. For the king is the honoured guest at his funeral banquet, his presence further made clear by a seated statue of himself amidst the festivities. So too a seated statue of the queen occupies a prominent place in the ceremonies that attend her death and burial. Feasting and sacrifices continue for several days. Then on Day 6, the bones are taken to what is called the *hekur*-house, their final resting place, and laid out on a couch. There are further offerings, and the feasting continues as the air is filled with the dirges of the musicians and the lamentations of wailing women, and is heavy with the aroma of fresh bread and roasting meats intermingled with the terror-soaked stench of sweat, blood and excrement of the sacrificed animals. These animals – cattle and sheep, horses and asses – will provide the king with livestock in his new world. A piece of turf, cut from the ground and taken to the burial place, symbolises the dead man's pasturelands, part of the king's estate in the next world where His Deceased Majesty will spend eternity in peace and comfort.

But this idyllic life-after-death was not entirely self-supporting, for the dead man's cult required a fair amount of upkeep from the king's survivors. Apart from the king's *hekur*-house, a tomb of stone – of which, alas, we have no firmly identifiable surviving examples – areas of land were set aside for the maintenance of the deceased, with livestock and personnel to go with them. The latter, lifetime employees, included gatekeepers, herdsmen, domestic servants and farm-hands. Entry to the king's tomb, however, was strictly limited to the dead man's immediate family. It was their responsibility, and above all the responsibility of the king's heir, to ensure the maintenance of a cult in his honour, involving regular offerings of sacrificed animals to his spirit.

So too at lower levels of Hittite society, ancestor cults were maintained in honour of the deceased, and sacrifices made to them, to keep alive their memory and help them maintain contact with the living members of their family. But like many of their fellow-Near Easterners, the Hittites seem to have had a pessimistic view of life after death – at least for the lesser members of society. The few Hittite texts we have which refer to the afterlife generally treat it as a gloomy, sunless netherworld region accessed by pits, holes, and shafts dug into the ground. And one of these texts tells us that when you get there, you have only foul water to drink and bits of mud to eat, and you don't recognise any of your relatives, including your mother or your sisters and brothers, nor they you.

But this one-off text may be unduly negative. Archaeological evidence gives a slightly more positive impression. We haven't found any royal tombs, but we *have* discovered a number of burial grounds, outside the cities (and dating mostly to the early Hittite period), containing the remains of mortals of lesser status. Cremation and inhumation were both used to dispose of bodies, sometimes in the same burial ground. Ceramic vessels stored the ashes of the cremated, and earth-graves in which the bodies were laid out intact were dug for those who preferred inhumation. Simple grave-gifts, like small pots, were interred with the bodies, sometimes along with the bones of animals, such as cattle, sheep, pigs, dogs and sometimes also horses and donkeys. Maybe these were intended purely as sacrificial offerings, maybe their purpose was to serve the dead in the next life. If the latter, then the Underworld may not have been quite as bad a place as the texts that refer to it would have us believe.

And as we have noted, the king and no doubt his family (or selected members of it) could apparently look forward to an afterlife of pleasurable ease, where they were endowed with meadowlands stocked with cattle and sheep, horses and mules, in something perhaps resembling the Elysian fields of Classical tradition, where Greek heroes, like their gods, could while away eternity in blissful ease. Indeed, Hittite kings actually joined the ranks of the gods after departing this life. This we learn when a king's son and heir refers to his father's death by saying: 'When my father became a god [. . .]'. Words meant quite literally – but with a qualification. Deceased kings didn't make it into the divine pantheon of the Hittite world. They were gods of a lesser order. But statues were made in their honour and set up in the temples of the Great Gods. Their spirits could enter these statues so that they continued to receive homage and tribute from all their subjects, not just their own family members. Ancestor cults were, as we've noted, common at all levels of society. But royal ancestor cults operated on a national scale.

Incidentally, the expression 'becoming a god' finds an echo in a much later age. Emperors of the Roman imperial period customarily had divinity bestowed upon them on their death. But

one of them, the down-to-earth, no-nonsense ex-military
commander Vespasian, was highly scornful of this deification
rubbish. And when he became aware that his own death was
imminent, he's reported to have brushed the thought of it aside
with the wonderfully cynical comment *Vae, puto deus fio*: 'Oh dear,
I think I'm becoming a god.' What a great exit line!

Of course, there were many societies which conferred divinity
upon their rulers, like the ancient Egyptians, or whose rulers
assumed divinity for themselves, during their lifetimes; the Roman
emperor Caligula and the Macedonian general Alexander the Great
spring to mind. And indeed the question arises as to whether some
of the late Hittite kings, specifically those of the last century of the
empire, also claimed divine status during their lifetimes. This
question is prompted by a significant development in the Hittite
visual arts in this period. From the reign of Muwattalli II, which
began about 1295, to the end of the empire, Hittite kings had
images of themselves carved on large stone surfaces – either cliff-
or rock-faces or surfaces of built stone. In these public monuments,
the king and sometimes the queen are depicted in ceremonial
priestly garb paying homage to one or more of their gods.
Sometimes the king appears kitted out as an armed warrior.
In other cases, he wears a skullcap, in his priestly capacity, but
sometimes a high conical hat, like the ones worn by male deities.
As a rule, the god can easily be distinguished from his mortal
worshipper by horns attached to his hat, a symbol of his divine
status. The more horns, the more important the god. But
sometimes the king in these reliefs also wears a horned hat. This
probably does not mean, as sometimes supposed, that he has
assumed divine status during his lifetime or that he is the spirit of a
dead, deified king. Rather, it is intended to set the living priest-king
apart from other priests by depicting him in garb virtually identical
with that of his patron deity, thus indicating his close identification
and intimate contact with the god.

That said, the third last king Tudhaliya IV *may* have claimed
divine status for himself while he was still alive, not just by wearing
the emblems of divinity but also in one inscription *apparently*
referring to a libation made to him – if the fragmentary text has

been correctly interpreted. Since libations were made only to gods, this would imply that Tudhaliya now presented himself to his people as a living god. The inscription is carved on stone blocks on a site, probably a sanctuary, now called Emirgazi. It is located in southern Anatolia on the Konya plain.[2]

So what do we make of all this? Why the appearance of these monuments, which dot the landscape of the Hittite realm in the last century of its history, and not before? Why the (suggested) assumption of divinity by a living king towards the end of this century? And there is something else I haven't yet talked about – the inscriptions which often accompany these monuments.

THE HIEROGLYPHIC INSCRIPTIONS

Let's deal with the inscriptions first. We should begin our discussion of these by going back to the nineteenth-century rediscoverers of the Hittites. You'll recall that Charles Texier and other explorers of the age found a mysterious hieroglyphic script carved on blocks of stone and cliff-faces at various sites in Anatolia and Syria. Later in the century, Archibald Henry Sayce concluded that the inscriptions written in this script represented the language of the people of a great empire – the Hittite empire. He believed that this empire was centred in Syria but spread to the westernmost parts of Anatolia. Now we've since established that what was actually the Hittite (strictly Nesite) language was written in a cuneiform script on clay tablets stored in the Hittite capital Hattusa and other administrative centres of the kingdom. But while Hittite/Nesite was the predominant language of the tablets, we've noted that a number of other languages written in the cuneiform script appear on the tablets as well. These include passages in Luwian, spoken by another of the Indo-European groups who settled in Anatolia.

But cuneiform was not the only script used for writing the Luwian language. In fact, Luwian written in a hieroglyphic script was the language used on the monuments scattered through Anatolia and Syria. In other words, the Hittite royal dynasty used not the Hittite language on the inscriptions of their public monuments, as Sayce and others had supposed, but the language, written hieroglyphically, of one of their subject populations – the speakers of Luwian. Already in the sixteenth century, this hieroglyphic script had begun to appear on seals, which were commonly stamped on documents for authentication purposes, or attached to larger objects to indicate ownership.

Later, it was used on the seals of kings and other members of his family for the same purpose. Indeed, one of the most impressive discoveries at Hattusa in recent years is an archive of almost 3,500 royal sealings, or seal impressions – far exceeding the total of all such pieces hitherto found. Typically, a king's name appeared in hieroglyphic form in the centre of the seal, and his name, and often that of his father and sometimes other royal predecessors, were written in cuneiform in concentric rings around the outer edge of the seal. But most significantly, the Luwian language in hieroglyphic form was the language used in inscriptions by the last century of Hittite kings, both in the capital and elsewhere in their empire, to proclaim their military achievements, their devotion to their religious duties, or sometimes just their names. These inscriptions were carved on stone blocks or natural rock surfaces, often with accompanying sculptures, for all to see.

But why use the language and script of their subjects, not their own language and script, for these public statements? The answer that immediately springs to mind is that a hieroglyphic script, with its picture-like signs, is much more appropriate for public display than the bureaucratically oriented cuneiform script. But there are other considerations as well. By the last century of the empire, Luwian-speakers were widely spread throughout the empire and were almost certainly the most populous of all its inhabitants. To speak to one's subjects, via public monuments, in their own language, might well have been considered an important means of bonding with these subjects, and reinforcing the spread of royal propaganda by proclaiming Their Majesties' close links with and devotion to the land's ultimate protectors – the gods.

There is another pragmatic consideration. Even the most illiterate of the king's subjects could have identified the names and titles of the inscriptions' authors when presented in their hieroglyphic form. So, for example, Tudhaliya IV could instantly be identified in his inscriptions by the hieroglyphic form of his name at the beginning of them – the figure of a god wearing a horned hat, with a mountain representing the lower half of his body, and below it an upturned boot. The name was commonly accompanied by the insignia of royalty: a winged sun disk above the figure, and the hieroglyphic symbols for 'Great King' and 'Labarna' on either side

Figure 11.3   Tudhaliya IV, Yazılıkaya.

of it. All this is depicted in the small group carvings in Figure 11.3. Similarly, a king's seal could instantly be recognised by the hieroglyphic form of his name in the centre of the seal, even if those who inspected the seal could not read the cuneiform inscription around its rim.

The great majority of the public monuments, carved in the last century of the empire and often decorated with both reliefs and hieroglyphic texts, have disappeared entirely. But there is little doubt that their widespread distribution throughout the Hittite realm was designed to promote the image of a firm, stable monarchy in this period. This was particularly important in the empire's last decades, as tensions increased between factions within the royal family, and as restiveness among the subject-states grew ever greater, intensified by the fear that the empire was close to disintegration. Visual propapaganda may well have been one of the means used by the last kings in an attempt to restore and maintain confidence in the ruling house of Hatti. In such a context, Tudhaliya may have sought to portray himself not merely as the one favoured by all the gods, but as a god himself.

Ultimately, it all proved to be of no avail. But that is a matter to which we shall return in our final chapter. For now, let us turn our attention to the events that followed the death of Suppiluliuma.

CHAPTER 12

KING BY DEFAULT

A 'MERE CHILD' ON THE THRONE

T he problems confronting Suppiluliuma's son and second
successor Mursili II could hardly have been more serious –
and they came in droves. Once more in his final years,
Suppiluliuma's preoccupation with mopping up the remnants of
the Mittanian empire prompted the Kaska tribes to launch new
waves of attacks on the Hittite homeland, destroying some parts of
it and occupying others. The king's sudden death *c*.1322 left the
new Kaska crisis unresolved. Fortunately, so it seemed, the Hittite
throne remained in good hands. The succession now passed to
Suppiluliuma's son Arnuwanda II, a battle-hardened, able warrior-
leader who had been well groomed for taking on the powers of
kingship. But then tragedy struck again. Within just a year or so of
his accession Arnuwanda fell ill and died. Both father and son were
probably victims of the plague which prisoners-of-war had brought
back to Hatti following Suppiluliuma's sack of Egyptian subject-
territory, in revenge for the death of his son Zannanza.

News that the new king Arnuwanda was terminally ill spread
rapidly through the kingdom. On his death, widespread uprisings
broke out among Hatti's subject-territories, and Hatti's enemies
mustered their forces for fresh invasions. All of them, enemies and
defecting allies alike, were the more encouraged to move in for the
kill when they heard who the new king was. Suppiluliuma's heirs
were running out. Zannanza had allegedly been killed on the way to
Egypt, Arnuwanda had just died, and two of the three surviving

Figure 12.1   Seal of Mursili II.

sons, Telipinu and Sharri-Kushuh, were fully engaged with the task of maintaining Hittite authority in Syria, where they had been appointed viceroys; any perceived slackening of Hittite control in this region would almost certainly have led to uprisings on a similar scale to those in the west. Perhaps even more seriously, a resurgent Assyria was beginning to pose a major threat not only to Hatti's subjects and allies east of the Euphrates, but also to Hittite territory west of the river. The conquest of Carchemish in particular was now firmly in the sights of the Assyrian king, as a first step to more extensive incursions into Hittite territory in Syria. Telipinu and Sharri-Kushuh could not afford to abandon their posts in the region.

That left only Suppiluliuma's youngest son, Mursili, to adopt the mantle of Great Kingship in Hattusa. As Mursili himself tells us, news of his accession was met with widespread derision, and enemy forces in ever greater numbers massed against the kingdom. Suppiluliuma and Arnuwanda were great warrior-kings, they all conceded. But what had they to fear now from a mere child with no experience of the battlefield, or anything else? But they gravely underestimated the new king. Inexperienced he may have been, but more than just a child. Already in his twenties at the time of his accession, he would certainly have already been blooded on the field of battle, perhaps many times. His father would have seen to that.

With all the courage, determination and ruthlessness of his greatest forebears, Mursili set about the task of defeating and repelling his enemies, bringing his rebellious vassals to heel and restoring to the kingdom its superpower status. The main account of all this is contained in the remains of Mursili's own Annals, which survive in fragmentary form in two series. One is a summary account of Mursili's own campaign achievements in the critical first ten years of his reign.[1] The other is a more detailed account of Hittite military campaigns covering this ten-year period but extending over some 27 years and including a record of the exploits of the king's military commanders. The two accounts are commonly referred to as the 'Ten-Year Annals' and 'The Comprehensive Annals' respectively. Unfortunately, much of the latter is now lost to us.

THE NEW ARZAWA CAMPAIGNS

But from what we can piece together from the remains of the Annals, we learn that Mursili spent the first two campaigning seasons of his reign driving the Kaska occupation forces from his homeland and carrying out punitive expeditions against them in their own territory. These were sufficient, it seems, to keep this perennial enemy subdued for the time being. That enabled their conqueror to set his sights on his western enemies and rebel states. Notable among these were the territories of the Arzawa lands. An added complication was that the leader of the most powerful of these lands, King Uhhaziti, ruler of what we have called 'Arzawa Proper', had formed an alliance with the king of Ahhiyawa, that is, with a Mycenaean king (if our Ahhiyawan-Mycenaean equation is correct). And the Land of Milawata (Classical Miletos) had done likewise. Milawata was brought to heel and destroyed by a Hittite expeditionary force despatched by Mursili. But the king himself led the main campaign army against his Arzawan enemy. He was joined by his brother Sharri-Kushuh with a contingent from Syria.

It took two years for Mursili to complete his Arzawan mission. But by the end of that time, Uhhaziti had abandoned his capital and fled to an offshore haven before the Hittite advance, his son who had taken over command of his army was resoundingly defeated in battle, and Mursili marched in triumph into his enemy's land. Ahhiyawa seems to have played no part at all in these operations, beyond perhaps providing asylum for Uhhaziti. Moral rather than military support may have been all it intended to offer anyhow to those who claimed alliance with it, especially with the arrival of a large Hittite army in the region.

Before returning to Hattusa, Mursili enforced the submission of other rebel states in the region, reducing them, or reducing them once more, to vassal status and subsequently drawing up treaties with their rulers. These treaties were an important element in the maintenance of Hittite authority over its vast empire. But we should note here that Mursili's main enemy, the ruler of 'Arzawa Proper', does not figure in any of the treaty arrangements. In fact, it's very likely that Mursili solved this particular 'Arzawa problem', by totally eliminating the kingdom – with a mass evacuation of its population back to the homeland (the king claims in his Annals that he deported 65,000 or 66,000 of the kingdom's inhabitants) – and probably by assigning its territory to the neighbouring state called Mira. Mira was also one of the Arzawa lands, and had appparently remained loyal to its Hittite allegiance when so many other states in the region had rebelled against it.

Deportation of the populations of conquered cities and kingdoms became a regular practice of Hittite kings, especially Suppiluliuma and Mursili in the wake of their conquests. The numbers of deportees varied from a few hundred in some cases to thousands in others – perhaps tens of thousands in the case of 'Arzawa Proper' (though the number may be exaggerated). These mass people-movements served two purposes: they reduced substantially the strength of a kingdom's human resources and thus reduced the likelihood of further uprisings by that kingdom, at least in the foreseeable future; and, very importantly, they helped restock the homeland's population – always a matter of pressing importance. Of course, the logistics of these deportations must have been enormous. They're something we'll consider later.

RENEWED PRESSURES FROM OTHER DIRECTIONS

Mursili's western campaigns were highly successful, not only because of the king's military victories in the region, but more importantly because of the stability which his campaigns left in their wake. But the king had little time to rest on his laurels, for there were further outbreaks of aggression to the north and northeast of his kingdom. Predictably, the Kaska people were prominent among the aggressors. Ruthless, retaliatory action by Mursili failed to subdue them for long. Hostilities often flared afresh in their lands shortly after they had been ravaged by the king's forces, sometimes within a couple of years.

But that was not the worst of Mursili's problems. Early in his seventh regnal year, trouble once more flared in Syria. This centred on the kingdom called Nuhashshi, whose ruler Tette had broken from his Hittite allegiance and called upon the pharaoh, then Horemheb, for support. Reinforcements for the rebel duly arrived from Egypt. Responsibility for crushing the rebellion was delegated by the king to his brother Sharri-Kushuh, viceroy in Carchemish. This left Mursili free to continue with his northern campaigns, and the utterly reliable Sharri-Kushuh succeeded in driving the Egyptian force out of Hittite territory and quashing the rebellion. For the time being.

But Mursili's problems were far from over. In the following two years, he was obliged to conduct further military operations against countries which threatened his northern frontiers. There were even more pressing concerns elsewhere. During his ninth year on the throne, Mursili left the management of his campaigns in the hands of deputies, while he himself travelled south to the city of Kummanni in Kizzuwatna. Kummanni was an important cult-centre and Mursili went there as a matter of urgency to celebrate an important religious festival, neglected by his father. But his stay in Kummanni served another purpose as well. For while there, he sent an urgent summons to his brother Sharri-Kushuh to meet him in the city.

We aren't told the purpose of the meeting, but it almost certainly had to do with a looming new crisis developing in Syria. This was due in part to the recent death of Telipinu, brother of Mursili and Sharri-Kushuh and Hittite viceroy at Aleppo. Telipinu's son Talmi-Sharrumma was ready to take his place, and may already have done so. But it was essential that the new viceroy be given every possible support by his uncles, to ensure that the change in leadership in Aleppo in no way signalled a weakening of Hittite authority in this vitally important part of the empire. How he could best be supported was very likely one of the major items of discussion in the meeting at Kummanni. Or was intended to be. But then an even greater blow fell.

While at Kummanni, Sharri-Kushuh suddenly fell ill and died. There is nothing in our records to suggest that foul play was involved, but we cannot rule it out. Sharri-Kushuh must have been a high priority target for disgruntled local Syrian rulers as well as for Hatti's foreign enemies. Both Assyria and Egypt had much to gain if this experienced and highly effective champion of Hittite interests in the region were eliminated. An agent acting on behalf of a local ruler, or the Egyptian or Assyrian king, could have abruptly ended the viceroy's career with the blade of a dagger or a poisoned chalice. Could Telipinu's death have been caused in the same way? The deaths of both viceroys probably within a few months, or even weeks, of each other, may well have been more than mere coincidence.

In any case, the passing of one so soon after the other seriously imperilled Hittite authority in Syria. Nuhashshi again rose up in revolt, and the city-state of Qadesh, where Suppiluliuma had appointed a vassal ruler, declared its independence. Worse still, the Assyrians fully exploited the Hittite crisis by crossing the Euphrates and capturing the viceregal kingdom of Carchemish. And to the northeast of the homeland the large and troublesome kingdom Azzi-Hayasa threw off its Hittite vassalhood and began attacking other Hittite subject-territories in the region called the Upper Land in Hittite texts. No doubt it was intent on carving out an even larger kingdom for itself in this region.

In the face of all this, Mursili once more displayed the true mettle of a great warrior-leader. Threats to the eastern part of his empire were met with prompt and decisive action. The king despatched an army under his experienced general Nuwanza to deal with the Azzi-Hayasan enemy in the northeast. His resounding success there resulted in the expulsion of all enemy forces from the Upper Land and the restoration of Hittite control over it. A second expeditionary force was despatched by Mursili under the command of his general Kurunta to deal with the Syrian rebels in Nuhashshi and Qadesh. Here too the campaign ended in decisive Hittite victories. Qadesh had been placed under siege, and victory over it was facilitated by the ruler's eldest son who killed his father and threw open his city's gates to the besiegers. Mursili himself undertook the reconquest of Carchemish. The Assyrians were driven out of the land, back across the Euphrates. Mursili installed Sharri-Kushuh's son on the viceregal throne. Then he proceeded to Aleppo where he formally installed Telipinu's son as viceroy.

For the rest of Mursili's reign, the region in Syria covered by Hittite vassal states seems to have remained relatively stable, no doubt due largely to the presence of the two viceregal kingdoms there. Both were ably managed by the current viceroys, as they had been by their fathers.

In the west, however, Mursili was confronted with new rebellions. These prompted further Hittite military operations, under His Majesty's direct command – though peace was finally restored to most of the region by diplomatic means, when Mursili concluded, or renewed, one-to-one treaties with the rulers of the Arzawa lands. Problems to the north of the homeland were not so easily resolved. Mursili spent much of the last half of his reign on regular campaigns in the north, where he claims to have led his troops further than any other Hittite king. But the campaigns were not always successful. And even when they were, Mursili had frequently to follow them up with further expeditions when the conquered lands quickly resurrected themselves, and rose again to cast off Hittite sovereignty. Not surprisingly, the Kaska people figure frequently in the king's northern campaigns. Despite all the efforts of Mursili and his successors, they would continue to harass, invade and plunder Hittite territory until the kingdom's very end.

PLAGUE

The account I have just given of Mursili's reign is confined largely to his achievements on the battlefield – understandably, because it is based on the king's Annals, which like all such Hittite records is essentially an account of the king's military campaigns and their outcomes. But we must insert into our story another important event not mentioned in the Annals. We learn of it not from bald historical records but from the king's prayers. In what are commonly referred to as the 'Plague Prayers', Mursili rebukes the gods for inflicting a devastating plague upon the Hittite land:

> O gods, what have you done? You have allowed a plague into Hatti, and the whole of Hatti is dying. No one prepares for you the offering bread and the libation anymore. The ploughmen who used to work the fallow fields of the gods have died, so they do not work or reap the fields of the gods. [...] To mankind, our wisdom has been lost, and whatever we do right comes to nothing. O gods, whatever sin you perceive, either let the Wise Women or the diviners(?) determine it, or let ordinary people see it in a dream! [...] O gods, have pity on the Land of Hatti! On the one hand it is oppressed by the plague, on the other hand it is oppressed by its enemies. [...] Now all the surrounding countries have begun to attack it![2]

As we have already noted, the plague was introduced into Hatti by prisoners-of-war brought from Egypt's Syro-Palestinian territories during Suppiluliuma's reign. It probably carried off both Suppiluliuma and his son and first successor Arnuwanda, and seems to have extended well into Mursili's reign. So we must add to the problems confronting Mursili, as he sought to reclaim Hatti's disintegrating empire in the early years of his reign, the likely substantial depletion of manpower available to him because of the effects of the plague. He says nothing of this in his Annals. But the prayer translated above leaves no doubt that, in Mursili's view at least, there was a direct link between the devastating impact the plague was having on his land and the encouragement this provided to Hatti's former allies to defect from it, and for all its enemies to renew their attacks upon it.

Unfortunately, though the Plague Prayers tell us about the consequences of the plague, they say nothing about its symptoms or manifestations. So what actually *was* the plague? There are a number of possible candidates. One is that it was an early form of tularemia.[3] Do you have any other suggestions? Mine, for what it is worth, is that it was bubonic plague, one of the forms of the 'Black Death' (pneumonic and haemorrhagic plague were other forms) which devastated the Byzantine world during Justinian's reign in the sixth century AD, Europe, Asia and Africa during the fourteenth century, and England in the seventeenth century. And that was not the end of it. In my home city Brisbane, Australia, there were outbreaks of this plague, carried by fleas on rats, in 1900 and every year after that until 1909, and again in 1921, with 115 cases and 63 deaths in total. (A small number, of course, compared with the vast numbers killed by it in the Byzantine and medieval eras.) According to the World Health Organization, bubonic plague is still killing people around the world. In 2013 there were 750 reported cases worldwide, with 128 deaths.

The name comes from the Greek word 'bubon' meaning 'groin' and reflects the most common physical manifestation of the disease – swellings in the groin area and swollen lymph nodes. In Old Testament tradition, the plague of festering boils, one of the ten plagues of Egypt inflicted by God on the country of the pharaoh who refused Moses' request to let the 'children of Israel' go, is quite possibly a biblical reference to bubonic plague (Exodus 9:9). Again in Old Testament tradition, the affliction the Philistines suffered by way of divine vengeance for seizing the Ark of the Covenant is described as 'an outbreak of tumours' or 'tumours in the groin' (1 Samuel 5:9). The actual cause of this affliction is indicated by the advice the Philistine priests and diviners gave for curing it: the ark was to be returned to the Israelites, along with a 'guilt offering', consisting of models of 'five gold tumours and five gold rats' (1 Samuel 6:4). By implication, the rats were associated with the disease itself. The linking of tumours and rats has led to the suggestion that the Philistines were suffering from bubonic plague. The handing over of expiatory offerings in the form of models of the chief agents of the disease would serve to remove it from its sufferers, by a form of sympathetic magic, a magical process by association, and through the grace of God.

Of course, we're talking here purely of biblical tradition. But we may reasonably suppose that bubonic plague was not unknown in the ancient Near East, specifically, for my proposal, in that part of it from which the prisoners-of-war were brought to Hatti in Suppiluliuma's reign. It was perhaps carried by flea-infested rats in the baggage brought to the Hittite homeland along with the prisoners, or by the prisoners themselves who could also be hosts for colonies of fleas. And all this happened because of Suppiluliuma's fury over the Egyptians' alleged responsibility for the death of his son!

In any case, the plague was regarded by Mursili as divinely inflicted. It could be ended only when Mursili had determined why the gods had imposed so severe a punishment on their own people – and to their own detriment. We'll come back to this in Chapter 24, when we'll be talking in more detail about the relationship between the gods and their mortal worshippers.

The man who became ruler by default over the vast Hittite empire must rank among the greatest of all Hittite rulers. Like his father and his grandfather, Mursili brought the Hittite kingdom back from the brink of annihilation against what appear to have been almost insuperable odds. What made his achievement all the more remarkable is that he did so at a time when his land was in the grip of a virulent plague. We should further stress that unlike his father who was a highly experienced warrior, spending many years in the battlefield, Mursili came to the throne as little more than a youth (though certainly more than a child) when the mantle of kingship was suddenly thrust upon him. In addition to everything I've said above, Mursili had other problems of a personal nature to deal with. These in themselves could have impaired significantly the effectiveness of his rule. (We'll refer to some of them elsewhere in this book.) Yet in spite of all, he passed on to his successor a kingdom in far better shape than the one he had inherited from his predecessors, when he became king by default.

But let's move on. My discussion of plague in this chapter prompts me to devote the next chapter to a more broadly based account of health and illness in Hittite society. What physical and psychological disorders did the Hittites suffer from? Who treated these disorders, and how?

CHAPTER 13

HEALTH, HYGIENE AND HEALING

WARDING OFF POLLUTION

The food preparation areas would have passed even the most rigorous health inspections today:

Those who prepare the daily loaves must be clean. They must be bathed and groomed, and their (body-)hair and nails removed. They must be clothed in clean garments. They must not prepare the loaves while in an unclean state. The bakery where the loaves are baked must be swept and scrubbed. Further, no pig or dog is permitted at the door of the place where the loaves are broken.[1]

But Hittite regulations went even further. Anyone found guilty of serving their guests food from an unclean vessel were forced to eat excrement and drink urine as a punishment. And kitchen-hands who prepared the food in an unclean state – by having sex the previous night and then failing to bathe at sunrise – suffered the death penalty.

Now we must hasten to add that the guests on the occasions referred to here were very special ones – gods who had been summoned to their temples and taken up residence in their statues. During the gods' residency, their mortal hosts were required to attend to all their physical needs – washing and anointing them and dressing them in clean garments on a daily basis, as well as providing them with food and drink.

Yet cleanliness was not only associated with godliness in the Hittite world. It was also associated with kingliness. Those assigned to looking after a king's physical needs were obliged to ensure that His Majesty was kept free of all forms of contamination, both physical and moral. Indeed the two were closely linked. Among other things, this meant a scrupulous check on what the king was given to eat and drink. Those who brought him water were required to strain it of all impurities before presenting it to him. Even the least oversight could have the most serious consequences. On one occasion the king discovered, to his horror, a hair in his water bowl. In response to his right royal outburst of fury, his terror-stricken attendants quickly identified the person allegedly responsible. He was subjected to some kind of ordeal (unknown to us) to establish his guilt or innocence. 'If he's guilty,' declared the king, 'he must die! But if he's found innocent, then let him go and clean himself up!'[2] Modern food inspectors would have similar concerns if they found traces of human (or animal) hair in food produced in commercial outlets – though the penalties now imposed for such infractions are rather less drastic than the Hittite ones.

Concerns about hygiene in food preparation and bodily cleanliness as demonstrated at the highest levels of Hittite society were no doubt reflected at lower levels as well. And bathing to remove all forms of pollution (including 'pollution' resulting from sexual intercourse, even when practised licitly) may have been a regular occurrence, especially among those in close contact with the king and those who had priestly duties. (More on this in Chapter 15.) Of course in a city like Hattusa which had a relatively small population and an abundant water-supply, bathing was no great chore.

Indeed, it must have been seen as one of the important means of warding off infection from diseases after contact with persons or objects already infected. The Hittites were well aware that diseases could be contracted from other persons already suffering from them, or even by having contact with objects the infectees had handled or clothes they had worn. They had no means of knowing that the transmission of infections was due to microbiological organisms. But they did understand that some sort of biological process was involved. This was painfully demonstrated by the plague described in Mursili's Plague Prayers. Whatever its nature, the Hittites could have had little doubt that it was linked to the prisoners-of-war brought back from Egypt's Syro-Palestinian territories. Indeed the Hittites themselves engaged in an early form of biological warfare by sending prisoners captured on their campaigns and obviously afflicted with some sort of disease back to their own land, to spread the contagion.[3]

But overall, their knowledge of the causes of diseases was extremely rudimentary – just as it was in most past civilisations. They had no clear understanding of what afflictions were contagious and what were not. Thus when Mursili II suddenly suffered a partial loss of speech during a thunderstorm – perhaps some sort of stroke which soon left him unable to speak at all – the most important part of his 'cure' (if in fact he was cured) began with loading onto a wagon all the garments he had worn and all the utensils he had used on the day his affliction first struck him. The wagon was then drawn by two oxen to a far-off location where the clothes and utensils along with the wagon and the oxen were burnt.[4]

In theory, the idea of putting to the torch everything an infected person had been in contact with was a sound one – but only, of course, in cases where the affliction was contagious. Many diseases, like that suffered by Mursili, were not. But even if Mursili's fellow-countrymen did have any awareness of such a distinction, they preferred to play it safe and assume that all diseases were infectious and needed to be dealt with by an appropriate set of procedures to ensure they did not spread to others. This also covered 'diseases' they regarded as purely or primarily moral in nature, including illegal sexual practices like bestiality and certain forms of incest. Moral as well as physical pollution could infect an entire community. (There are many today who would agree with that!)

Sexual deviancy could attract the death penalty, thus eliminating the source of the pollutant before it spread more widely. But other ills afflicting members of Hittite society could be disposed of by an appropriate ritual, involving the use of substitute animals, like oxen (as in Mursili's case), asses, birds, donkeys, sheep and pigs. Live animals were better, but budget-constrained sufferers could make do with replicas of these animals instead. Ritualists would be hired, often women who were specialists in ritualistic practices, to carry out the necessary procedure.

THE RITUALIST

Conventionally known as the 'Old Women', which may falsely give the impression of a bunch of cackling old crones, the Hittite term is better translated as 'Wise Women'. This group of healing professionals, who were probably literate and had a knowledge of several languages, would provide all the necessary equipment for the ritual of cure, including the animals for sacrifice, and chant the appropriate ritualistic formulae, in the appropriate language or languages. In the course of the performance, the client's affliction would be transferred to the sacrificial victims, who served as substitutes. The transfer could be made by a number of means; the client might touch the victim or spit into its mouth, or the victim might simply be waved over the client's head. In this way a cure would supposedly be effected. Not only for physical ailments, but also for many psychological or behavioural disorders, as illustrated by a ritual for restoring harmony to a dysfunctional family torn apart by domestic strife. And for all we know, the mesmerising rituals, with their potent mix of sight, sound and smell, might well have proved successful in actually effecting cures, especial for those ailments which were pyschological or psychosomatic in nature.

At least some ritualists seem also to have specialised in sex therapy. One of them tells us her cure for what *may* have been impotence. Part of her treatment reads:

> I place a spindle and a distaff in the patient's hand, and he comes under the gates. When he steps forward through the gates, I take the spindle and distaff away from him. I give him a bow and arrows, and say to him all the while: 'I have just taken the femininity away from you and given you

masculinity in return. You have cast off the (sexual) behaviour expected (of women); you have taken to yourself the behaviour expected of man.'[5]

But we should tread carefully here. In today's Western world, ritual exhortations for a man to cast off his femininity could be regarded as politically incorrect, especially if they risk eradicating the man's genuine sexuality – causing him further confusion about his sexual identity. In this context, we might note that there is not a single clearly identifiable reference to homosexuality in Hittite texts, though one scholar has interpreted the text just quoted as a ritual antidote to homosexuality.[6] Undoubtedly there was a homosexual element in Hittite society. But the fact that there is no mention of it even in the Hittite Laws, which include a long list of banned sexual activities, indicates that it was not on the list of proscribed sexual offences.

THE HOLISTIC APPROACH

The Hittite world's curers of diseases included physicians in the conventional sense. Most of these were men, but we hear of a few women doctors as well. All were very likely among the relatively small group of literate members of Hittite society, for a number of texts describe the procedures to be followed by doctors in the treatment of such ailments as wounds, eye diseases, intestinal and throat problems, and in the preparation and administering of drugs. And many of the straightforward conditions requiring medical treatment, like minor injuries caused by assault, could be dealt with by basic medical procedures with prescriptions for healing salves, potions and poultices made from various plant extracts, minerals (like lead) and animal products (like blood, bones, milk, fat and tallow), administered orally, anally, or externally.

But Hittite medicine often involved a comprehensive, 'holistic' approach to the treatment of patients. Practical medical procedures were complemented or replaced by rituals, which included the application of spells and incantations, and sometimes also by direct appeals to the gods. Physicians and incantation priests often worked together to effect a cure, in particular when a case presented complex problems. As Albert Einstein once said,

> Seeing with eyes of wholeness means recognizing that nothing occurs in isolation, that problems need to be seen within the context of whole systems. Seeing in this way, we can perceive the intrinsic web of interconnectedness underlying our experience and merge with it. Seeing in this way is healing.

An essential element in the curing of diseases was the role the gods played in both inflicting them in the first place, and providing cures for them in the second. This was in accord with the belief that many of the afflictions suffered by humankind, both medical and otherwise, resulted from punishments imposed by the gods on their mortal worshippers for offences they had committed. Included amongst these offences were ones against the gods themselves, such as the neglect of their sacrificial ceremonies. Thus when no other reason could be found for an ailment which afflicted either an individual, from the king downwards, or all the inhabitants of the Hittite land, divine displeasure was suspected. Specially qualified priests or priestesses were called upon to ascertain who the displeased deity was, and the reasons for his or her displeasure.

This was done by consulting the oracles, often through the examination of a sacrificed animal's entrails. First of all, the god whose wrath had been provoked had to be identified. This in itself could be a protracted process, given the Hittite world's multiplicity of gods. And once the god had been identified, the reason for the offence he or she had taken had to be established. Then appropriate remedial action could be initiated, to appease the god and effect a cure. But even then oracular enquiry could be a long, drawn-out process since the gods were not particularly helpful in their responses to the consultant's questions. When the patterns on an animal's entrails were examined for a sign from above, the enquirer could expect only a 'yes' or 'no' answer to their question when they suggested a possible cause of offence. If the answer was 'no', the process of sacrificing an animal and examining its entrails had to be repeated – and then again until an affirmative answer was obtained. Collaboration between physician, incantation priests and specialists in oracular enquiry was often essential if health was to be restored to the victims of divine wrath.

But some afflictions were beyond cure, even after appeals to the gods. Thus King Hattusili III was a chronic sufferer of an indisposition his wife Puduhepa called 'fire-of-the-feet'. She did so in her appeal to the goddess Lelwani for a cure. I once wrote that the disease in question was possibly gout. Two neuro-surgeons, one from Turkey and one from France, responded with the same suggestion: almost certainly the king was suffering from a painful disease called neuropathy. If you yourself suffer from this condition, you'll know that your feet really do feel as if they are on fire when you walk. Despite this problem, Hattusili seems to have been actively involved in military campaigns for most of his long career, though presumably his wife ensured that he didn't have to do much walking on these campaigns. (She was very influential in the kingdom's affairs, as we shall see.)

DOCTORS ON LOAN FROM ABROAD

Despite what appears to have been a high level of medical expertise available in the Hittite world, there were times when Hittite kings, Hattusili III in particular, asked their Egyptian and Babylonian Royal Brothers for a loan of their medical experts. Most famously, Hattusili appealed to the pharaoh Ramesses II to send one of his doctors to Hatti to help his sister become pregnant. She was married to a man called Masturi, ruler of the important western vassal state Seha River Land. Offspring of the union would ensure that future rulers of this land would have Hittite blood in their veins. But the marriage had so far failed to produce fruit. Hence Hattusili's last-resort appeal to Ramesses. He confessed that the task of making the princess fertile was a challenging one: she was now 50 years old, or so he claimed. Ramesses knew better, and made this clear in his reply to the request. 'You say your sister is fifty. Fifty? She's sixty! But whether she's fifty or sixty, I'll send a physician and an incantation priest to see what they can do.' Arrogant and unchivalrous though this reply was, Ramesses was almost certainly correct, as my calculations of just how old the princess was make clear. If anything, he was erring on the side of generosity. As far as we know, the princess never produced a child.[7]

HITTITE BIRTHS AND MIDWIVES

Speaking of births, let's finish this chapter with a special category of health professionals – the midwives of the Hittite world. As with other categories of health management, birthing involved a combination of both ritual and practical procedures. If in the first place a woman who sought to become pregnant had been unable to do so, she could try spending a night in the shrine of an appropriate deity, in the hope that during her sleep the god would come and have intercourse with her and cause her to conceive. Maybe Hattusili's sister had already tried this before her brother called on the services of an Egyptian doctor. Once conception had occurred, whether by natural means or divine intervention, the pregnancy might be celebrated with a special festival honouring the mother goddess. Then just to be on the safe side, there might be oracle enquiries to ensure the mother was in a spiritually fit state to give birth, with remedial action taken, by means of sacrificial offerings, if the oracular response was negative.

If all went well with the pregnancy, a midwife was summoned to assist with the birth. She had all the practical expertise, made sure all necessary equipment was available, and assisted with the birth and washed the baby clean when it emerged. The birth itself took place while the mother was seated on two cushioned stools, with her legs apart, and as her baby was born, the midwife caught it in a blanket positioned between the mother's legs and above a third cushion, to make doubly sure of a soft landing for the new infant. During and after the birthing, the midwife chanted incantations, as did others in attendance, including doctors and priests whose duties were primarily ritualistic.[8]

What sort of world was the new child entering? Let's imagine that he or she was born into a family lower down the social scale than those who formed the elite class of Hittite society. In the next three chapters, we'll get a few glimpses into the life of the ordinary citizen of Hittite society, and further down the scale of those who formed its lowest class, the slaves and the compulsory migrants to the land of Hatti, prisoners-of-war acquired by Hittite war leaders on their campaigns abroad. What were the norms and values of the society in which they lived? What were the rules governing their conduct? What rights and responsibilities did they have? As we shall see, Hittite society presents us with a few surprises, illustrated by some of its marriage provisions. Our best source of information on all this is a set of laws, which give us a number of important insights into the daily lives of the people of whom Hittite society was composed.

CHAPTER 14

JUSTICE AND THE COMMONER

THE HITTITE LAWS

A collection of 200 laws provides us with our best source of information on how Hittite society worked, and on the daily lives and moral and social values of its members. The collection was copied many times, and though none of its copies have survived intact, we can put together an almost complete version of it by piecing together the various bits and pieces that still exist.[1] In many respects, the Laws are modelled on the so-called 'Code' of the eighteenth-century Babylonian king Hammurabi. Carved on a basalt stone column, the one surviving (largely complete) copy of Hammurabi's Laws is now on display in the Louvre in Paris. One thing we do need to stress is that it's quite misleading to use the term 'Code' to apply to either the Babylonian or the Hittite Laws, since they're no more than a sample gathering of legal precedents, cherry-picked from a large number of cases dealing with similar matters brought to court and judged on previous occasions.

Both the Babylonian and the Hittite collections of laws cover a wide range of activities of both a civil and a criminal nature. And like their Babylonian predecessor, the Hittite Laws are expressed as conditional statements: *If* (someone does/suffers something), *then* (this will be the consequence). No doubt each official presiding in a court of justice had a copy of the Laws at his disposal, to see what decisions were made in the past on cases similar to one now before him. But, like their Babylonian predecessor, the Hittite Laws served purely as guidelines, not as prescriptive rulings, leaving much to the judge's own discretion. And the highly selective nature of the Laws left untouched many areas where legal action could arise. Either these were covered elsewhere, or were decided purely on their merits by whoever happened to be the presiding judge.

In regional and rural districts of the homeland, the administration of justice was one of the responsibilities performed by town or village authorities known as Councils of Elders. Their membership probably drawn from the heads of prominent local families, these councils were obliged to work closely with the regional governor, called the BĒL MADGALTI. The governor's many duties included the oversight or dispensation of justice in the region where he was appointed. Though the local councils may have had authority to deal on their own with cases of a minor nature, the more serious cases were probably referred to the governor during his regular tours of inspection of his region. On such occasions, he no doubt presided over local courts with the mayor and members of the village council acting as his advisers.

One major difference between Hammurabi's Laws and the later Hittite collection is that the former were supposedly divinely inspired, particularly by Shamash, god of justice, who appears in company with Hammurabi at the top of the Louvre column. Divine endorsement is also bestowed on the Babylonian document in both the prologue and the epilogue attached to it. In the latter, Hammurabi emphasises one of his Laws' most important purposes, to ensure that the strong do not oppress the weak, and that justice is provided for the waif and the widow – that is, for the most vulnerable members of society.

By contrast, there is no explicit social or philosophical rationale appended to the Hittite Laws, nor any suggestion that they were divinely inspired or endorsed. They are a plain, straightforward secular document, without prologue or epilogue. Nonetheless, their underlying social and moral intent is often implicit in the nature of some of their specific clauses. The obligations and responsibilities imposed upon the local governor as the administrator of justice in his region emphasised the importance of his acting fairly and impartially, not favouring the strong over the weak, being sure to protect against exploitation the interests of vulnerable members of society, like widows and slaves:

> Into whatever city you return, summon forth all the people of the city. Whoever has a suit, decide it for him and satisfy him. If the slave of a man, or the maidservant of a man, or a bereaved woman has a suit, decide it for them and satisfy them. Do not make the better case the worse or the worse case the better. Do what is just.[2]

In 'doing what is just', regional governors were also obliged to take full account of local customs, ensuring that the judgments they pronounced and the penalties they imposed were consistent with the region's customary laws. If cases arose where judgments contained in the Laws were at variance with local law, precedence was to be given to the latter. This was why it was very important for a governor to consult closely with his district councils. The advice they provided on local laws and traditions helped ensure that his judgments did not run contrary to these. Indeed, there might well have been cases where local legal tradition prescribed harsher penalties for offences than those laid down in the Laws. In such cases, the governor was obliged to follow the local tradition:

> As it has been from olden days – in a town in which they have been accustomed to imposing the death penalty, they shall continue to do so. But in a town where they have been accustomed to imposing exile, they shall continue that (custom).[3]

Later versions of the Laws indicate an increasing shift towards local communities becoming as self-regulatory as possible, with correspondingly less involvement in their affairs by the kingdom's central authorities. The basic principle was that in communities which have their own customary laws, the members of these communities should be tried in accordance with them. In attempting to sort out the many crimes and misdemeanours and disputes that arose in the course of daily life in regional communities, the Laws might have been regularly consulted in the search for precedents. But the Laws were not prescriptive. Ultimately, it was up to the local governor as judge and the local councils who advised him to decide what judgments were appropriate in the cases brought before him.

Criminal activities dealt with in the Laws include homicide, manslaughter, robbery, theft, arson, witchcraft and various categories of forbidden sexual liaisons. One of the advantages of the Laws being purely secular is that the provisions they contain could be changed over the centuries, corresponding no doubt to changing perceptions of the gravity of certain crimes. Milder penalties for offences often replace earlier harsher ones. Distinctions came to be made between offences committed with deliberate intent to cause injury, and offences in which damage suffered by the victim was an unintended consequence. If in fact the gods had given their *imprimateur* to the original Laws, these could not have been so easily altered to accommodate changing perceptions of crime and punishment.

THE PRINCIPLE OF COMPENSATION

The most important feature of the Laws is the principle of compensation which underpins them. This marks a striking departure from Hammurabic law, one of whose defining features is the *lex talionis* principle – i.e. revenge for revenge's sake, or in biblical terms, 'an eye for an eye, a tooth for a tooth'. Thus:

> If a builder constructs a house for a man but does not make his work sound, and the house he constructs collapses and causes the death of the householder, that builder shall be killed.[4]

In Hittite law, the emphasis is not on retributive justice or vengeance for its own sake, which is rarely of any material benefit to the victim, but on compensatory justice. An offender will have satisfied the demands of justice once he has discharged his legal obligations to his victim by paying him appropriate compensation. Thus:

> If anyone injures a person and temporarily incapacitates him, he shall provide medical care for him. In his place, he shall provide a person to work on his estate until he recovers. When he recovers, his assailant shall pay him 6 shekels of silver, and shall pay the physician's fee as well.[5]

Punishment purely for punishment's sake has little place in Hittite law.

The Laws also draw a distinction between various categories of manslaughter. But what of cases of actual murder – homicide with deliberate intent? Here again the Laws seem to have changed over time in favour of more lenient punishment for the offender. In earlier times, the fate of a murderer seems to have lain in the hands of the victim's family who could demand the death penalty. In later times, the death penalty appears to have been ruled out. Except in districts where capital punishment had the sanction of customary law, the only choices available to a murdered person's family seem to have been either compensatory payment by the murderer or his enslavement to the family.

Arson, house-breaking, burglary, theft of livestock and damage to or interference with another man's property are dealt with in many Hittite laws. Thus:

> If anyone carries embers into a field while it is in fruit, and ignites the field, he who sets the fire shall himself take the burnt-over field. He shall give a good field to the owner of the burnt-over field, and he (the new owner) will reap it.[6]

This prompts me to make a general point. The high percentage of laws dealing with theft of or damage to property, and the penalties which such offences attract, clearly reflect the importance which Hittite society attached to the protection of individual property rights, particularly in an agricultural context. The farmer who loses his crops or livestock or equipment through someone else's negligence or malice risks losing his livelihood, which is ultimately to the detriment of Hatti's land-based economy. Penalties had to be sufficiently high to prevent this, or to ensure adequate compensation for the victim. Even though in later versions of the Laws compensatory payments for damage to agricultural property or livestock were generally much smaller, sometimes 50 per cent smaller, than in earlier versions, the prescribed compensation was still up to five or ten times greater than the actual loss suffered by the victim. Livestock were a particularly important asset, and the laws which deal with theft of or injury done to them reflect the value Hittite society placed on them – especially animals which had been trained to do important, specific jobs. Trained working animals like sheep- and cattle-dogs were valuable assets. Strike and kill an ordinary farmyard dog, and you will pay its owner one shekel of silver. But if you strike and kill a herdsman's dog, you will pay 20 times that amount.

On His Majesty's Service?

The Hittites were not a great trading people, and references to actual Hittite merchants in our texts are very rare. Foreign intermediaries conveyed most of the goods imported into the kingdom, ranging from essential commodities to luxury items. Sometimes these goods were tribute from the kingdom's vassal states or 'gifts' to Hittite kings from their international Royal Brothers. Even within the land of Hatti, we have very little evidence of merchants or traders hawking their wares between cities or in local markets. Indeed, the Hittite word for a merchant, unnattallaš, is rarely found, and even when it does occur it refers only to wealthy and important men who conducted the business of international trade with allied countries, as His Majesty's agents and acting under his protection.

Many of these agents came from the port city of Ura on Anatolia's southeastern coast and seem to have played a major role in arranging shipments of goods from Ugarit on the eastern Mediterranean coast to the homeland. Grain originating in Egypt or Hatti's Syrian vassal states was amongst the most important of these shipments in the last decades of the empire. Large numbers of livestock including cattle, sheep, horses, mules and asses made up part of the consignments whose despatch to the Hittite homeland or other parts of the Hittite realm was undertaken by 'merchants'. As was the conveyance there of valuable metals and other precious wares such as gold, silver, lapis lazuli, and carnelian, and commodity metals like copper, bronze, and tin. Slaves and high quality horses, linen garments and dyed wool also figure among the items transported to various destinations in the Hittite world. Trading links via intermediaries extended as far afield as Babylon, and Assyria in the southeast, and Egypt in the south. But we have very little evidence for trading links with the western Mycenaean world.

So the Hittites were certainly enmeshed in the world of international Late Bronze Age trade, but to judge from the rarity of references in the texts to merchants or traders of their own, they seem to have left trading enterprises mainly in the hands of others. Indeed the large scale of many of the attested enterprises very likely indicates that the 'merchants' who engaged in them were royal agents hired by the king to escort the goods to their destinations, no doubt with substantial armed backup, rather than private entrepreneurs. Of course there must have been plenty of small-time operators. But our texts appear not to deal with them.

Whether acting in a private capacity or as royal agents, those involved in the transportation of goods often ran considerable risks of robbery and death in the course of their expeditions. On land they were vulnerable to brigands and rapacious local rulers through whose territories they passed. By sea they risked both attack by pirates, who infested the eastern Mediterranean and its coastlands, and sudden storms to which their ships and cargoes often fell victim.

This brings us to the reason I've included merchants and traders in this chapter. Hittite kings attached considerable importance to the protection of merchants, given the vital role they played in supplying the Hittite world with a wide range of goods often originating from distant locations. Severe penalties were imposed on anyone who stole from them. Sometimes the thieves were of high status. A case in point is a king of Ugarit accused of seizing 400 donkeys, worth 4,000 shekels of silver, from a merchant caravan passing through his land. He was fined the substantial sum of one-and-a-third talents of silver for this offence.[7] Indeed, many of the cases judged in the courts of the Hittite viceroys concerned crimes against merchants, including robbery, hijacking and murder. If the offenders were not caught, the inhabitants of the districts, or their authorities, where the crimes were committed, were obliged to pay substantial compensation.

We are given a clear indication of the importance attached to the safety of merchants from one of the few explicit references made to these persons in the Hittite Laws. The penalty for murdering a merchant is set at 4,000 shekels of silver (plus in Hittite lands replacement of his goods) – far higher than the penalties imposed for most other offences in the Laws. The relevant clause (§5) clearly refers to intentional and premeditated homicide by the perpetrator, the motive undoubtedly being to rob the merchant of his goods. Interestingly, serious though the crime is, the primary concern in this clause is not with the actual homicide. It is the seizure of the merchant's goods rather than his murder for which the penalty is prescribed. Which illustrates a significant feature of Hittite law – its emphasis on the protection of property, and on obtaining compensation for a crime rather than punishment for its own sake. Indeed, a later version of the clause stipulates that if the merchant is killed without his goods in a quarrel or accidentally – that is, robbery is not the motive for the offence – the penalty is substantially reduced, to 240 and 80 shekels of silver respectively. If the merchant is killed with his goods, the perpetrator will pay, in addition to a substantial fine, compensation worth three times the goods' value.

A FASCINATING GLIMPSE INTO THE WORLD OF THE COMMONER

The Laws provide important insights into many aspects of the daily lives of those who inhabited the lower echelons of Hittite society. *Their* world was one of which we have only faint glimpses from other sources, for the Laws are above all concerned with the activities and disputes that arose between the common people of the Hittite world – those who laboured on the land, engaged in trades and crafts, thronged the streets of Hittite cities and villages, and refreshed themselves in the local taverns. This is the world of 'the villager injured in a tavern brawl or in a dispute with his neighbour over boundaries, the small farmer seeking to buy some pigs or a small orchard, the hired labourer, the herdsman, the cattle rustler, the slave, the local romeos and lotharios, the participants in family weddings, the partners in mixed and common law marriages. There was potential for conflict and litigation in every aspect of life in the village and farming communities, and no doubt the "city-gates", the venue of the local courts, were thronged with clamorous appellants, seeking justice for real or supposed wrongs, laying claim to stray livestock which their discoverer has refused to hand over, demanding compensation for a crop trampled by a neighbour's unsupervised cattle, or for a favourite working dog brained by an irate neighbour for savaging his ducks.'[8] All this is far removed from the world of elite Hittite society, which dominates both the archaeological and the written record. It was a common everyday world of farmers, labourers, craftsmen and tradesmen, of slaves as well as free. For this reason in particular, the collection of Hittite Laws is one of our most valuable social documents dating to that period, especially because of the light it throws on life and society at its lower levels in the day-to-day activities of the peoples who inhabited the kingdom of the Hittites.

In the next two chapters, we'll have a further look at the workings of Hittite society. We'll focus particularly on attitudes to sex, the roles women played in society at various levels, the institution of marriage, and the status, functions and rights of slaves.

CHAPTER 15

NO SEX PLEASE, WE'RE HITTITE

This title should not of course be taken too literally. If it were strictly true, the Hittite kingdom would never have got going, let alone lasted 500 years. But a number of sexual practices were strictly forbidden in the Hittite world, and others permitted only with clear conditions attached. Violations met with severe punishment.

THE HORROR OF INCEST

Incest was regarded with particular abhorrence, at least by Hatti's royal authorities. King Suppiluliuma I makes this perfectly clear in his treaty with one of his vassal rulers. Provoked by reports of hanky-panky between closely related family members in the vassal state, he bans the practice and issues a grim warning:

> For Hatti it is an important custom that a brother does not have sex with his sister or female cousin. It is not permitted. Whoever commits such an act is put to death. But your land is barbaric, for there a man regularly has sex with his sister or cousin. And if on occasion a sister of your wife, or the wife of a brother, or a female cousin comes to you, give her something to eat or drink. Both of you eat, drink, and make merry! But you must not desire to have sex with her. It is not permitted, and people are put to death as a result of that act.[1]

The fact that this is the only known occasion when a Hittite king interferes in the customs and domestic practices of one of his vassal states highlights the strong stand Hittite authorities took against incest, wherever in Hatti's territories it occurred.

A large number of clauses in the Hittite Laws are devoted to sexual offences of this and other kinds. Bans on sex between family members extended from those mentioned above to sexual relations between mother and son, father and daughter, father and son, stepmother and son (unless the son's father is deceased), son-in-law and mother-in-law. But there were exceptions. The law allowed a man to sleep with slave women who were sisters, and with their mother as well, without committing an offence. It also condoned sex between in-laws – in cases where the husband or wife of one of them had predeceased their spouse. Indeed it positively encouraged, if not actually mandated, what appears to be marriage between a widow and a male member of her husband's family. Thus:

> If a man has a wife, and the man dies, his brother shall take his widow as wife. (If the brother dies), his father shall take her. When afterwards his father dies, his (i.e. the father's) brother shall take the woman whom he had.[2]

This recalls the biblically attested custom of levirate marriage (from the Latin *levir*, 'brother-in-law'). Deuteronomy 25:5 – 6 tells us that if brothers are living together and one of them dies without a son, his widow must not marry outside the family but become the wife of another of the brothers. The first son of the new union must bear the name of the first husband 'so that his name will not be blotted out from Israel'. The purpose of the corresponding Hittite law is not made clear, but it's very likely intended to ensure that the deceased's family takes responsibility for his wife's future welfare.

Such a provision may well have had practical application many times, given the frequency of Hittite military campaigns and the inevitable battle casualties that resulted from them, leaving behind many a widow and no doubt fatherless children. If the marriage with an in-law were one in the full sense of the word, then another reason for the state's endorsement of it was to ensure that a wife so taken in a second marriage continued to produce offspring if she were still of child-bearing age. Given the chronic shortage of Hittite manpower, the continuing patter of tiny Hittite feet, especially male ones, despite the death of a woman's first husband, was no doubt a welcome sound in the Hittite kingdom.

Adultery

Of course, there must have been many instances where a man who was obliged to marry an in-law's widow was already married. Such cases would provide the only examples of polygamy or concubinage clearly attested in Hittite society outside the elite circle of royalty where kings had several or many concubines as well as a chief wife. There *may* have been other instances at sub-royal social levels that we don't know about. But by and large Hittite society (unlike Babylonian society as reflected in Hammurabi's Laws) seems to have been a monogamous one, with several of the laws concerned with adulterous behaviour.

Let's consider clause 197 of the Laws. It begins thus:

If a man seizes a woman in the mountains (and rapes her), it is the man's offence, but if he seizes her in her house, it is the woman's offence: the woman shall die.

The rationale behind this distinction, not spelt out in the Hittite text, is provided by a passage in Deuteronomy, which almost certainly derives, directly or indirectly, from Hittite law. Part of it reads:

If out in the country a man happens to meet a girl pledged to be married and rapes her, only the man who has done this shall die. Do nothing to the girl; she has committed no sin deserving death [...] for the man found the girl out in the country, and though the betrothed girl screamed, there was no-one to rescue her.

(Deut. 22:25–27).

That is to say, the woman was considered innocent if she were attacked in circumstances where she was unable to summon assistance. In contrast to this situation, the second part of the Hittite clause implies that if the act occurred in a place where the woman could have called for help from others nearby (as would allegedly have been the case if the offence was perpetrated in her own home) but failed to do so, this would imply consensual sex. And she must pay the penalty for it.

What penalty? It is clear that the law is referring specifically to a married woman, for the second part of clause 197 states that if the woman's husband catches his wife and her lover in the act, he can kill them both without suffering any penalty. That is to say, the law condoned if not actually legitimised his action. By implication, if he failed to do this in the heat of the moment, he could not later take the law into his own hands, but had to refer the matter for judgment to the king's court. This is made clear in Clause 198:

> If (the husband) brings (the adulterous pair) to the palace gate (i.e. to the royal court) and says 'My wife shall not die', he can spare his wife's life, but he must also spare the lover [...]. If he says: 'Both of them shall die,' [...] the king (or presumably his delegate) may have them killed or he may spare them.

Note the important proviso: the cuckolded husband cannot ask for his wife to be spared and her lover executed; it had to be both or neither. If both, the final decision rested with the king or his delegate, who no doubt investigated the circumstances of the illicit liaison before making the decision.

Overall, the range of offences for which capital punishment was prescribed was relatively small in the Hittite world, and indeed became even smaller as the Laws were revised over time. This is in marked contrast to Hammurabi's Laws where the death penalty is stipulated for a wide range of offences, including some we might regard as trivial. So those offences which did attract the death penalty in Hittite society had all the greater significance because of their relative rarity.

BESTIALITY

Notable in the list of such offences were those involving what was regarded as sexual deviancy. Incest and certain types of bestiality figure a number of times among offences punishable by death. The latter included intercourse with pigs, dogs and sheep. Thus Clause 199 of the Laws begins by stating that anyone who has sexual relations with a pig or a dog commits a capital offence. The matter is to be judged by the royal court. But the clause then goes on to say that the king has the final say on the verdict and *may* decide to spare the lives of both the animal and the human. Whatever his decision, 'the human shall not approach the king' – so the clause continues. What precisely is the significance of this?

Firstly, it seems that bestiality was not in all cases deemed a capital offence, or even a punishable one. Thus Clause 200a tells us that it is not an offence for a man to have sex with a horse or mule, though anyone who does so may not approach the king or become a priest. The reason why horses and mules are excluded from the bestiality provisions remains a mystery to us. (Do you have any suggestions?) In any case, in this and in a number of other respects, Hittite law was at variance with biblical law which has a blanket prohibition on all forms of bestiality. But even when sex with certain animals was not banned by Hittite law, persons who indulged in any form of bestiality were forbidden to enter the king's presence. This almost certainly has to do with the concern that such persons had rendered themselves unclean, and thus unfit to appear before the king, who might be contaminated by contact with or even proximity to them. That could have terrible consequences for the king and indeed his whole kingdom, if the gods took punitive action.

EVEN LICIT SEX COULD POLLUTE

And there were certain prohibitions that applied to all forms of sex, licit or otherwise. Even a king, Mursili II, was instructed to refrain from intercourse with a woman the night before he embarked upon a ritual designed to cure him of a speech affliction, for fear that by engaging in sex so soon before the ritual he would jeopardise a beneficial outcome from it.[3]

Officials on temple duty had to be in an absolutely pure or sterile state before they entered the presence of the god. It was OK for them to have sex beforehand, but they must then spend the night in the temple, presumably after they had thoroughly cleansed themselves from their sexual activity as well as from any other form of pollution. An official who spent the whole night with his wife and thus came unclean before the god forfeited his life. The death penalty was also prescribed for cooks and kitchen-hands who prepared food for the gods 'in an unclean state', an offence they would have committed if they'd had sex the night before. Well, having the sex was allowable, *provided* those who so indulged bathed themselves at sunrise, to remove all contamination before having contact with the god's food. And if you knew of someone who prepared the gods' food without having had a bath after sex, and failed to report it, you too would be executed.

The belief in the polluting effects of sexual activity, whether licit or illicit, was not confined to the Hittites in the Near Eastern world. Similar beliefs, and the bans and penalties associated with them, are also found in Egyptian and Mesopotamian societies. And *illegal* sexual activity such as, in Hittite law, certain types of bestiality, could have widespread ramifications, threatening the well-being of an entire community where the pollution occurred. Hence the severity of the penalties imposed for such activity, in contrast to the often much milder penalties for many other crimes, including homicide, which affect a much smaller number of persons.

WHAT WENT ON IN THE ARZANA-HOUSE?

To finish off this chapter, let's turn our attention briefly to an institution called the *arzana*-house. The few references we have in the texts to institutions so called indicate that they were places of music and merriment which served food and drink, and also provided overnight lodgings for their guests.[4] Who were their customers? Did soldiers frequent these establishments?

For all that our texts tell us about what Hittite soldiers did in the performance of their duties, they say almost nothing about what they did in their time off. But it doesn't take much imagination to work this out. Drinking, eating, singing and patronising the world's oldest profession must have played a large part in a Hittite soldier's R & R leave. And where lots of soldiers are gathered together, taverns and inns and brothels quickly spring up. One of the Hittite texts refers to 'hostels' in towns in the frontier zone with the Kaska lands. Very likely these were commercial establishments like taverns and inns which served both the local populace and Hittite troops stationed in the area. But with no further information about them, we can't be sure.

So what about the *arzana*-houses – places of eating, drinking, music and merriment and 'overnight lodgings'? One of them is associated with a group of women designated by the logogram KAR.KID. This term crops up also in the Laws and was long believed to refer to prostitutes. In the text which refers to this particular *arzana*-house, the crown prince is present, and he features in a curious ritual. He has a meal of bread, cakes, porridge, milk and beer, and a drink called *marnuwan*. His dinner companions are 12 KAR.KID women. Later that night, he lies down, and priests place loaves of bread on either side of his head and feet and pour beer in a circle around his body. Then the KAR. KID women are brought in. Do they now initiate the prince into the delights of puberty, as once suggested? Unfortunately, the first tablet of the text which contains the relevant information ends here, and its sequel has not yet been found. So what did happen next?

Firstly, KAR.KID women were almost certainly not prostitutes. Rather, says the Hittite scholar Bille Jean Collins, the term was used for single women who were not under the guardianship of a father or husband. Indeed, as Collins and other scholars have pointed out, the whole notion of sacred prostitution in the Near East has been discredited. The other thing is that it's unlikely that *arzana*-houses were taverns or brothels or drinking-houses. Rather, what we know about them suggests that they were cultic establishments, associated with sacred rituals and festivals. And that has prompted the suggestion that the ritual for the prince in the *arzana*-house wasn't some sort of sex initiation ceremony but rather what has been called a 'dream incubation'.[5]

So we must, alas, finish on a negative note. We have no evidence of the robust sexual activities in which Hittite soldiers, like other soldiers, must have engaged at every available opportunity. We cannot even find a single identifiable reference to prostitution in our texts. But this simply illustrates one of the big gaps in our information about daily life in the Hittite world which neither textual nor archaeological evidence can fill. It is a classic example of the old adage that absence of evidence is not evidence of absence. The discovery of a building that could be clearly identified as a brothel, perhaps in a Hittite city yet to be unearthed, along with some tablets relevant to the building's use, would be a most welcome addition to our information about the seamier side of the world of the Hittites.

CHAPTER 16

WOMEN, MARRIAGE AND SLAVERY

THE WOMEN OF THE EMPIRE

A t the top level of Hittite society, women could and sometimes did wield considerable influence in the management of their kingdom's affairs. But what about all other women in Hittite society? What roles did they play? What rights did they have? How did they fare in relation to their male counterparts? Let's now address these questions.

When soldiers were inducted into the Hittite army, they were threatened with a humiliating punishment if they broke their military oaths:

> Whoever breaks these oaths and does evil to the king and the queen and the princes, let these oaths change him from a man into a woman! Let them change his troops into women, let them dress them in the fashion of women and cover their heads with a length of cloth! Let them break the bows, arrows, and clubs in their hands and let them put in their hands distaff and mirror![1]

In another text, a king rebukes his troops for their cowardice in failing to take a city by siege:

> Why have you not given battle? You stand on chariots of water, you are almost turned into water yourself(?) [. . .] You

had only to kneel before him and you would have killed him or at least frightened him. But as it is you have behaved like women![2]

Such demeaning references to women are a feature of many societies in many ages. 'Frailty, thy name is woman!' declares Shakespeare's Hamlet. And in his *Julius Caesar*, Cassius compares Caesar to 'a sick girl', for his whimperings and cowardly behaviour when he narrowly escapes drowning. Until quite recent times, generic put-downs of women in expressions like 'the weaker sex' were commonplace in Western society.

So how did women fare in the Hittite world? Like almost all other societies, ancient and modern, this world was a strongly patriarchal one, from the royal family down. Kingship passed from one male to another, men did all the fighting, men held all the important offices of state, and men were far more prominent than women in the professions and the general workforce.

But the picture is not totally one-sided. From our texts it's clear that women at all levels of Hittite society had certain rights which were denied them in many other societies. Let's take a look at the institution of marriage.

TILL DEATH US DO PART?

To judge from their Laws, the Hittites' approach to marriage was a comparatively enlightened, liberal, and practical one. De facto as well as formal marriages were recognised. Pre-nuptial agreements were often entered into, divorce was apparently not uncommon, and divorce proceedings could as easily be initiated by a woman as by a man. Particular concern was given to what happened to the children of a marriage in the event of a divorce, and what their inheritance entitlements were. There were provisions to ensure that a widow was adequately cared for if her husband died first. And if, following their father's death, his widow's sons failed to take care of her, she had the right to disinherit (and reinstate) them.[3]

Much of this we learn from the Laws' numerous clauses relating to marriage, divorce and inheritance. Property rights figure largely

Figure 16.1 A Hittite wedding?

in these clauses. Understandably, since many marriages were arranged, and in the nature of business contracts between the bride's and groom's families. These contracts involved the transfer of property, often probably quite considerable, from one contracting party to another. So pre-nuptial agreements acted rather like insurance policies which would take effect in the event of a divorce or the death of one of the marriage-partners.

A broad distinction is made, however, between 'formal' marriages, and marriages based purely on cohabitation. Whether or not property transference was associated with the union seems to have been a significant aspect of the distinction. In the 'formal' variety, it was customary for the prospective bridegroom to present his bride-to-be or her family with a gift before an engagement became official, and then a more substantial 'gift' as part of the betrothal procedures. This second gift was known as a *kusata*, a term generally translated as 'brideprice'. Prior to the wedding, the bride's father presented his daughter with a dowry. This was her share of the family estate, and it remained hers for the rest of her life. Her husband may have become the formal custodian of the dowry, but he gained ownership of it only if she died before him. The *kusata* was an important, indeed perhaps an essential, way of conferring formal status upon a marriage, as distinct from unions which, regardless of whether they were permanent or long-lasting, were of a more informal nature. Did this matter in practical terms? It probably did, as we shall see.

Given that at least 'formal' marriages, were often in the nature of business contracts, there doesn't seem to have been much scope for romantic love as the basis of such unions. Nor is this reflected in any of the terminology used of marriage; the Hittite language contains no specific word for 'marry' – a new husband is said to 'take' his wife, and henceforth to 'possess' her, as in the nursery rhyme where 'the farmer takes a wife'. We have very few references to love as the basis of marriage. One is in a hymn to Ishtar, goddess of love: 'You, Ishtar, have decreed that a man and his wife should love each other and carry their love to fulfilment.' Another appears in the *Apology* of King Hattusili III (see Chapter 19), where Hattusili tells us that when he married his wife Puduhepa, Ishtar gave the couple 'the love of husband and wife'.

But the course of true love does not always run smooth – nor ever did – and the Laws envisage a situation where two young lovers elope after the girl has been promised to someone else, and the prospective bridegroom has already made payment of 'gifts' to her family as part of the pre-nuptial formalities. Thus:

> If a daughter has been promised to a man, but another man runs off with her, he who runs off with her shall compensate the first man for whatever he gave. The father and mother of the woman shall not make compensation.[4]

The full implications of this clause are not entirely clear. But it seems that the girl's mother and father have no legal claim over her as far as her marriage is concerned. She's free to marry whomever she will, the only stipulation being that her new (?) lover make full compensation to the jilted groom for any investment he has already made in the marriage. The girl's parents themselves are not held accountable for their daughter's conduct, evidently because she's a free agent, entirely independent of parental authority.

As we might expect, there were a number of cases where marriages which did go ahead failed and ended in divorce. Divorce proceedings could be initiated by either the husband or the wife, though the actual grounds for such action are never spelt out in the Laws. Presumably adultery provided one of these grounds. And perhaps as in Hammurabic law the failure of a wife to present her husband with children was another. Of course, the wife may not have been the one at fault. But there were no tests for sperm counts in those days, and erectile dysfunction seems not to be mentioned in any of the texts – though that *may* have been one of the problems addressed in rituals whose *commonly assumed* purpose was to cure impotence (but see Chapter 13). In any case the Laws' chief concern with divorce is with its property implications, and above all with the arrangements made for the children, if there were any, of a divorced couple.

The situation is often particularly complicated in mixed marriages – marriages in which one of the partners is a slave and the other free. Such marriages were by no means exclusive to the Hittite world. (Hammurabi's Laws cover a number of such cases in Babylonian society.) And before discussing such marriages, we should look briefly at the institution of slavery in the Hittite world.

THE UNFREE IN HITTITE SOCIETY

Let's begin with a general comment on slavery. Slaves were a component of virtually every society in the ancient world. Indeed, I know of only one group of people who believed that the enslavement of a fellow human being was morally wrong – the Essenes at Qumran. Can you think of any other ancient peoples who believed likewise? And what of today's societies? Officially, slavery no longer exists. Unofficially, there are more slaves in the world now, some 46 million according to a recent Global Slavery Index, than there have been *in total* in all past eras. Indeed slaves are far worse off today because in many past societies, like Hittite society, there were laws governing their treatment and their rights. There are no such laws today because officially slavery no longer exists!

Hittite male slaves were designated by the logogram ÌR in the Laws and other texts. This term basically means 'servant', and could be applied to anyone who was subordinate to someone else. Thus the king is the ÌR of the gods, and each of the king's subjects, from the highest to the lowest, is an ÌR of the king. Most commonly, however, the term designates a male slave, and GEME a female one. Persons reduced to this status could be bought from slave traders, who may have acquired them on foreign markets or kidnapped them from foreign lands. But slaves were sometimes of local origin, and originally free. A person who had committed a particularly serious crime could be punished by his enslavement to the victim's family, though he might have the option of producing another member of his family to take his place (if one could be persuaded or coerced). Other persons suffered reduction to slavery because of their failure to pay a debt. If the debt was substantial, other members of his family could have been forced to surrender their freedom as well. But debt-slaves were released after a few years – though we can't be sure precisely how long they remained slaves, or what if anything they had to do to regain their freedom.

By far the largest number of unfree persons were the 'booty-people' brought back to the homeland as part of the spoils of conquest by Hittite armies abroad. Officially designated by the logographic term NAM.RA.MEŠ, some were kept by the king and recruited into his armies or workforces, or served as temple personnel, some were allocated to the king's military officers to work their estates and some were used to repopulate sparsely inhabited or depopulated frontier areas of the homeland. In all cases, they were virtually owned by those to whom they were given, had no freedom of movement, and were forced to undertake all duties assigned to them. To all intents and purposes, they too were slaves, and they too could earn their freedom, sometimes for services rendered to their masters, and sometimes by accumulating sufficient property and goods to buy their way out of servitude.

We have noted that in many ancient societies, the treatment of slaves was subject to legal oversight. Hammurabic and Hittite society provide clear examples of this. Both had laws to ensure that slaves as well as all other members of society were justly treated. But like its Babylonian counterpart, Hittite justice was far from blind. Slave and free were clearly distinguished in the meting out of penalties for offences committed against or by them. Thus a person who blinds a slave or knocks out his tooth or breaks his arm or leg or bites off his nose, or tears off his ear pays only half the amount, or less, of the compensation imposed for inflicting the same injuries on a free person. Punishments for thefts of a fairly trivial nature committed by a slave (or by a free person for that matter) were fairly lenient. But when a slave committed a serious offence, he suffered a much severer penalty than a free person. Thus a slave found guilty of arson had his nose and ears cut off. A free person who committed the same offence was obliged to pay full compensation to his victim. But his bodily features were left intact.

MATRILOCAL AND MIXED MARRIAGES

One of the distinctive features of Hittite society was the *antiyant*-marriage. The Hittite term, which literally means 'one entering into', refers to a marriage in which a husband enters into his wife's family, rather than what is traditionally the other way round. We've seen that at society's topmost level, provision was made for the husband of a king's daughter to enter into the royal family as the king's adopted son and successor to the throne. Provision was made for this in the event of a king having no sons, or suitable sons, of his own to fill the position of heir designate. The term 'matrilocal' is used to refer to such marriages.

Similarly at lower social levels, the Laws indicate a number of cases where such marriages were contracted. One obvious reason for a family seeking to bring a son-in-law within its fold was to help ensure the continuation of a family line which had been weakened by the loss of at least some of its own male members on military campaigns. Alternatively, or in addition, such marriages boosted the supply of males available for physically demanding, labour-intensive activities like work on a family estate. One imagines that the incentives offered to a prospective son-in-law for joining his wife's family were not inconsiderable

This brings us back to the matter of mixed marriages. Though slaves were clearly inferior in status to the free members of society, they were in some circumstances able to contract marriages with women of free status. As in Hammurabic society, there seems to have been no legal impediment to a slave marrying a person of free status. One assumes that the slave-owner's consent would be required for the marriage to go ahead, but the Laws have nothing to say about this.

Several clauses envisage the possibility of a free woman marrying a slave, which almost certainly indicates that such marriages did take place. This raises several questions. Firstly, what effect did a marriage of this kind have on the legal status of the couple? Let's look at two clauses from the Laws which appear to answer this question. As elsewhere in this book, translations of the Laws are by Harry Hoffner:

> If a male slave pays a brideprice for a woman and takes her as his wife, no-one shall free her from slavery (§34).
>
> If a slave pays a brideprice for a free young man and acquires him as a son-in-law, no-one shall free him from slavery (§36).

If these translations are correct, then it would appear that free persons of either sex lose their freedom and become slaves if they marry slaves – provided a brideprice is paid. Hoffner comments that by accepting the brideprice, the parents of a free son or daughter relinquished the right to redeem their offspring from slavery. But this leaves open the question of *why* such a marriage was contracted in the first place.

We can only speculate – always bearing in mind that each law was very likely inspired by a particular case in the past whose details are unknown to us. It's possible that the slave in question had accumulated a tidy nest-egg, perhaps by acquiring land from a generous owner, or earning and saving funds as a tenant farmer of his owner. He might then have been able to afford to 'buy' a free wife or son-in-law, offering a sufficiently large brideprice to his prospective parents-in-law to make the proposition attractive to them. In such a case, parents would be effectively selling their sons or daughters into slavery. But they might have done so if they were in straitened circumstances and needed funds raised by the brideprice to pay off a debt or meet some other financial commitment. As we have seen, debt-slavery was not unknown in the Hittite world, the Near Eastern world in general, or indeed in the Classical world.

But then we must ask what did a slave, or a slave's father, have to gain from such an arrangement if the bride or bridegroom, originally free, was thus also reduced to slave status?

We could avoid this question if an alternative interpretation of the last part of the two clauses referred to above were accepted: Instead of 'no-one shall free her/him from slavery', the translation 'no-one shall change her/his social status' has also been proposed; that is to say, free marriage-partners would retain their free status after marrying slaves – provided the marriage was formalised by the payment of a brideprice. In this case, it's likely that a slave's descendants by his free wife or his free son-in-law would be born and remain free, even if he himself retained his slave status. Throughout the ages, the two greatest aspirations of slaves have been to die free, and to have children or descendants who are born free.

I am reminded that in Roman society there were a number of cases of a male slave marrying a free woman because in Roman law the offspring of a free woman were always freeborn, regardless of the father's status. But much closer to home, we have several Hammurabic laws which deal with marriages between slaves and free women. From the Babylonian clauses, it is clear that the free woman retained her free status and children of the marriage were born free.[5]

As far as the Hittite Laws are concerned, if Hoffner's translation of the two clauses discussed above is correct, I really cannot come up with any satisfactory motives for the mixed marriages, apart from what I have already suggested. Perhaps by looking at the matter afresh you may do better. Suggestions welcome!

There is of course another possibility we haven't considered – the possibility of a love-match between two people of unequal status. *Amor omnia vincit* as the saying goes, and the Hittite Laws are humane enough to recognise and provide for this.

The Laws are also aware that the course of true love, or arranged marriages, did not always run smooth and sometimes ended up in divorce. What is to happen to the children of a terminated marriage? That depends on the status of the marriage-partners. In the case of mixed marriages, the Laws inform us that if the husband is free and his wife a slave, the property they have accumulated is equally divided between them, but the wife takes only one of the children and her husband all the rest. If on the other hand, the woman is free and her husband a slave, she is the one who gets all except one of the chidren. This we learn from Clauses 31 and 32 of the Laws. In neither of these cases is any reference made to a brideprice as part of the original marriage settlement. Perhaps this is why a free partner in such a marriage apparently retained his/her free status – as these clauses clearly imply. At least such an explanation would be consistent with Hoffner's interpretation of Clauses 34 and 36, which we've just discussed.

ROYAL BRIDES

To my way of thinking, the women most to be pitied in Hittite society are those belonging to the most elite level of this society – the daughters of the king. These were valuable diplomatic assets, to be despatched to the marriage-beds of the king's foreign peers or important vassal rulers. Marriage-alliances generally involving Hittite princesses (occasionally Hittite princes) were an important means of forging or consolidating alliances between Hatti and its contemporaries. Thus in the wake of the 'Eternal Treaty' concluded in 1259 between Hattusili III and Ramesses II, Hattusili sent one of his daughters to Egypt to marry the pharaoh. The king's wife Puduhepa, who acted as royal matchmaker on a number of occasions, made the preparations for the princess' journey to Egypt for the marriage.

We know this from letters exchanged between Puduhepa and Ramesses. Some of the exchanges were acrimonious, with the pharaoh rebuking Puduhepa for undue delays in sending him his princess. Puduhepa in return accused the pharaoh of being mercenary: he was interested only in the gifts he'd receive from Hattusa as part of the marriage-settlement.[6] (At least that is what she originally wrote. But the version we have of her letter is only a draft, and she may well have toned down her language in the letter's final version.)

But all arrangements were finally completed, and the princess despatched to Egypt where Ramesses received her with all due pomp and ceremony. Indeed, he wrote in rapturous terms about her to her parents.[7] Unfortunately, the royal couple did not live happily ever after. Besotted though he may have been with his Hittite bride at the outset, Ramesses did not make her his chief wife, as Hattusili and Puduhepa had expected from the marriage-settlement. And to Hattusili's great disappointment the union produced no heirs. In a thinly veiled criticism of Ramesses' manhood (or lack of it), Hattusili complained of the union's failure to bear fruit, suggesting that the pharaoh was not up to the job. Quite unfairly! The pharaoh's loins proved extremely fruitful on many other occasions, as evidenced by the well over 100 offspring sired by them, at times when they weren't girt for battle. But as far as we can tell, nary a one of them had a Hittite mother. Indeed, it seems that the Hittite princess later disappeared into obscurity, consigned to a royal harem in the Faiyum Oasis west of the Nile. There is no trace of her existence when some years later a second daughter of Hattusili was sent to Egypt to wed the pharaoh.

Let's spare a thought for these royal women. In a sense, they were little better than glorified sex slaves, used as mere tools to advance the affairs of state, ending up, after a secluded and privileged life in their father's court, in totally alien locations, knowing nothing of the local languages or customs, and probably relegated to a harem-like existence where obscurity was probably the least cruel of the treatments to which they were subjected. There were of course obvious exceptions to all this, most notably Suppiluliuma's Babylonian queen who dominated and disrupted the royal household through the last years of her husband's reign, the reign of her stepson Arnuwanda and part of the reign of her younger stepson Mursili, before she was finally banished from the palace.

We hear of other instances where royal marriages came to a bad ending. That was the fate of a marriage-alliance between two of Hatti's vassal kingdoms, Amurru and Ugarit. In an effort to bind more closely together these neighbouring kingdoms, a princess of Amurru had been wed to Ammishtamru (II), the recently installed king of Ugarit. The marriage ended in divorce – apparently because the princess had been found guilty of some serious offence, perhaps adultery. She had been sent back to Amurru in disgrace. But after she'd gone, her ex-husband kept brooding about her behaviour and concluded that she had got off too lightly. He promptly wrote to his ex-brother-in-law, the king of Amurru, demanding that his sister be returned to Ugarit for appropriate punishment; if the demand was refused, the aggrieved ex-husband declared he would go to war with Amurru to enforce it.

The Amurrite king was in a bit of a dilemma. He didn't want war, but then again if he sent his sister back to Ugarit, he knew she would almost certainly suffer a horrible death. Tudhaliya IV was the Hittite king at this time, and the last thing he wanted was a war between two of his most important Syrian vassals. Compromise was essential, and Tudhaliya came up with one that both sides accepted. The Amurrite king was to send his sister back to Ugarit, in exchange for whom he would receive from Ugarit's king a one-off payment of 1,400 shekels of gold. That would help soothe his grief as he farewelled his sister on her way back to her death in the land of her ex-husband.[8]

WOMEN IN THE WORKFORCE

Our texts provide us with very little evidence about women engaging in professional activities in Hittite society. We learn of no women scribes or bureaucrats (preserves almost certainly exclusive to the male sex, and very largely to male members of particular family groups). And though there were certainly priestesses who made up the personnel of many religious establishments and were

participants in many religious festivals, the positions they occupied
were probably well down the priestly hierarchy – even in cases
where a particular cult was dedicated to a female deity, like the
goddess Ishtar or the Sun Goddess of Arinna.

There are occasional references to women's involvement in
various lower-level occupations, as bakers, cooks, weavers and
fullers. They were also hired as seasonal farm-labourers, alongside
male labourers, though their rate of pay, as specified in the Laws,
was only half that of men, or even less. Payment was often in kind.
Thus Clause 158 of the Laws tells us that in the harvest season:

> If a free man hires himself out for wages, to bind sheaves,
> load them on wagons, deposit them in barns, and clear the
> threshing floors, his wages for three months shall be fifteen
> hundred litres of barley. If a woman hires herself out for
> wages in the harvest season, her wages for three months shall
> be six hundred litres of barley.

Of course as we have noted, the Laws served merely as guidelines,
not as prescriptive rulings. And the value of women in the workforce
no doubt increased substantially at times of severe shortages of
manpower due to plague, the redeployment of males on public
works projects, or the absence of males on military campaigns. Their
rates of pay may have varied considerably depending on the
circumstances which led to their employment.

But women did play a major role in the various healing
professions. We know that a number of women practised as
physicians, perhaps as many as one to four male physicians,[9] and
women were very prominent in other healing arts. Midwives figure
in a number of our texts – firstly to assist with the birth of a baby
and then in uttering incantations designed to ensure that the baby
would be healthy and enjoy a long life. We've discussed this at
greater length in Chapter 13.

We have no idea of infant mortality rates in the Hittite world.
But in view of the importance that must have been attached to
population renewal, a great deal of attention was very likely focused
on keeping these rates as low as possible – through the attention
of specially trained midwives and other health professionals in

combination with all appropriate rituals to gain the goodwill of the gods. Given that the kingdom of Hatti almost certainly suffered chronic shortages in its labour and defence forces, a newborn child must have been one of its most valuable assets.

Such an asset was essential to the maintenance of Hatti's status as a great military power. And that brings us to the reign of Mursili's son Muwattalli, and the decisive showdown with the king's Royal Brother from the land of the Nile.

CHAPTER 17

WAR WITH EGYPT

THE AMURRITE TERRORIST CLAN

B efore reading any further, have a look again at Map 6.1, and note the locations of Amurru, a mountainous region lying between the Orontes river and the Mediterranean coast, and a bit further south the city-state of Qadesh on the east bank of the Orontes. These lands were key components of the events leading up to the final showdown (more precisely showdowns) between the Great Kings of Hatti and Egypt. In the past, both lands had been subject-territories of Egypt. But during the reigns of the pharaohs Amenhotep III and his son Akhenaten, Amurru had become a wild and anarchic region, taken over by a terrorist-clan led firstly by a ruthless brigand called Abdi-Ashirta. This man built himself a formidable military force by recruiting large numbers of predatory semi-nomadic groups called Habiru, promising them rich plunder in return for their services. Having secured their support, he not only set about robbing hapless groups of travellers who passed through the open countryside he controlled, but also let loose his bands of thugs on the cities and settled populations of the region. In so doing, he risked bringing upon himself the wrath and military might of Egypt, for these peoples and cities were subjects of the pharaoh.

But he kept staving off Egyptian military retaliation by protesting in response to the pharaoh's complaints that he was His Majesty's devoted subject, and that all his actions were carried out to protect his interests and eliminate those elements who were disloyal to him. He got away with this for quite some time until his career was suddenly ended. We don't know the details but it's likely that he pushed his luck too far with the pharaoh, probably Amenhotep III, who sent a strong Egyptian expeditionary force to Amurru and captured and no doubt executed the miscreant. But that failed to solve the problem in Amurru. For Abdi-Ashirta's shoes were rapidly filled by his son Aziru, under whose leadership the terrorist-clan continued to harass, plunder and seize for themselves the cities and territories of the pharaoh, now Akhenaten.

Like his father, Aziru protested that in all he did, he was merely acting as his overlord's agent, particularly by keeping out Egypt's most dangerous enemy – the Hittites. For Amurru was a frontier state adjacent to Hittite subject-territory in Syria, and there were ominous signs of a large build-up of Hittite forces in the region. The Hittite threat and Aziru's representations of himself as a bulwark against it, were apparently sufficient to ward off any action by a deeply suspicious pharaoh, and despite a constant stream of complaints by the rulers of other Egyptian vassal states in the region. Most vocal among these was the king of Byblos, whose city-state was in imminent danger of falling to Aziru.

All this we know from the letters exchanged between the terrorist leaders, their victims, and the pharaoh – one of the most interesting groups of letters found in the Amarna archive.[1] From these letters we learn too that while pledging his allegiance to the pharaoh, Aziru was establishing alliances with states that had already gone over to the Hittite side, including the ruler of Qadesh which bordered on Amurru's territory. 'You are at peace with the ruler of Qadesh. The two of you take food and strong drink together. Why do you act so?' Akhenaten demanded to know.

And as Aziru's acts of treachery became ever more blatant, and the cries of his victims ever more shrill and desperate, the pharaoh's patience ran out. Aziru was summoned to Egypt to explain himself in his overlord's presence. 'If for any reason you plot evil treacherous things,' Aziru was warned, 'you and your entire family shall die by the axe of the king!' Aziru realised his bluff had been well and truly called. Though he had complied with the pharaoh's demand that he come to Egypt for a thorough briefing on an earlier occasion, this time he realised that if he returned to Egypt, the likelihood of his being detained there indefinitely – or worse – was considerable. Best not to risk it. Instead, he declared his allegiance to King Suppiluliuma of Hatti.

THE LOOMING SHOWDOWN WITH EGYPT

Henceforth, both Amurru and Qadesh as well as other former Egyptian territories remained firmly in Hittite hands – for the time being. But there was no doubt that Egypt wanted them back, and would take the first opportunity it could to wrest them from Hittite control. That opportunity presented itself with the emergence of a powerful new dynasty in Egypt, the Nineteenth or so-called Ramesside dynasty, named after its founder Ramesses I. This Ramesses reigned only briefly before dying and leaving the throne to his son and successor Seti I (1294–1279). Seti soon made it clear that one of his major aims was to get back Amurru and Qadesh. At that time the Hittite throne was occupied by Muwattalli II (c.1295–1272).

Muwattalli's father and predecessor Mursili had left him a relatively stable kingdom throughout the length and breadth of its territories. But the new king realised that matters would soon come to a head with Egypt, and very likely began making comprehensive preparations for a major war with his Egyptian Royal Brother shortly after his accession. This meant building a substantial military force, to be taken deep into Syrian territory and probably stationed there for a long time. Which was not without its problems. Hittite history had given repeated lessons about the dangers of stripping the kingdom's military resources for major campaigns far from the homeland, and thus leaving Hatti's core territory vulnerable to hostile neighbours, particularly the Kaska tribes. How was Muwattalli to ensure the security of his homeland, especially the royal capital, while taking the bulk of his army to Syria for a war with Egypt?

A NEW ROYAL CAPITAL

This provides the context, and probably at least part of the explanation, for an astonishingly bold decision Muwattalli made – to shift the seat of his empire to a new location several hundred kilometres to the south of Hattusa. It was called Tarhuntassa.[2] Virtually unknown until then, Tarhuntassa lay somewhere in the western part of the region which the Greeks and Romans called Cilicia. You'll recall that once before a Hittite king had left Hattusa and set up his administration in another place, probably the city called Samuha located to the east, or in the eastern part, of the homeland. But this was done under duress and was intended to be no more than a temporary move. Almost certainly Muwattalli's new royal seat was to become the permanent new capital of the empire. The fact that Hattusa's gods and ancestral spirits were transferred there from Hattusa is seen as a clear indication of this.

Why precisely Muwattalli decided to take such a radical step has led to much debate. One suggestion is that Hattusa was simply too vulnerable as a royal capital, especially if Muwattalli planned to move a large part of his military forces to Syria. But there may well have been a number of reasons for the move, both practical and strategic, which we're unaware of. And there was no intention on Muwattalli's part to leave the northern part of his kingdom to fend for itself. The former capital Hattusa continued to function as a regional centre of the kingdom under the administration of a chief bureaucrat appointed by Muwattalli. And to secure all the homeland's territories to its northern frontier, Muwattalli converted it into a largely autonomous kingdom within the empire, and placed it under the command of his brother Hattusili (later to become Hattusili III).

Hatti thus became essentially a diarchy, with sovereignty over its northern regions conferred upon Hattusili who bore the title LUGAL 'king'.[3] Most importantly, Hattusili was charged with the responsibility of repopulating abandoned or sparsely inhabited areas within his kingdom, resurrecting ghost towns and resettling areas which had been largely occupied by the Kaskans. It's likely that many of these settlers were drawn from the substantial pool of deportees brought back in their thousands from lands conquered by Mursili. This was one of the most tangible legacies Mursili left to his successor.

NEW PROBLEMS IN THE WEST

Muwattalli had also to deal with unwelcome new developments in the west. One of these was the emergence of an insurrectionist called Piyamaradu – possibly a former Hittite subject of high status and maybe even related to the royal family. After apparently losing favour with his royal master, Piyamaradu had set about building a power-base for himself in western Anatolia. He may have gained temporary control over at least two Hittite subject-states in the region, Wilusa and Seha River Land, before an expeditionary force sent by Muwattalli drove him out of the occupied territories and restored them to Hittite rule. Some time later, Muwattalli drew up a treaty with the king of Wilusa which was designed to strengthen the Hittites' hold over their western territories. This still surviving treaty is commonly known as the Alaksandu treaty, after the vassal king who ruled it at the time.[4]

But Piyamaradu remained on the loose, and would continue to threaten Hittite interests in the west for many years to come. What made him all the more dangerous was that he operated in cahoots with the current king of Ahhiyawa. This king (name unknown) continued to advance Ahhiyawan interests in at least the western fringe territories of Anatolia, and indeed appears to have achieved a major success in his endeavours. In all probability, the land and city of Milawata (Classical Miletos) which had already tried unsuccessfully to ally itself with Ahhiyawa early in Mursili's reign, now became subject-territory of the Ahhiyawan king. We have no textual record of a Mycenaean/Ahhiyawan takeover of the city and surrounding region, but we do have material evidence of a substantial Mycenaean presence there at this time, including Mycenaean architecture, burials and common domestic artefacts.

THE BATTLES OF QADESH

A first clash between Hittite and Egyptian forces took place probably not far from Qadesh during Seti I's reign. On his war monument in the temple of Karnak in Egypt, Seti claimed a great victory for himself and a smashing defeat for the Hittites. He does so with lots of rhetorical bombast, but even shorn of this, his account very likely does reflect a major Egyptian victory. We know that in the wake of the battle, the territories over which the Royal Brothers were in dispute, Amurru and Qadesh, both reverted to Egyptian control. But the Seti–Muwattalli clash was just a curtain-raiser to the main event, the famous battle of Qadesh fought between Muwattalli and Seti's son and successor Ramesses II. This was in 1274, the fifth year of Ramesses' reign.

The pharaoh's version of events, culminating in the battle itself, is recorded in both words and pictures (the latter with accompanying captions) on the walls of no fewer than five Egyptian temples.[5] Unfortunately, we have no corresponding Hittite account, to balance the blatantly biased Egyptian version. But we can sort out some of the basic facts, reading between the lines of what Ramesses tells us. You will find modern accounts of the actual battle and the events which preceded it in many sources.[6] So let us here just briefly summarise some of its main features.

Ramesses' army was made up of four divisions, each recruited from an Egyptian city named after a prominent Egyptian god – Amun, Re, Ptah and Sutekh. From his capital Pi-Ramesse in the Egyptian Delta, the expedition set out, with Ramesses commanding the first of these divisions. Muwattalli for his part had recruited an army 47,500 in number, including some 3,500 chariotry (with three men per chariot; see next chapter) and 37,000 infantry. This is what Ramesses' account tells us, the Hittite numbers swelled by many foreign troops serving as mercenaries; the land of Hatti was stripped of silver to pay for them, according to Ramesses.[7] As they travelled northwards, the Egyptian divisions became increasingly spread out and separated from one another. Ramesses was not concerned about this, particularly when two apparent defectors from the Hittite army came to him with the news that Muwattalli and his forces were at that time still far to the north of Qadesh, in the land of Aleppo. Incredibly, the pharaoh sought no verification of their story, but in leisurely fashion started setting up his camp with the Amun division, across the Orontes and northwest of Qadesh city.

Figure 17.1 Ramesses II, Abu Simbel.

But then came horrifying news. Two genuine Hittite scouts sent to spy out Ramesses' position were captured, and under torture revealed that the entire Hittite army was in a concealed position the other side of the Orontes, poised to attack. And attack they suddenly did, smashing into the Amun division while it was still making camp, and charging into the Re (Second) Division which was still crossing the river to the south. The other two Egyptian divisions were too far away to be of any use at all to Ramesses. A total rout of the first two divisions and the capture or death of the pharaoh, seemed inevitable. But luck was with the Egyptians. Believing the victory was already won, the Hittite forces discarded all discipline and set about plundering the Egyptian camp. This afforded the Egyptians an opportunity to regroup, their morale boosted by the arrival of a large number of reinforcements from the west, probably from Amurru. Ramesses claims that he won the battle, and did so singlehandedly. Yet at the end of the day neither side was able to claim victory, and when fighting resumed on the morrow the outcome was still a stalemate.

Nevertheless, with the wisdom of hindsight we must declare the Hittite king Muwattalli the ultimate winner of the contest. Qadesh and Amurru once more reverted to Hittite control, and the pharaoh's retreating forces were pursued by the Hittite army to the region of Damascus. Damascus-city and the territory attached to it, which had hitherto been firmly under Egyptian control, were now occupied by Muwattalli's forces and placed under the command of the king's brother Hattusili. Subsequently, Damascus was returned to Egypt, and a de facto boundary between Hittite and Egyptian territory was established just to the north of the city.

Of course, you wouldn't have been aware of any of this if your time machine had taken you back to Ramesses' Egypt, and the pharaoh had given you a tour of the five temples where *his* version of the Qadesh engagement was recorded. He would have relished pointing out to you his alleged resounding defeat of his opponent's forces and the abject surrender of the Hittite king, 'the wretched one of Hatti'. Even with the wisdom of hindsight, would you have dared challenge his version of events while you were his guest?

In subsequent years, Ramesses did in fact try to bolster his international reputation by further campaigns which took him deep into Hittite subject-territory, and posed further threats to the security of the Hittites' Syrian states. But there was never another major battle between the two Great Kings. Indeed, the casualties on both sides had been so heavy that neither could afford another such engagement. Even so, tensions between the two powers remained high, not to be resolved for some years to come. And all the while Assyria lurked menacingly on the sidelines.

CHAPTER 18

ALL THE KING'S HORSES AND ALL THE KING'S MEN: THE HITTITE MILITARY MACHINE[1]

H ow did they do it? Before explaining what I mean by this question, let's look at some figures.

THE SIZE OF THE ARMY

As we've noted, Ramesses' inscriptions tell us that in the Qadesh engagement the Hittite king put 47,500 warriors into the field. He claims that this total included a massive horde of mercenaries hired by his Hittite adversary. It's possible that Hittite kings did hire mercenary troops to swell their ranks for major military operations (despite the fact that no Hittite texts make mention of them) – though Ramesses may have exaggerated the size of the mercenary component at Qadesh. But even if he did, his overall figures are probably fairly accurate. Indeed, a warrior-king is more likely to overestimate than underestimate the size of his enemy, to enhance his military reputation if he wins a battle, or to have a ready excuse if he loses it. In any case, both armies were probably quite evenly matched in numerical strength. And undoubtedly

Muwattalli did muster all the forces he could for the engagement, especially after his earlier defeat by Ramesses' father on the same battlefield.

Allowing for the possibility of a mercenary element in his army at least for this battle, we can probably put the size of Muwattalli's *own* troops at Qadesh at somewhere around 40,000. Of course, he would have needed to leave a sizeable defence force behind him in Anatolia, both within the Hittite homeland, as well as in the south in the region around his new capital Tarhuntassa. (This is on the assumption that he had shifted his royal capital there prior to Qadesh.) Already several of his predecessors had learnt from bitter experience the dangers of exposing their homeland regions to enemy invasions by failing to leave an adequate defence force there while they were engaged on major campaigns in distant lands. At a guess, I suggest that a force of at least 10,000–15,000 troops would have been left to defend core regions of the empire. Many of these were probably 'reservists', who had other occupations as farm labourers etc., but had also been given military training and could be quickly called up from their usual jobs if and when the need arose. The total size of the Hittite army around the time of the Qadesh engagement would thus have been around 50,000 to

Figure 18.1   Hittite Warriors (locals used in Ekip Film's *The Hittites*).

55,000 (give or take a few thousand) – plus mercenaries if and when hired, and levies from subject-states if and when called upon.

THE COMPOSITION OF THE ARMY

The core of the army was a professional standing force on all-year-round duty. They lived in military barracks, and were on constant standby, for immediate military action. But generally, military campaigning was a seasonal activity, carried out between spring and early autumn. In 'off-seasons', full-time soldiers could be employed on public projects, like the construction and maintenance of roads, public buildings and defence works, and on policing activities. Many members of the standing army were probably recruited from the subject-territories. Sometimes, certain states, like Tarhuntassa, were granted exemption from the obligation of providing their own youth for full-time service in the Hittite army. Otherwise, local officials were responsible for recruiting young men from their districts and sending them to Hattusa for military training. One can imagine that many lived in dread of a knock on the door by the local recruiting agent. And once selected, there was no way out, nor any chance of paying someone else to take your place, even if you could afford it. A mild consolation for reluctant draftees was that they joined units made up of other draftees from their own regions, and served under officers also recruited locally.

To the above recruitment pool we should add a significant number of the deportees brought back as spoils of war from Hittite military conquests. As we've noted, many were assigned as farm labourers to agricultural estates and to various other labour-intensive activities, but many also helped swell the ranks of, or make up for shortfalls in, the military forces – some as part of the standing army, some as reservists called upon as the need arose.

The king was the army's commander-in-chief and often led campaigns in person, in keeping with his image in royal ideology as a great warrior-leader. But he sometimes deputised his command to other family members, notably the crown prince, or one of the king's brothers. This happened especially at times when Hittite armies were obliged to fight campaigns in several different regions simultaneously or when campaigns of a relatively minor nature were undertaken. When the king himself led a campaign force, the crown prince and other able-bodied royal males often served as divisional leaders under His Majesty's supreme command. In battle as in daily life, the king was protected by an elite bodyguard of spearmen known as the *MESHEDI*, led by another member of the royal family, called the GAL.*MESHEDI*, one of the most prestigious appointments in the imperial administration.

Next in the military hierarchy came a cadre of officers drawn from the aristocracy. Land-owning barons and other dignitaries provided the officer class. But for them as for all other Hittite warriors, fighting was a part-time occupation. Most of it was carried out during a campaigning season which generally extended between spring and early autumn, as we've noted. Whenever possible, it was important to get the fighting over in time for the army to return home before the winter snows set in. The part-time officer class was made up predominantly of the owners of large grazing and farming estates, often bestowed on them as royal land-grants. In return, they were obliged to render military service to the king during the campaigning season, and were further rewarded for this by the king who allocated a portion of the spoils of military victories to them, in the form of deportees, or prisoners-of-war, and cattle and sheep. The deportees boosted their owner's agricultural workforce, the cattle and sheep his herds and flocks. Very likely when called upon for a military campaign, the land-owning officer was obliged to bring many of his male farm labourers with him to swell the army's infantry ranks. It was a double quid-pro-quo system.

On most campaigns, infantry probably made up at least 90 per cent of the army's total force. The remaining 10 per cent consisted almost entirely of an elite chariot corps, drawn primarily from the officer class. (The chariotry at Qadesh apparently formed a much greater percentage of the overall Hittite force.)

WEAPONS AND BATTLE DRESS

We have a fairly clear picture of how a Hittite infantryman was armed and equipped from the famous relief of a warrior-god,

Figure 18.2 Warrior-God with detail of upper torso, 'King's Gate', Hattusa.

2.25 m high, carved on the inside of one of the main gates of Hattusa, the sculpture that had so puzzled Charles Texier. The warrior-god's armaments clearly represent those of his mortal worshippers. His head is encased in a leather helmet, to which cheek- and neck-flaps are attached and at the back a long plume. On the lower half of his torso, he wears a short kilt. He *may* have worn a shirt of mail, as perhaps indicated by the wiry-looking coils on his upper torso. These coils have also been interpreted as a thick mat of hair, but there are other indications of a mail-shirt protective covering, including bits of scale-armour, found in Hattusa.

Interestingly, the Hittite charioteers depicted in Egyptian relief sculptures of the battle of Qadesh are all clothed in neck-to-ankle sleeved garments. These garments were probably made of linen and leather over which chain mail was sewn. Leather shoes with toes upturned seem also to have been regulation issue for Hittite troops. Basic defensive armament was provided by several types of shields, the standard one made of leather stretched over a wooden frame, large enough to protect the body from neck to thigh.

Hittite weaponry for infantrymen are represented by the battle-axe which the warrior-god clasps in his right hand and a short sword with curved blade which the god wears at his waist. Short, ribbed stabbing swords with crescent-shaped pommel, some with slighly curved blades, and longswords used for thrusting, were standard issue to Hittite troops. The first were particularly suitable for close-in or hand-to-hand fighting in mountainous terrain or forested areas. The longsword was more effective in battles fought on open ground, which the Hittites preferred and were better at, as was also the long spear, more than 2 m in length, regular army issue at all levels. Bows and bronze-tipped arrows were the principal weapon of the chariotry.

CHARIOTS AND HORSES

Chariotry was first used in campaigns after the horse was introduced into the Hittite world, probably around 1600. Detailed information about the preparation of Hittite horses for chariot combat is provided by a still surviving training manual, allegedly the work of a prisoner-of-war brought back by the Hittites as a deportee from Mittani.[2] The horse-training manual covers a period of 214 days, 32 of which deal with night-training manoeuvres so that the animals would be accustomed to combat in night operations. The horses were trained for their speed, strength, their prompt reaction to commands, and above all their stamina. A rigorous culling of animals was carried out before the programme began, so that only the strongest and fittest were accepted for training.

There was an apparently significant development in Hittite chariot warfare when the chariot crew was increased from two men to three, the standard team of driver and fighter (armed with spear and bow and arrow) now augmented by a third member, a shield-bearing defender. The defender's sole job was to protect the driver and the fighter, fending off enemy spears and arrows, and thus leaving the driver free to manoeuvre his vehicle and keep it upright, and the fighter to attack the enemy. We see these three-man chariots depicted in Egyptian reliefs of the battle of Qadesh. Made of leather stretched over a wooden frame, the chariot had to be strong enough to support three fully armed warriors in extreme

Figure 18.3   Three-man Hittite chariot, Luxor.

battle conditions. To give greater stability to the heavily loaded vehicle, the axle was shifted from the vehicle's rear to its middle.

I should say that apart from the record of the Qadesh engagement, we have no evidence of the use by the Hittites of three-man chariots in warfare. This leads me to suspect that the three-man crew was purely a one-off tactic – an attempt to give the Hittites an edge over their opponents after their first apparently disastrous encounter with Egyptian forces at Qadesh some years earlier during Seti I's reign. We have no indications that the three-man chariot was ever used again by the Hittites after Qadesh.

Despite the theoretical advantages of the three-man chariot, there were obvious significant limitations to its use in battle. The main one was that it must have been slower, less manoeuvrable, and less stable than its two-man counterpart – much more likely to spill its occupants if it had to make a sharp turn, however great the driver's skill. Very likely, then, it was used primarily at the beginning of a battle, with a chariot contingent acting like a modern tank formation, travelling at speed before the other troops, crashing into and creating mayhem among the enemy forces, and thus paving the way for the infantry to move in for the kill. The speed of a chariot contingent in full attack mode has been estimated at 45 km (about 28 miles) per hour. It's interesting to recall the words of a number of Hittite kings that their gods 'ran before them into battle'. If taken literally, the gods could thus have outperformed many a modern Olympic athlete! But of course if you're a god, why not?

There is also the question of how the chariots were actually transported to distant battle sites, often hundreds of kilometres away, over rough terrain, and still be in a sound enough state to carry their warriors in full battle gear into the heat of the fighting without the risk of their falling apart. I find it hard to believe that they were actually *driven* to distant theatres of war, with all the wear and tear they would have suffered on the way. Rather, in my opinion, they were *carried* there – in wooden carts, perhaps after being disassembled. As the army approached the battlefield, the chariots could quickly be unloaded, reassembled if necessary, and thus still be in first-rate battle condition. (Part of a chariot-team's training may well have been to learn the prompt reassembling of their chariot as they drew near to enemy territory.) There would obviously be benefit in this for the chariot-horses as well – for without having to drag a chariot and a driver over very long distances they could be kept in as fresh a condition as possible before facing the rigours of armed conflict.

What about cavalry? In fact we have no clear evidence that the Hittite army regularly included a cavalry contingent, though cavalry detachments and small groups of armed horsemen may have played some role in Hittite military operations, and we have occasional references to mounted troops being despatched against cities, towns and enemy forces.[3] It's likely that mounted horsemen were involved primarily in reconnaissance activities, and in escorting deportees and captured livestock back to the homeland. (We do incidentally have indications that the Egyptians used small numbers of cavalry in their military forces.)

ARMY DISCIPLINE

Though we have few details, military training and discipline within the army must have been harsh and rigorous. This was a necessity given the large distances the expeditionary forces frequently had to cover, in as short a time as possible and often in harsh environmental conditions. All the while they needed to be in peak physical shape, fully prepared to meet at short notice enemy attacks along the campaign route as well as at the final destination. Deserters were referred directly to the king for punishment. Those found guilty were almost certainly executed, probably after they'd been paraded before the troops in women's clothes as a sign of their cowardice. Failure to report acts of disloyalty by officers or by those in the ranks also incurred the death penalty. In one particularly serious crisis, a king threatened his officers stationed in one of the homeland provinces with blinding or execution for failing to respond promptly to his commands: 'Say to Kassu and Zilapiya: "As soon as this letter reaches you, come with all haste before His Majesty. If not, (my men) will come to you and blind you on the spot!"'

How did they do it?

This brings me back to my initial question. How did they do it? What I mean is this. Despite their limited resources, Hittite kings managed to build an empire which at its peak in the fourteenth and thirteenth centuries stretched from the western coast of Anatolia, right across the Anatolian peninsula to the Euphrates river, and down south through Syria as far as the northern frontier of Damascus. It was a kingdom made up of a myriad of disparate vassal states which largely retained their independence in their local affairs, and often rebelled against Hittite overlordship. How did the rulers of Hatti keep control of this vast region, while still ensuring that their homeland had sufficient troops to defend it when the main army was on campaign? They had also to ensure that Hatti's foodlands remained productive to their maximum capacity. Food production was a highly labour-intensive activity, and would be seriously affected if a large proportion of the land's agricultural workforce were reassigned to military service – especially at peak periods of the agricultural year. We've estimated the size of the Hittite fighting force, including reservists, at around 50,000 or not much more, plus subject-state levies. Not a large number when you look at the vast territory over which Hatti's armed forces were expected to maintain control. Back then to our question. How did they do it?

Let's begin with a brief consideration of the logistics of a campaign. One of the most important of these was ensuring that your troops had enough food and drink to sustain them on their marches, often through arid and semi-arid lands, sometimes occupied by enemy populations or populations sympathetic to them. Basic food supplies were brought from the homeland. They consisted primarily of rations of flour and bread (called 'soldier-bread') packed into oxen- or horse-drawn carts forming part of the baggage train, or carried in sacks slung over the backs of donkeys. These supplies were supplemented by the contents of food silos, called 'seal houses', which were built on a number of campaign routes, at strategic intervals within the subject-territories, for reprovisioning both the army and its animals. Provisions were also requisitioned from local rulers subject or friendly to Hatti, through whose territory a Hittite expeditionary force passed. The Hittite king guaranteed that all requisitioned goods would be paid for in full. But when the army marched through enemy or neutral territories, its troops were were given free rein to loot whatever they could from the towns and villages and foodlands to supplement their rations.

Then there was the question of the return home after a successful campaign. On the outward journey, the well-trained, physically fit troops could move with considerable speed to their destination. But the return must have been much slower. This was because of the large number of deportees forcibly transplanted to the homeland, along with large numbers of cattle and sheep, as part of the spoils of war. Sometimes, according to Hittite records, the numbers of deportees ran into the thousands – men, women and children; the livestock, we're told, were too numerous to count.

The upside of all this was that the deportees became an important, indeed perhaps at times a vital, supplement to the homeland population, particularly after the great plague which broke out in the final years of Suppiluliuma I's reign, and the livestock significantly built up the homeland's herds and flocks. The downside was that the movement of the deportees and livestock would have considerably slowed the return journey, substantially more food had to be found to sustain both the human as well as the animal booty, and all the booty had to be closely guarded to prevent defections by the human part of it, and the rustling of the animal part of it by local raiders. Dire warnings issued by the king against any state which provided asylum for escaping deportees, and extradition clauses in the vassal treaties covering the return of fugitives who had reached the state of a vassal ruler appear to have been reasonably effective in keeping the attrition rate low.

Then of course there is the question of how quickly and effectively the deportees were assimilated into the Hittite population. We have no information about this. But given that Hatti's population was such a heterogeneous one to begin with, new elements could more rapidly be absorbed into this population than if it had been structured on more clear-cut ethnic lines. As far as we're aware, issues of racial discrimination or claimed racial superiority over newcomers by longer established elements in the homeland never arose. And apart from the rebellion of the thousands of prisoners-of-war early in the fourteenth century (see Chapter 7), the deportees assigned to the agricultural workforce and military service seem to have adapted fairly readily, perhaps under a great deal of compulsion, to their new lives. At least we hear nothing to the contrary.

But while attempting to answer our question 'How did they do it?', let's ask another one: 'Were there times when they tried to *avoid* doing it?' Though royal ideology required a king to demonstrate his prowess as a military leader with impressive conquests and stacks of plunder, and though a warrior culture was deeply embedded in Hittite society, the Great Kings of Hatti often committed themselves to military ventures beyond their home-land *only* when they appear to have had no other option. They were well aware of the costs and risks that these enterprises entailed. Particularly so, given the limited manpower on which they could draw, and the necessity of doing so without seriously affecting the supply of able-bodied men available for working the land and for other major projects, like the construction and maintenance of city fortifications.

These considerations help explain why Hittite kings some-times seemed excessively indulgent in their treatment of wayward vassals, and in their attempts to come to terms with regional insurrectionists rather than take military action against them. We've seen in Chapter 8 how reluctant two successive Hittite kings were to use military force against their manipulative, treacherous protégé Madduwatta, even though he was consorting with the enemy and building a small empire of his own in the west. Later, the western renegade Piyamaradu defied Hittite authority repeatedly, until a Hittite king, probably Hattusili III, was forced to lead a campaign against him; even while on the march, Hattusili tried unsuccessfully to end Piyamaradu's insurrectionist activities in Hatti's western states by diplomatic rather than military means.

THE ROLE OF THE TREATY

Yet diplomatic activity often provided the Hittites with a relatively successful means of maintaining their authority through the lands they won initially by force. After deporting many of a defeated country's inhabitants, thus weakening the country's potential for future uprisings, a Hittite king sought to seal his authority over it by a treaty which bound its ruler to him as his vassal. Vassal treaties were one-to-one compacts drawn up by the Hittite king and imposed upon his vassal, either one who had ruled his state before it was conquered, or one newly appointed by the Hittite king. In both cases, the ruler was of local origin. He was granted a large measure of autonomy in the way he administered his own kingdom. And in return for fulfilling his obligations to his overlord, he was guaranteed not only his own rule in his state but also that of his rightful successors to the throne. The guarantee was backed by an assurance of Hittite military support, if this proved necessary. In return, the vassal swore unconditional allegiance to his overlord, and his rightful successors.[4]

Thus in his treaty with Alaksandu, vassal ruler of the western Anatolian state Wilusa, Muwattalli states:

You, Alaksandu, (must) benevolently protect My Majesty. And later protect my son and grandson, to the first and second generation. And as I, My Majesty, protected you, Alaksandu, in good will because of the word of your father, and came to your aid, and killed your enemy for you, later in the future my sons and my grandsons will certainly protect your descendants for you, to the first and second generation. If some enemy arises for you, I will not abandon you, just as I have not now abandoned you. I will kill your enemy for you.[5]

This provision emphasises a definitive feature of the treaties: they were agreements concluded not between two states but between two persons. This meant that a new treaty had to be drawn up every time a new Great King or a new vassal ruler ascended his kingdom's throne.

Amongst other important features of the vassal treaties was the requirement that a vassal must provide his overlord with troops whenever called upon – most likely when the king was on campaign against other states in his region. In the western states in particular, the vassals were obliged to act as local watchdogs for their overlord, advising him of any developments within their region – or outside it – prejudicial to Hittite interests, like the brewing of insurrectionist activity in a neighbouring state. Thus King Mursili II warns Targasnalli, one of his Arzawan vassal rulers:

> If you hear in advance of some evil plan to revolt, and either some Hittite or some man of Arzawa is at fault [...] and you do not quickly write in advance to My Majesty, but ignore these men, and think as follows: 'Let this evil take place', then you will have violated your oath.[6]

Advance warning of such activity enabled the king to take appropriate pre-emptive action – preferably diplomatic, but military if necessary.

The treaties sometimes specify an annual tribute to be paid by the vassal ruler to Hattusa on behalf of his kingdom. And this no doubt constituted a not insignificant contribution to Hatti's revenue. But as much as anything else, the treaties were intended to minimise the need for regular Hittite military action in the regions where they were located. And if the Hittite king was obliged to conduct military campaigns in these regions, he could call upon the vassal for both military support and the provisioning of his troops with food and other necessities of life.

Hittite garrisons were never established permanently in the vassal territories to ensure their loyalty and good behaviour. This could be seen in part as a diplomatic measure in itself, intended to make clear that a vassal state was still virtually autonomous despite its obligations and nominal subjection to the Hittite crown. But more importantly, it was a matter of pragmatism. The Hittite king simply did not have the resources to deploy garrison forces of sufficient strength to keep under control each of the states over which Hatti held sway. Garrison forces were occasionally used, but only in cases where a state continued to be troublesome after conquest, and then only until the troubles had subsided.

The surviving preambles to the treaties often provide useful information about past relationships between the vassal state and its overlord, and can thus make a valuable contribution to our attempts to reconstruct Hittite history. But there is an important *caveat*: the 'facts' they contain are presented purely from the overlord's point of view, and in many cases may be adapted, distorted, cherry-picked and perhaps even falsified to give whatever spin the overlord wishes to the events leading up to the treaty. Sometimes, the king uses the preamble to praise the loyalty of the current vassal's predecessors, to serve as a model for the vassal's own behaviour. Sometimes, the king speaks of the disloyalty and treachery of a vassal's father and predecessor, to emphasise his forebearance and readiness to 'forgive' and accept the new ruler. (Remember that a son can rightly be held responsible for the 'sins of his father'.) Of course, we need to take claims like these with the proverbial grain of salt. The king accepts the new vassal purely because it is in his own best interests to do so.

There were a number of occasions when Hittite kings sought to win over their subject-rulers by displays of clemency rather than by threats and intimidation. Here is an example: The Hittite king Mursili II was preparing to invade a rebel vassal state, Seha River Land, whose ruler Manapa-Tarhunda had persistently defied Hittite calls upon him to surrender. In accordance with the 'rules' of warfare, if a king was compelled to take a land or city by force then he and his troops had free rein to sack and plunder it and massacre or take prisoner all its inhabitants. On this occasion, Mursili was on the verge of doing just that when a terrified Manapa-Tarhunda sent a delegation of old men and women to him, led by the rebel ruler's own mother, to offer his surrender and to plead on the rebel's behalf. Mursili was won over, or so he says: 'Because the women fell down at my feet, I had mercy on them and so I did not enter the Seha River Land.'[7]

While this is clearly propagandistic stuff, it does exemplify a characteristic desire of a number of Hittite kings to project an image of chivalrous, compassionate behaviour rather than of brute force to win over a subject-people. Mursili must have welcomed the rebel's final submission without the need for military action – especially as the campaigning season was rapidly drawing to a close. It was a happy ending all round. The king was spared the necessity of spending more days or even weeks capturing and subduing the rebel land by force, he could represent his decision as the act of a benevolent and merciful conqueror, and the land and its people were spared inevitable and brutal destruction.

There were a number of occasions when vassal rulers broke their allegiance and rebelled against their overlord, or when loyal vassals were overthrown by local rebels. Expeditionary forces had often to be despatched to bring the rebels to heel. But by and large the vassal system seemed to work pretty well. Many local rulers remained loyal to their allegiance and to the treaty obligations to which they swore, or at least long enough for their overlords to divert their resources to other regions in more urgent need of attention and action. Undoubtedly we should attribute the success of the Hittite empire as much, or almost as much, to the treaty system and the diplomatic skills of its rulers, as to the prowess of its troops on the battlefield.

But in the empire's closing decades, troubles within the subject-territories became increasingly frequent, and attempts to reassert authority over them imposed an ever greater drain on His Majesty's resources. The empire's decline and fall were inevitable. And all the king's horses and all the king's men couldn't put Hatti together again.

CHAPTER 19

THE MAN WHO WOULD BE KING

THE PATHWAY TO GREAT KINGSHIP

He was a sickly child, with only a few years of life left to him. That was the prognosis for this the fourth son of King Mursili. But then came the good news. While the king slept, his oldest son, the future king Muwattalli, came to him in a dream with a message from the goddess Ishtar: If the king dedicated his ailing son to Ishtar's service, he would live. And so it came to pass. Not only did this sickly child, another Hattusili, survive his childhood, but he went on to live to a ripe old age, and in the process became the most important man in the Hittite kingdom.

All this we learn from a document commonly referred to as *The Apology*.[1] The term 'Apology' is not used as an expression of regret or repentance, but rather as a justification for what Hattusili achieved and a defence of the way in which he rose to the highest office in the land. For Hattusili eventually became the Great King of Hatti, not through the normal process of succession, but by seizing the throne from the prince who had occupied it after his father's death – Urhi-Teshub, son of his brother Muwattalli.

But that was some years in the future. In his early adulthood and with his health apparently restored, Hattusili proved to be one of his brother's most able and loyal supporters. His abilities, both military and administrative, came early to the fore when Muwattalli appointed him governor of the Upper Land. It was an appointment that earned Hattusili a crop of enemies, for it meant displacing the current governor Arma-Tarhunda. This man was also a member of the royal family and bitterly resented being cast aside to make way for the king's brother. Many others flocked to his support and various charges were brought against the new appointee in an attempt to discredit him. Hattusili vigorously defended himself against the charges, with the backing and guidance, he claimed, of his patron Ishtar.

He then went on to justify his appointment by conducting a series of resoundingly successful campaigns against the kingdom's enemies in the lands entrusted to him. As a war-leader, his abilities were severely tested when Muwattalli's shift of his royal capital to Tarhuntassa prompted widespread rebellion and enemy attacks on Hittite territory in its northern regions. With Ishtar leading the way into battle, Hattusili tells us, he confounded his enemies and restored Hittite control over the northern states. Muwattalli was delighted when he received the good news. In recognition of his brother's achievements, he conferred upon him the title LUGAL, 'king', and established the seat of his power in the (as yet unlocated) city of Hakpis. This gave Hattusili authority over the whole northern part of the kingdom, including perhaps the former capital Hattusa. And it appears that Hattusili exercised his powers and responsibilities in the region with exemplary diligence – at least according to his own account in the *Apology*.

Yet we also learn from the *Apology* that the Hittites' hold on the region remained fragile. This became evident when Hattusili joined his brother in Syria for the showdown with Ramesses at Qadesh. Hattusili commanded one of the divisions in the Hittite army, and was subsequently placed in charge of the Damascus region. We don't know how long Muwattalli left him there before handing the region back to Ramesses. But news from northern Anatolia, about further Kaskan invasions and an uprising in Hakpis, made it imperative that Hattusili return to his kingdom at the earliest opportunity.

On his way home, however, he interrupted his journey to visit a city called Lawazantiya in the land of Kizzuwatna. Lawazantiya was

Figure 19.1   Puduhepa.

an important cult centre of the goddess Ishtar, and her protégé
thought it appropriate to pay his respects to her in the city. This
would renew her goodwill and support for him, before he
confronted the potentially dangerous situation awaiting him on
his return home. But while he was in Lawazantiya something
happened that was to change the course of his life, and indeed
was to play no small part in Hatti's future. For in what appears to
have been a whirlwind romance, he met and married the daughter
of a priest of Ishtar. Her name was Puduhepa. Of course, we don't
really know whether we have one of those 'love at first sight'
moments, or whether in fact the marriage had been pre-arranged
and was the reason for Hattusili's visit to Lawazantiya on his
homeward journey. In any case, Puduhepa became her husband's
main support for the rest of his life, and wielded great influence in
the kingdom for many years after his death.

Once back home, Hattusili promptly set about ridding the
land of its enemies and restoring his authority over Hakpis,
where his new bride was installed as queen. But the uprisings in
his kingdom left him in no doubt that there were many who

continued to resent his appointment. Notable among them was Arma-Tarhunda, the sacked governor of the region, who took advantage of Hattusili's absence in Syria to bring an indictment against him. He allegedly even resorted to witchcraft as he relentlessly sought his successor's overthrow. Hattusili responded with a counter-indictment, and won his case. Muwattalli informed him that he could now do what he liked with the loser. This was an excellent propaganda opportunity. 'I did not respond with malice,' he tells us in the *Apology*. 'Rather, because Arma-Tarhunda was a blood-relative, and was moreover an old man, I took pity on him and let him go free.' Hattusili says that he freed his son as well. He later had cause to regret doing so. Far from being reconciled with Hattusili by this act of mercy, Arma-Tarhunda's family remained implacably hostile. Time would make that very clear.

The ill-fated reign of Muwattalli's son

On Muwattalli's death *c*.1272, the succession passed smoothly to his son Urhi-Teshub. The new king was the offspring of a secondary wife, a concubine, since presumably the king had no heir, or no suitable one, from a first wife. Urhi-Teshub's appointment accorded perfectly with the royal laws of succession, and was fully supported by the young man's uncle Hattusili. Indeed, in his *Apology* Hattusili claims credit for actually putting him on the throne. Maybe he made this claim to help justify the actions he later took against the king. Or just possibly Muwattalli did in fact die without formally proclaiming Urhi-Teshub his heir and it was left to Hattusili, now the most senior office-holder in the land, to formalise the appointment. In any case, there is no doubt whatever that Urhi-Teshub was now the legitimate Great King of Hatti. And perhaps to emphasise this, he took on the throne-name Mursili, the name of two of his most illustrious predecessors.

In the early years of the reign, nephew and uncle seem to have got on well together. And to be fair to Hattusili, ruthless schemer though he turned out to be, he may initially have had no intention of changing the status quo. But a momentous decision by

Urhi-Teshub (we'll retain his birth-name to avoid any confusion) may have served as a catalyst to change all this. Some 20 years after his father had relocated the royal capital in Tarhuntassa, Urhi-Teshub decided to shift it back to Hattusa. Tarhuntassa was not abandoned. In fact, it became one of the most important regional centres of the Great Kingdom, under the immediate authority of a ruler of high rank, perhaps always a member of the royal family, with a status virtually equivalent to that of the Syrian viceroys.

There were other changes as well made by Urhi-Teshub which ran counter to his father's actions. For the most part, Hattusili seems to have gone along with these, and in some cases actively supported or even instigated them. But then tensions arose between the pair when Urhi-Teshub started stripping his uncle of the substantial powers bestowed upon him by Muwattalli – particularly his sovereignty over the northern part of the kingdom. Hattusili had continued to be an effective ruler of this region after his brother's death. Indeed, one of his crowning achievements in the early days of his nephew's reign was his recapture and rebuilding of Nerik, one of the holiest cities of the Hittite realm. Two centuries or more earlier, it had been sacked by the Kaskans and left in a ruined state. Its reoccupation and restoration was without doubt a major feather in Hattusili's cap.

But the unprecedented power he wielded in the kingdom made Urhi-Teshub increasingly uneasy. And quite apart from this, Urhi-Teshub might well have believed that his return to Hattusa reduced significantly the justification for having a de facto co-regent ruling regions north of the restored capital. Increasingly, Urhi-Teshub began acting independently of his uncle and ignoring his advice. But when he started stripping him of the powers Muwattalli had bestowed upon him, the relationship between the pair was irretrievably broken. According to Hattusili, he initially resigned himself to his reduced status – because of his own sense of right conduct and out of respect for and loyalty to his brother's memory. But the final straw came when Urhi-Teshub tried to take away from him his most prized possessions – Hakpis, his administrative centre, and Nerik, which was very close to his heart after his repossession of the holy city.

Mounting tensions between nephew and uncle erupted into civil war. In his *Apology*, Hattusili does his best to convince us that this conflict should not be seen as a rebellion by him against his rightful king. Rather, it was a just and legitimate contest which would be decided by divine judgment. 'Come! Ishtar of Samuha and the Storm God of Nerik shall decide the case for us!' Of course, claims by war-leaders that they have their god or gods on their side in their 'righteous' wars against their enemies is a commonplace of history. And despite all Hattusili's protestations, he had absolutely no legitimate basis for going to war against Hatti's duly appointed Great King. There is no reason for believing that Urhi-Teshub was not an able and conscientious ruler in his brief tenure – about seven years – on the throne, and that the war provoked by his uncle (who tried to downplay Urhi-Teshub's legitimacy by never referring to him by his throne-name Mursili) was simply a power struggle between two men – one the rightful king, the other a potential usurper. The struggle was a brief and bitter one, with support for both contenders extending from the homeland through to the western Anatolian states. It ended when Hattusili gained the upper hand, captured Urhi-Teshub, sent him into exile and put himself on the Hittite throne in his place.

THE USURPER SEEKS ENDORSEMENT BOTH AT HOME AND ABROAD

Then came one of the biggest challenges of his career. He had to convince both his own subjects and his foreign peers that he was now truly the rightful Great King of Hatti. It was no easy task. Acknowledging that the conflict had divided the population of Hatti (there may even have been rioting in the capital), Hattusili sought to reunite all his subjects under his rule by attempting to justify to them his seizure of power, and by promising there would be no retribution against those who had supported Urhi-Teshub.

At least as great a task was winning endorsement from his international Royal Brothers. If they were prepared to acknowledge him as Great King of Hatti, this might help him win acceptance from his own subjects. But the exiled Urhi-Teshub remained a serious obstacle. He had been banished to Nuhashshi in Syria and given some administrative responsibilities there, to keep him busy and out of mischief. It didn't work. Urhi-Teshub was determined to get his throne back, and appears to have sought at least diplomatic support from both the Assyrian and the Babylonian kings for this purpose.

Relations between Hatti and Assyria had become strained when Assyria's king Adad-nirari attacked the land of Hanigalbat. This was what was left of the old Mittanian kingdom, and until recently it had been a Hittite puppet state, though nominally independent. Adad-nirari reduced it to Assyrian vassal status, and then annexed it. This was while Urhi-Teshub was on the Hittite throne. Not wishing to pick a fight with Hatti, Adad-nirari had made peaceful overtures to Urhi-Teshub, and been rebuffed. Now Hattusili, seeking to distance himself from his nephew's regime, sought to establish friendly ties with Adad-nirari, firstly by getting the Assyrian to acknowledge him as the legitimate king of Hatti. But his overtures to Adad-nirari failed, at least initially. We conclude this from a letter Hattusili wrote to him, complaining that he had snubbed the usurper's coronation:

> When I assumed kingship, you did not send a messenger to me. It is the custom that when kings assume kingship, the kings who are his equals in rank send him appropriate greeting gifts, clothing befitting kingship, and fine oil for his anointing. But you have not done this.[2]

Hattusili also had difficulties in establishing diplomatic relations with the Babylonian king Kadashman-Enlil II, despite the fact that the king's father had made an alliance with Hattusili shortly before his death.

Thus, and probably with many misgivings, the usurper felt he had no option but to cultivate the goodwill of his former arch-enemy Ramesses. To be acknowledged by the pharaoh as Hatti's rightful king would significantly add, he hoped, to his credibility among his own subjects. But there was a major complication. Urhi-Teshub had fled his place of exile in Syria and taken refuge in Egypt. Hattusili wanted him back. There was a flurry of letters between the Hittite and Egyptian royal courts concerning the whereabouts and eventual fate of Urhi-Teshub. The tone of these letters is acrimonious. Ramesses claimed that he couldn't deliver up Urhi-Teshub because he didn't know where he was. Hattusili and Puduhepa didn't believe him. But what made the pharaoh's responses to their demands particularly galling was his claim that Urhi-Teshub had actually left Egypt, and returned to Hittite territory. Hattusili strenuously denied this: 'Urhi-Teshub is *not* in Aleppo or Qadesh or Kizzuwatna,' he declared. 'Otherwise my own subjects would have told me!' 'Your subjects are not to be trusted,' sniffed the pharaoh in reply.

Peace at last!

The Urhi-Teshub affair seems to have dragged on for many years. But despite their acrimonious exchanges about it and other matters, Ramesses and Hattusili came to a mutual understanding that the greater good would be served if they settled their differences by concluding a peace treaty. And so they did, in the year 1259, 15 years after the battle of Qadesh. It is called the Eternal Treaty because the treaty-partners pledged 'great peace and great brotherhood between themselves forever'. Two independent versions were composed, one in Hattusa, the other in Pi-Ramesse. Each presented its author's own perspective on what was agreed to, though generally the variations between the two are minor.

The Hittite version was originally written in Akkadian, from a first Hittite draft, inscribed on a silver tablet and then sent to Egypt where it was translated into Egyptian. Copies of this version were carved on the walls of the temple of Amun at Karnak, and the temple of Ramesses called the Ramesseum, which lay across the Nile from modern Luxor. Correspondingly, the Egyptian version was first composed in Egyptian, and then translated into Akkadian on a silver tablet before being sent to the Hittite court.[3] (Thus the version of the treaty written in Egyptian represents the original Hittite version, and the version in Akkadian the original Egyptian version.) Seen as an inspiration for peace and harmony throughout the world for all time, a translation of the treaty has been mounted at the entrance to the Security Council in the United Nations building in New York.

Let's be a bit cynical about all this. The treaty itself in both its versions reflects not a broad ideology of peace and harmony between nations, but a set of narrow self-interests. It's much more concerned with things like guarantees of military support for each treaty-partner in the event of an attack by a third party, and contains provisions for extraditing refugees from one kingdom seeking asylum in the other. And very significantly, the Hittite version contains a provision which has no corresponding clause in the Egyptian one: If the people of Hatti rise up against Hattusili, Ramesses must send troops to his aid. This clause leaves no doubt that Hattusili still felt insecure on his throne, and was now signalling his readiness to call on foreign military aid in the event of fresh uprisings against his rule.

So from Hattusili's point of view, the treaty was important in confirming the pharaoh's endorsement of his regime in Hattusa, and also in securing a promise of Egyptian military support should his regime be challenged by his own people. For Ramesses, one of the incentives for concluding the treaty may well have been its propaganda value to him; he could represent it as a settlement sought by the Hittite king now abjectly suing for peace. This could have provided a useful boost to the pharaoh's credibility as a warrior-king, given that his military ventures in the Syro-Palestinian region had achieved little of lasting value, especially when compared to the great exploits in the region of former Egyptian warrior-leaders like Tuthmosis III. The ever-increasing threat posed by Assyria to the subject-territories of both kingdoms, if it decided to launch an invasion across the Euphrates, may also have been a factor in persuading the former arch-enemies to come to terms. Fear of a common enemy as much as, or more than, a desire for lasting peace and harmony may well have provided the essential foundation of the Eternal Treaty.

You might bear all this in mind when you read the inscription on your next visit to the United Nations. But perhaps we shouldn't be too cynical. Though tensions still simmered between the Hittite and Egyptian courts, the two kingdoms remained at peace for the rest of the Bronze Age. And most importantly, the treaty established a basis for much greater stability in the Syrian and Palestinian regions. No doubt the boundaries between the two kingdoms were sorted out, and the alignments of the various cities and kingdoms which fell within these boundaries confirmed.

THE DEFIANT RENEGADE

What made this particularly welcome to Hattusili was that disturbing new developments in his Anatolian territories called for urgent attention. Once more the Kaskans were menacing Hatti's northern frontiers, and regular campaigns were needed to keep them at bay. But more disturbing were fresh outbreaks in the west. From the few surviving fragments of the king's *Annals*, we learn that rebels from the Lukka Lands in the southwest of the peninsula had set about conquering large parts of Hittite subject-territory in their region. The situation was serious enough for the king to lead a campaign in person to the west. And it may be to this context that one of the most famous Hittite documents belongs.

Commonly known as the 'Tawagalawa letter', the document was addressed by a Hittite king to his counterpart, the king of Ahhiyawa.[4] It's so called after Tawagalawa, the brother of the Ahhiyawan king, who had come to Anatolia to take delivery of refugees from Hittite authority. The letter originally covered three tablets, of which only the last has survived. The names of both its author and his addressee would have appeared on the first tablet, and have thus unfortunately been lost to us. However, most scholars attribute the document to Hattusili.

Also, the main subject of the letter is not Tawagalawa, as once believed, but someone we've already met – the renegade Piyamaradu. This man who had long eluded Hittite authority had now been gathering up Hittite subjects, mainly from the Lukka lands, and handing them over to Tawagalawa, probably for resettlement in Ahhiyawan territory. Some may have gone voluntarily, but it seems that others had remained loyal to their Hittite allegiance and were taken against their will. Most likely they were to be recruited into their new homeland's workforce, like many of the deportees captured during Hittite campaigns and transported to the Hittite homeland. In any case, Hattusili wanted all of them back, and their retrieval was at least one of the reasons for his western campaign.

Putting paid to the activities of Piyamaradu was clearly one of the main objectives of this campaign. But it was not easily achieved. Fully aware of the support Piyamaradu commanded in the west, including at least tacit backing from the king of Ahhiyawa, Hattusili tried to bring him to heel without resorting to force. While on his march to the west, he sent messengers to Piyamaradu, to open up communications and attempt a peaceful settlement with him. But Piyamaradu was not interested. He rejected his former overlord's advances on the specious grounds that he had failed to follow proper diplomatic procedures in the approaches he made to him. A resolution of the matter by armed conflict was now inevitable.

Hattusili continued his march westwards, and Piyamaradu and his supporters were pursued all the way to the coast. Though offering some stiff resistance before they got there, they were finally overwhelmed by their pursuers, and Piyamaradu was left defenceless. His enemy had still to lay hands on him, but he could not hope to remain free for long. There was just one option left. He fled to the city of Milawata and sought refuge in it. He would be safe here, he thought, for Milawata was at that time under the control of Ahhiyawa. Surely the Hittite king would respect Ahhiyawan sovereign territory and keep out. It was a false hope. Now that he was so close to capturing his quarry, Hattusili ignored diplomatic niceties, and ordered his troops to enter the city and seize Piyamaradu. The renegade's career was about to come to an abrupt end, so it seemed. But Hattusili had underestimated his instinct for survival, for once more Piyamaradu eluded his pursuers. He escaped from Milawata by ship and found safe haven elsewhere in Ahhiyawan territory, out of the Hittites' reach – probably on an island under Ahhiyawan control off the Anatolian coast.

Frustrated and virtually empty-handed, Hattusili returned home. He wrote to the Ahhiyawan king about the whole affair, blaming him for supporting or at least conniving at Piyamaradu's activities. But the letter was couched in largely conciliatory terms.

He offered what amounted to an apology for entering Milawatan territory, but declared that this was only to capture the fugitive and was not intended as an act of hostility towards Ahhiyawa. What he asked now was that his correspondent keep Piyamaradu on a leash, preventing him from using Ahhiyawan territory as a base for provoking further uprisings against Hittite authority in western Anatolia, or – better still – hand him over to Hittite authority. More generally, the letter sought to win the Ahhiyawan king's cooperation in stabilising the west, above all by not interfering in Hittite subject-territory, or encouraging or supporting his acolytes like Piyamaradu to do so.

In his attempt to butter up his correspondent and make him more amenable to his requests, the Hittite king referred to him as a 'Great King' and called him 'My Brother'. These terms were generally strictly reserved for the genuine Great Kings of the Near Eastern world, the pharaoh and the kings of Hatti, Assyria and Babylon. On the assumption that the king of Ahhiyawa in the Tawagalawa letter was the ruler of only one of many Mycenaean states contemporary with the Late Bronze Age Near Eastern kingdoms, it was a pure diplomatic fiction to accord him such a status. After all, Mycenaean states, like Mycenae and Thebes, were tiny in comparison to the Great Kingdoms which ruled the vast stretches of land to their east. But in view of the capacity of the Ahhiyawan king, whoever he was, to cause significant disruption in the Hittites' western world, it was worth flattering him by according him a status far above his actual worth in the hope of winning his cooperation. And of course we must allow the possibility that Hattusili had very little knowledge of the kingdom of Ahhiyawa. He may really have believed that its size and resources warranted its ruler's membership in the Club of Royal Brothers.

We don't know the outcome of the Hittite appeal, but it seems not to have worked. For Piyamaradu continued to harass Hittite territory in the west for years to come. And Ahhiyawa continued to play a subversive and probably an increasingly active role, politically and perhaps also militarily, in western Anatolian affairs.

That was but one of the problems inherited by Hattusili's successor Tudhaliya IV, who came to a throne which still bore the taint of illegal occupation. There were still disgruntled elements of the royal family, especially those who believed they had been robbed of their rightful inheritance. Urhi-Teshub had now faded from the scene, but there was already emerging upon it a man whose name sounds like a drumbeat – Kurunta (Kuruntiya). The brother or half-brother of Urhi-Teshub, Kurunta was to play an important role in the history of the kingdom as it entered its final decades.

We'll return to these matters in Chapter 23.

CHAPTER 20

PARTNERS IN POWER: THE GREAT QUEENS OF HATTI

A unique feature of Hittite society was the position held by its First Lady. As we have seen, she is sometimes specifically designated by the term Tawananna. Perhaps of Luwian or Hattian origin, this term may originally have been the personal name of the first Hittite queen, the female equivalent to Labarna. But subsequently it came to be used as a title for a number of her successors. The Tawananna's primary role was that of Chief Priestess of the Hittite realm. This in itself bestowed considerable power and authority on her, in a state where secular and religious authority were closely intertwined. She was also manager of the royal household. This role too brought with it great power and influence, for it gave her authority over the king's harem of concubines and the numerous offspring resulting from it, as well as responsibility for the day-to-day running of the palace's domestic operations. What made her position all the more powerful was that she held it for life. She may have started off as the wife or chief consort of the reigning king. But if her husband died before her, she remained Tawananna until her own death. This meant that she could have been both a king's wife and a new king's mother, or occasionally his sister or aunt or some other female relative. And if the new king had a wife of his own, she would have had to wait for the old Tawananna to die before she herself assumed the title and became First Lady.

Under normal circumstances, that is. The anomalous position of the Tawananna in an otherwise strongly patriarchal, male-oriented society had the potential for causing much disruption within and beyond the royal household. Especially if the bearer of the office exceeded the bounds of her authority, or engaged in corrupt and criminal practices. A couple of the Tawanannas allegedly did so. But justice eventually caught up with them, as we shall see.

A RULER IN HER OWN RIGHT?

The first historical reference we have to a Tawananna occurs in the introductory words of Hattusili I's *Annals*. It was common practice for a king to identify himself, at the beginning of important documents or on his royal seals, by using his royal titles, and by stating his relationship with one or more of his royal predecessors (son of x, grandson of y etc.). Thus in his *Annals*, Hattusili proclaims himself 'Great King, Tabarna, Hattusili, King of the Land of Hatti, ruler of the city of Kussar', and then adds that he was 'son of the brother of Tawananna'.

These last words are unique in Hittite royal titulature, and there have been many attempts to explain them. Do they, for example, indicate some sort of avunculate system whereby the succession passed from uncle (or aunt in this case) to nephew? Can you think of other possibilities? Here's an idea of my own. It is pure speculation, and other scholars will disagree with it. I'm by no means firmly wedded to it myself, but I don't know of any argument that categorically rules it out. So let me do a spot of limb-climbing.

I've already suggested that Tawananna was originally the personal name of the highest-ranking female member of the royal family. A seal in the shape of a Maltese cross, which records the genealogy of the late fourteenth-century king Mursili (II) extending back at least eight generations, names the first Labarna and a Tawananna as a royal couple.[1] According to my own reconstruction of events, the coup in Sanahuitta which overthrew and probably killed Labarna's son and likely successor, the new Labarna, may have left the king without a male heir. The king himself decided (I believe) who his successor would be, and called upon his subjects to honour his decision. Generally, he would choose a successor from his own immediate family, unless circumstances forced him to select someone from a collateral line, typically a nephew, to be his heir.

In these circumstances, if Labarna I no longer had any sons to succeed him, did he choose a daughter, who now assumed the name Tawananna as a formal title, to become the kingdom's new ruler? And was she the immediate royal predecessor of Hattusili? This could explain why she was named in his titulature. If she had no sons of her own, or no suitable sons, the royal succession could still be kept within the same family group if it passed to her nephew, her brother's son. This brother, I suggest, was the first Labarna's son who was originally destined to rule the kingdom but may not have survived the uprising in Sanahuitta. King Telipinu was later to rule that the husband of one of the king's daughters could become his adopted son and successor. But we have no evidence that such a provision existed, or was ever put into practice, before Telipinu.

An obvious objection to my idea is that there was never a later occasion in Hittite history when the kingdom was ruled by a queen, nor is there any other reference to this supposed female ruler in any other text. But female rule was not entirely without precedent in the history of the region. Already in the Assyrian colony period, we learn from the merchant texts that queens sometimes ruled over the cities through which the traders' caravans passed. And a mythological tradition preserved in Hittite records has as one of its main characters a 'queen of Kanesh', who accomplished the prodigious feat of bearing 30 sons in a single year.[2] Fairytale though this part of the text is (it becomes progressively more historical later on), it nevertheless indicates that the notion of a ruling queen was not entirely inconceivable. And if we want a historical parallel from another Great Kingdom, we need only go to Egypt where against all tradition and precedent a woman became ruler more than 150 years after Tawananna's 'reign' – the pharaoh Hatshepsut. After her death, her successor Tuthmosis III set about erasing her images and other records of her reign. Was the name of the Tawananna also later expunged from official Hittite records, for reasons unknown to us?

There is just one other reference to a Tawananna in Hattusili's reign. This one is the subject of a virulent decree:

> In future let no-one speak the Tawananna's name. Let no-one speak the names of her sons or her daughters. If any of the sons of Hatti speaks them they shall cut his throat and hang him in his gate. If among my subjects anyone speaks their names he shall no longer be my subject. They shall cut his throat and hang him in his gate.[3]

Who was this person who so aroused the king's wrath? Perhaps it was the king's wife, who may have been accorded the title after her husband's accession. If so, then it was her children, at least two of whom had been disowned by their father for their treachery, who were included in the *damnatio memoriae*. But it's possible that for one reason or another the office of Tawananna had been held by Hattusili's sister. Her son had now been rejected as her brother's successor. And she herself, along with all her children, had constantly set themselves against the king. Perhaps she and her family were the objects of the decree.

THE WICKED STEPMOTHER

In any case, the office itself survived. Some of the later Tawanannas may well have performed their duties loyally and inconspicuously – so much so that we don't even hear about them. But others proved highly problematical. Most notorious among them was the Babylonian wife of Suppiluliuma, who was accorded the title Tawananna, and used it also as a personal name. The circumstances of her marriage to Suppiluliuma remain uncertain. It appears, however, that Suppiluliuma had put aside (perhaps banished?) his former wife Henti, the mother of his five sons, to make way for his new marriage. No doubt reasons of state were a prime motive for his actions. In any case the Babylonian Tawananna outlived him, and continued to enjoy all the privileges and powers of her office through the brief reign of his first successor Arnuwanda II and part of the reign of Arnuwanda's brother and successor Mursili II.

Mursili has left us a damning account of her abuse of power. He speaks of her domineering behaviour in the royal palace and beyond it, her extravagance, her habit of stripping the palace of its treasures to lavish on her favourites, and her introduction of undesirable foreign customs into the land. His father apparently did nothing to rein her in, probably because of his preoccupation with campaigns abroad, and after his death she continued all her destructive, disruptive practices: 'As she governed the house of the king and the Land of Hatti in the lifetime of my father, likewise in the lifetime of my brother she governed them', Mursili complains. But even after his own accession, he did little to curb her behaviour – until his own beloved wife fell gravely ill and died. That was the final straw. Holding his stepmother directly responsible for her death (and she may indeed have seen her stepson's wife as a threat to her dominance of the royal household), he put her on trial for murder. She was found guilty and banished from the palace.[4] (Hittite kings were extremely reluctant to punish errant members of their family with more than banishment, even those who were guilty of the most serious crimes.)

But she was not the last of the Hittite royal consorts to prove a disruptive influence in the kingdom, or at least within the royal court. Indeed not long after her fall from grace, another Hittite queen called Tanuhepa (Danuhepa) fell foul of the king. She may have been a later wife of Mursili, or else the wife of his son and successor Muwattalli. In any case, she became embroiled in a dispute with Muwattalli, apparently over acts of profanation which she had committed, and was placed on trial by the king. Like the Babylonian Tawananna, she was found guilty and sent into exile.

THE FORMIDABLE PUDUHEPA

But the most powerful and most famous Hittite queen of all was the wife of Mursili's son and third successor Hattusili III. Her name was Puduhepa. As we've noted in the previous chapter, she was the daughter of a Hurrian priest in Kizzuwatna, and became the wife of Hattusili when he was returning home from Syria. The Hittite throne was still at that time occupied by Muwattalli, and the succession passed from him to his son Urhi-Teshub. But as we've seen, Urhi-

Teshub lost his throne a few years later to his uncle Hattusili. Puduhepa now became First Lady of the Hittite empire. Probably a good deal younger than her husband, she wielded enormous influence in the kingdom, not merely as the power behind the throne, but as a power actually on the throne, at her husband's side.

She co-signed treaties with Hattusili, including the famous treaty with Egypt, she exchanged letters with the pharaoh Ramesses, and received from the pharaoh copies of his letters to her husband, she regularly appeared with her husband in making offerings to the gods and in participating in religious festivals, and she served as judge in important legal cases. No doubt her power and influence increased as the years took their toll on her husband and the illnesses which may have afflicted him since his childhood became increasingly debilitating. Of course, one of her chief responsibilities was the supervision of the royal household, no simple job since we are told that probably already on her arrival in Hattusa as Hattusili's bride she found the palace full of the offspring of her husband's concubines. Later, she played a major role as matchmaker in marriage-alliances contracted between Hittite princesses and foreign or vassal rulers.

Overall, the power and influence wielded by Puduhepa seems to have served the kingdom well. But inevitably she made enemies within palace circles, and hostility towards her may have increased after her husband's death. Her son Tudhaliya had married a princess from Babylon, probably a marriage arranged by Puduhepa herself. But after Tudhaliya's accession, there appear to have been clashes between him and his wife on the one side and his mother on the other, as Puduhepa continued to wield the powers she had enjoyed during her husband's reign. An oracle text of the period indicates factions among the women of the court who had divided themselves into supporters and opponents of a Great Queen. We can't be entirely sure, but the Great Queen in question was almost certainly Puduhepa. Indeed, it's possible that as a result of royal family feuds Puduhepa was expelled from the palace.[5] But if so, she seems eventually to have emerged victorious over her opponents, and very likely continued to be a major influence in both the kingdom's foreign as well as its domestic affairs until the end of her life. She may have been at least 90 when she died.

CHAPTER 21

CITY OF TEMPLES AND BUREAUCRATS: THE ROYAL CAPITAL[1]

THE GREAT RAMPART, POSTERN GATE AND CITY-WALLS

An impressive sight greeted visitors as they approached the Hittite royal capital: a great earthen rampart some 250 m long and 30 m high paved with limestone and dazzlingly bright in the reflected rays of the harsh Anatolian sunlight. It is called Yerkapı today, meaning 'Gate in the Earth'. The reason for the modern name is that there is a tunnel through it (actually built before the rampart) now called the 'Postern Gate', which provided access to the outside world. Hattusa has a number of other posterns as well ('postern' is derived from the Latin word *posterula* meaning 'side- or back-gate'), but this is the only one you can still walk through. The tunnel is made up of layers of roughly hewn stone blocks, each slightly overlapping the one below, in a technique known as corbelling. Exactly the same building technique can be seen in contemporary architecture of the Mycenaean world. The galleries of the Mycenaean palace centre at Tiryns, dating to *c.*1200, provide an excellent example. It's not unlikely that the technique originated in the Hittite world and was transmitted westwards to Anatolia's Aegean coast, and thence across the sea to mainland Greece.

The 71 m long Postern Gate was once closed by double wooden doors. What its actual purpose was remains a mystery. Entrance

Figure 21.1 Yerkapı, Hattusa.

Figure 21.2 Tiryns gallery.

Figure 21.3   Postern Gate, Hattusa.

gates were the weakest parts of a city's fortifications, and all needed
protection by the city's defence forces against enemy attack. Could
the postern have been used as a sally port for surprise counterattacks against a besieging force? Almost certainly not. The highly
conspicuous tunnel would have been obvious to any such force,
and in any case extended too far out from the walls for defenders
atop them to provide counter-attacking troops with covering fire.
What do you think? Can you suggest any practical purpose the
Postern Gate might have served?

Let's return to the rampart. From its top, at the southernmost –
and highest – part of the city, Hattusa's entire fortification system
was on display. And this part of the system could be accessed
simply by climbing up flights of stairs at either end of the rampart.
Clearly, it was built not for defensive purposes but for show – to
impress the capital's visitors, whether merchants, foreign dignitaries,
or travellers on any other business, with a foretaste of the city's
grandeur and splendour.

At its greatest extent, the royal capital covered an area of
181 hectares, one of the largest cities of the ancient Near Eastern

world. Its fortification walls were more than 9 km in length. The outer wall, which surrounded the city, was 6.6 km long and punctuated by outward-protruding towers or bastions at roughly 30 m intervals. The base of the walls was made of roughly hewn stone blocks which in parts may have risen 3–4 m above ground level. Above this, mudbrick walls extended the height of the fortifications to perhaps 8 m, with the towers rising several metres higher. Rounded triangular crenellations topped off the walls and towers, helping shield the city's defenders from enemy missiles fired from below, as well as adding to the impressiveness of the whole fortification complex. Particularly given the rugged terrain on which the city was built, its fortifications alone which stretched far into the distance as they came into the visitor's view were a massive architectural and engineering achievement, an explicit statement of the kingdom's might and grandeur as much as it was of the capital's defence capabilities.

THE SPHINX GATE

Even today you can climb Yerkapı's staircases, which will lead you to one of the city's main gates – the so-called Sphinx Gate. Once, four sphinxes embellished the gateway, two facing towards the city, two facing the outer world. Unlike Egyptian sphinxes, which provided their artistic inspiration, Hittite sphinxes are female. (Remains of a number of other monumental sphinxes have been found both in Hattusa and at other Hittite sites, notably Alaca Höyük.) Unfortunately only one sphinx, an exterior one, is still in its original position, and it's badly worn. The two inner sphinxes have survived, in a much better condition, one housed in the Near Eastern Museum in Istanbul, the other until recently in the Near Eastern Museum in Berlin before arrangements were made for its return to Turkey. Human-headed and with the bodies of winged lions, these hybrid creatures represent divinities. We know this from the horns, symbols of divinity, appearing on the helmets of the 'inner sphinxes', which are carved almost completely in the round, their lions' bodies ending in a cat's tail. They smile benevolently upon the city below.

Figure 21.4 Sphinx, Alaca Höyük.

There are a number of entrances to Hattusa through the city's fortification walls, but the Sphinx Gate was almost certainly not an ordinary entrance, partly because of the narrowness of the staircases which were the only means of access to it from the outside. Archaeologists working in the royal capital have commented that the gatehouse flanked by the two inner sphinxes has a shrine-like feel to it; through it on special occasions priests may have emerged bearing the image of a god, with the rampart serving as a kind of gigantic stage for the celebration of religious rites before the assembled throngs below. But for any visitor allowed to mount one of the staircases the gate would have provided an excellent vantage point for viewing the entire city, enclosed within its massive fortifications which seemed to stretch almost endlessly into the distance.

THE UPPER AND LOWER CITIES

From where you stood, at Hattusa's highest point, the city's terrain sloped gradually downwards. It was rugged terrain, marked here and there by large outcrops of rock and spurs, interspersed with flat areas, hollows and large ponds of water. As your eye travelled north down the rugged slope, across a complex of mudbrick-on-timber-frame buildings, it would see, beyond further rocky outcrops, a wall which partitioned off another large area of the city. Numerous tunnels, what we have called posterns, inserted in the wall provided access between both parts of the city – hence the modern name for this wall, the 'Postern Wall'. Archaeologists now refer to the southern, higher part of the city as the 'Upper City', and the lower, northern part as the 'Lower City'. In the southeast corner of the Lower City was an elevated plateau, today called Büyükkale ('Big Castle') which had fortifications of its own. This was the royal citadel, location of the palace of the Great Kings of Hatti. And to its northwest lay an enormous sprawling complex, the largest temple in the Hittite world. Commonly referred to as the Temple of the Storm (Weather) God, it contained two shrines in its innermost recesses, in contrast to most other temples that contained only one. For this reason, it is believed to have been dedicated to two deities – the most important ones in the Hittite pantheon – the Storm God and his consort, the Sun Goddess of Arinna.

THE CITY'S TEMPLES

We'll look in more detail at some of these features as we inspect the city at closer quarters. But let's now return to our original vantage

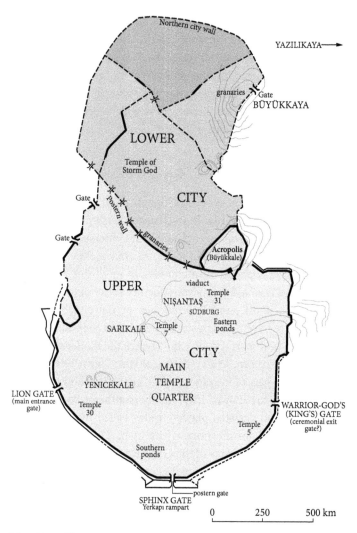

Map 21.1 Hattusa.

point, the Sphinx Gate, and proceed from there down the western staircase to what was undoubtedly the main entrance to the city. This was the so-called Lion Gate, flanked by two roaring lions and located to the northwest of the Sphinx Gate. Almost all visitors to the city, whatever their mission or purpose, entered and departed the city via this gate. To the east of it, and north of the Sphinx Gate, lay a

Figure 21.5 Acropolis, Hattusa.

complex of mudbrick buildings similar to other buildings located in various parts of the Upper City. Comparable in concept, though with many variations in detail, these buildings were temples, sacred structures wherein were housed the statues of the 'thousand gods' of Hatti (or at least some of them).

Figure 21.6 Temple of the Storm God, Hattusa.

Figure 21.7 Lion Gate, Hattusa.

All temples were made of sundried mudbrick on timber frames. Their walls would have been coated in a mud plaster, both inside and out, and in at least some temples the interior walls would have had painted decoration. Apart from the Temple of the Storm God, the temples ranged in size from around 400 to 1,500 sq. m. All of them featured an open courtyard which provided access to a portico and then via a series of anterooms to the innermost shrine.

Figure 21.8   Upper City temples, Hattusa.

This was the temple's most sacred area, for it housed the statue of the temple's deity, life-sized or larger and gleaming in the gold and silver plating with which the statue's wooden core was coated. The courtyard provided a venue for rites associated with the worship of the god. But attendance at these and indeed access to any part of the temple was restricted to the priests in the god's service, including of course the king and the queen who were by reason of their office the chief priest and priestess of the Hittite world. Many rituals and festival events must have taken place in the temple's courtyard, including perhaps royal coronation ceremonies.

A total of 31 temples have been discovered so far within the city (more may come to light). All are in the Upper City, with the exception of the largest and most important of them, the Lower City's Temple of the Storm God (and probably the Sun Goddess). In its latest known phase, the temple has been dated to the fourteenth–thirteenth centuries, though beneath the terrace on which it was built there are almost certainly remains of earlier phases of its existence. The gods' statues stood on bases at the rear of their shrines, and in contrast to the dim windowless interiors of the shrines of Greek deities, were bathed in light by windows which reached almost to the floor. No doubt window-screens were installed to give privacy to the deities when this was deemed appropriate.

Beyond their most sacred spaces, their shrines, porticoes and courtyards, Hittite temple-complexes incorporated many subsidiary areas as well. Like other Near Eastern temples, those of the Hittite world were often rambling, multifunctional structures, in contrast to the simple, single-functioned, symmetrical temples which were a hallmark of Western architectural tradition, beginning with the Classical Greeks. Both Near Eastern and Classical temples had an inner sanctum which housed the statues of their patron deities, and where sacred rites were performed. But the largest of the Hittite and other Near Eastern temples also contained within their boundaries storerooms for housing the clothes and equipment used in sacred ceremonies, kitchen areas where bread, meat and other foodstuffs were prepared for the gods and priests, and rooms for scribal staff and tablet archives.

The Temple of the Storm God, covering 2,730 sq. m, provides the archetypal example of all these features. The single-storeyed temple proper was surrounded by at least 82 storerooms, and probably as many as 200 if the storage areas were two or three storeys high. Many of these were no doubt used to house the robes, the ritual vessels, musical instruments and other equipment used in ceremonies and festivals associated with the temple when they were not in use. Some of the rooms were used for storing, on wooden shelves, the temple's clay tablet archives, which contained many of the most important documents to survive from the Hittite world. These included copies of international and vassal treaties. Working space had also to be provided for the temple's scribal staff, as well as for numerous other personnel associated with the temple, including deportees assigned to various temple duties. Other storage areas contained huge pottery vessels sunk into the ground. Hundreds of these were found, each with a capacity of up to 2,000 litres, their contents consisting of foodstuffs like cereal grains, beans, oil and wine. Butcheries and bakeries must also have figured in the temple complex, providing food for the gods as sacrificial offerings, as well as sustenance for the temple personnel. The total complex of which the temple-proper was the nucleus extended over 14,500 sq. m.

On a smaller scale, many of the other temples, both in Hattusa and elsewhere in the Hittite world, had a similar range of functions beyond the purely sacred and ritualistic. Tablet-finds in a number of Hattusa's temples indicate that these religious institutions often owned food-producing land, which enabled them to contribute to Hatti's food supply and economic development; the institutions themselves sometimes provided storage facilities for at least part of their produce for redistribution purposes.

Overall, Hittite temples functioned very much like mediaeval monasteries in the complexity and range of activities, both secular and religious, in which they engaged.

ROCKS AND PONDS

Given the special sacred significance attached to rocks in the Hittite world, several large rocky outcrops within the Upper City – especially those now known as Sarikale (Turkish 'Yellow Castle'),

Figure 21.9   Yenicekale, Hattusa.

Yenicekale ('Newish Castle') and Nişantaş ('Marked Rock') are of
particular significance. Their locations indicated on the city-plan,
they were once incorporated into building complexes. Thus
Sarikale has some preserved masonry and the remains of a cistern,
and at Yenicekale, you can still see a well preserved 7 m high wall;
the building complex within it was erected on the outcrop's levelled
summit. To the south of Yenicekale, near Hattusa's highest point,
five ponds were dug, to serve as reservoirs for the city's water
supply.

Notable among the remains at Nişantaş are fragments of two
sphinxes, like those of the Sphinx Gate at Yerkapı, which were
carved into an entrance gate. The gate was reached by a ramp
which gave access to a substantial building complex on top of the
outcrop. A long hieroglyphic inscription was carved on the side of
the outcrop (hence the Turkish name 'Marked Rock') during the
reign of the last king Suppiluliuma II. The inscription, now badly
weathered and almost illegible, probably listed the main
achievements of Suppiluliuma's reign. It's generally believed that
these rock complexes were the locations of religious institutions,
perhaps what Hittite texts refer to as 'rock-crest' structures, which
were associated with the cults of dead kings.

To all these features which serve to emphasise the special sacred
character of the royal capital, we can add two more ponds or
artificial lakes, with paved embankments and watertight bottoms
of plastered clay. The so-called 'Pond 1', with a surface area of
60×90 sq. m, was separated by a dam from the slightly smaller
'Pond 2'. Fed by a number of springs, and thus providing part of
the city's water supply, the ponds also had a sacred significance.
This is indicated by two domed chambers, one located at the
western corner of Pond 1, and one at the northern corner. The two
chambers, providing us, incidentally, with the oldest known domed
stone structures in the Near East, were discovered in 1988, just
south of the royal acropolis.

'Chamber 2' is of particular interest because of its well preserved
reliefs and inscription. The reliefs depict a deity, the Sun-God, and
the last Hittite king Suppiluliuma II, the inscription is a record of
Suppiluliuma's military exploits in southern and southwestern

Anatolia. Though it was once thought to be Suppiluliuma's tomb, the scholar David Hawkins concluded, with widespread scholarly assent, that this structure served as a symbolic entrance to the Underworld – what Hittite texts call a KASKAL.KUR. Here cult ceremonies were performed in honour of the deity, and in this way the built chambers were linked with the artificial lakes, which not only served a practical purpose in supplying water for the city, but also, like lakes and springs in many parts of the ancient world, provided passageways to the Underworld.

THE PALACE

On the plateau now called Büyükkale located at the southeast end of the Lower City lay a large architectural complex which, though not identified by inscriptions, must have been the palace of the Great King of Hatti. This was the very heart of the Hittite world. Isolated and heavily protected from the rest of the city by its own buttressed fortification wall, it covered some 31,185 sq. m. What remains of it today dates mostly to its last renovation phase, some

Figure 21.10   Entrance to acropolis, Hattusa.

time in the late thirteenth century. Persons granted entry to the complex via a southern gate (visiting dignitaries and diplomats, palace personnel etc.) passed through a series of courtyards, connected by gateways and surrounded by colonnades and groups of rooms, which led to various parts of the palace, including the great Audience Hall. In this Hall, the king held court, with envoys from foreign kings, rulers of his vassal states and his own high-ranking bureaucrats and military leaders. It was probably located on a second storey, above a large central court. Many of the buildings around a 'lower court' to the southeast probably provided residences for the most important palace officials, guest accommodation for VIPs and quarters for the king's special bodyguard, the 'Men of the Golden Spears'. A large proportion of the king's extended family – and by the thirteenth century there were a lot of them when you take into account all the collateral branches of the family – may also have resided within the palace area.

WHO ELSE LIVED IN HATTUSA?

Capacious though the palace was, there must have been many lesser luminaries who were connected with the palace but lived beyond its walls. But where? So far, few residential areas in the city have come to light. The most significant of these is in the Lower City, close to the Temple of the Storm God, and thus within easy commuting distance of the palace. It seems to have been an elite residential area, with multi-roomed houses, some with their own plumbing systems, and ovens and open fireplaces. Architectural fashions changed over time. Earlier courtyard houses featuring an open-air inner court were later replaced by vestibule houses with living areas completely roofed in. As with the temples, the houses were made of mudbrick built on timber frames and mud-covered flat roofs.

We can imagine that this area was inhabited primarily by bureaucrats, priests, core security and defence forces (square structures that may have been military barracks have come to light in the Upper City, near the Sarikale outcrop), and the most highly skilled specialist craftsmen and artisans, whose services were of crucial importance for the material maintenance of Hittite society.

Other beings of lower social status, builders' and agricultural labourers, farmers etc., lived outside the city, in no doubt numerous peripheral villages, hamlets and farmsteads clustered close enough to the city's walls for their inhabitants to be able to come within the walls in times of threatened enemy attacks. So far, however, the existence of such peripheral communities has yet to be determined by archaeological investigation, and it may well be that even small traces of them will be difficult to find.

Estimates of Hattusa's population have ranged from about 9,000 to 15,000 inhabitants. These figures seem extremely modest for the population of the capital of one of the Great Near Eastern Kingdoms. But if they come close to the truth, they could be explained by the fact that Hattusa was primarily a city of administrators, diplomats and priests, with no significant trading centres or merchant class, no significant industrial or manufacturing activities. That was beginning to change in the last decades of the empire's existence when some of the temples in the southernmost parts of the Upper City fell into disuse.[2] Their sites were occupied by a number of smaller dwellings and workshops, as more of the lower class elements originally living outside the walls managed to relocate inside them. They no longer had confidence in the protection the king's forces could provide to unfortified settlements.

Grain storage depots

One critically important role that Hattusa played in the Hittite state, beyond its religious and administrative functions, was as a grain-storage and redistribution centre. Excavations by Jürgen Seeher's team brought to light two main storage complexes. One of these was on the long high ridge lying to the northeast of the Lower City and separated from it by a deep river valley. It is today known as Büyükkaya ('Big Rock'). In Hittite times, it was enclosed by a fortification wall, dating to the thirteenth century. Here Seeher uncovered an enormous granary, dating from the sixteenth century onwards. Seeher's excavations revealed 11 subterranean rectangular pits. These pits, or silos, were used primarily for the storage of grain, mainly einkorn (a hulled or glume wheat) and barley,

Figure 21.11   Büyükkaya granaries, Hattusa.

intended for redistribution in the capital and other parts of the homeland. Seeher's excavations also uncovered a second storage complex of the same period in the Lower City. Just behind the postern wall, 32 semi-subterranean chambers divided into two parallel rows were found. Many thousands of tonnes of grain, mostly barley and some wheat (einkorn) were stored in these facilities, for several years if necessary, in an oxygen- and vermin-free environment. Grain silos have been found at other locations in the Hittite homeland as well, and no doubt more will be discovered. These storage facilities must have made an important contribution to ensuring the adequacy of the Hittite homeland's food supplies not only for the current year, but also for a significant period beyond, in anticipation of a season or successive seasons of poor harvests, due to enemy action, drought, or other devastating weather conditions.

THE WARRIOR-GOD'S GATE

A number of gates provided access to the city through its walls. Three in particular stand out. All are at the southern end of the Upper City. They are the Sphinx Gate, which may have provided a backdrop to ceremonial performances, the Lion Gate, which was the main public entrance into the city, and directly opposite in the eastern part of the wall the Warrior-God's Gate (sometimes referred to, inappropriately, as the King's Gate). As we've noted in Chapter 18, the last of these features a sculpture, 2.25 m high, on the inside of the gate depicting a warrior wearing a tasselled helmet and a short kilt; he's armed with a short sword and battle-axe (see Figure 18.2).

This figure completely mystified Charles Texier when he came upon it in 1834. And a number of explanations of it were offered in the years that followed. Its beardless cheeks, enlarged nipples and soft round chest contours suggested to some that it was a female warrior. If so, perhaps this strange place was the city of the Amazons! That theory used to pop up quite regularly once upon a time, but has long been discredited (in case you're thinking of reviving it). Most likely the figure represents the god Sharrumma, the patron deity of Hatti's third-last king Tudhaliya IV, and was sculptured during his reign. His divinity is indicated by his horned helmet.

Note that the god appears on the *inside* of the gate, and has his left arm held upwards with his fist clenched. I suggest that this was the gate through which Hittite armies marched as they set out on their campaigns. The clenched fist makes me think of sports contestants today who clench their fists as a sign of victory, or of confidence in a victory still to be achieved. I believe that the god is signalling a farewell to departing troops, with an assurance that victory will be theirs. Of course, the gate may also have been used for other purposes, such as the exit point of diplomatic missions or of a king setting out on a religious pilgrimage to the holy places of his land, or for cultic processions.

Close by lie the remains of Temple 5. It is one of the largest of Hattusa's temples, not much smaller than the Great Temple, and like it contains two inner shrines, indicating that it was dedicated to two deities. I suggest that this too is a temple of both the Storm God and the Sun Goddess of Arinna, and is indirectly linked with the Warrior-God's Gate. Perhaps here in the temple's innermost sanctuary a departing king paid his respects to these deities as he

Figure 21.12   Temple 5, Hattusa.

embarked on his enterprise abroad before receiving the final farewell at the departure gate from the deities' son Sharrumma.

Any other suggestions?

RECONSTRUCTING HATTUSA'S WALLS[3]

The first sight to greet you when you visit Hattusa today, via the ticket office located just to the north of the Great Temple, is a stretch of 65 m of fully intact city-wall, complete with two crenellated towers, 20 to 25 m apart, flanked by three stretches of curtain wall. It is an impressive entrée to your tour of the city. But it's a reconstruction, just a few years old.

In a project lasting from 2003 to 2005 (and extending over 11 months in total work-time), the archaeological team working at Hattusa under Jürgen Seeher's direction, with assistance from local authorities and a labour-force of 65 workmen, built from scratch this section of the walls. The mudbricks of which it was composed were made in what the archaeologists believe was the traditional manner, and each brick was laid manually, without mechanical

Figure 21.13   Reconstructed wall, Hattusa.

assistance. Small clay models of Hittite walls and towers and other evidence from the Hittite period were used as a basis for the reconstruction. The casemate wall, built on stone bases called socles, reach a maximum height of 8.3 m above ground level, the towers 12.8 m. 'Casemate' is the term applied to walls consisting of parallel outer and inner shells (each $c.1.5-2$ m thick) like two parallel courses of cavity brick in modern houses, linked to each other by crosswalls. These crosswalls created chambers called cists. In other fortification systems, cists could be used as storage rooms, for food and military equipment. But there was no evidence of this at Hattusa, and the cists in the reconstructed fortifications are packed with earth. The width of the walls, inclusive of the cists, ranges from 3–5 m. The mudbricks themselves were made of loam tempered with straw and pebbles – essential to ensure that the bricks would not crack while drying out, or crumble under pressure. They were moulded in wooden frames with dimensions of 45 × 45 × 10 cm. Each brick weighed around 34 kgs.

The brick-making was carried out during the driest part of the year, from June through September. Of course even in these

Figure 21.14   Reconstruction in progress.

months heavy rainfalls sometimes occur, and large sheets of plastic were used to cover the newly made bricks when dark clouds began to appear on the horizon. Very likely, the Hittites made their bricks during the same months, using sheets of straw-matting to cover them when rain threatened. From experimentation, the project team concluded that it took 12 days of curing in open sunlight for the bricks to reach their maximum strength, depending on temperature and other weather conditions. The bricks could then be stored or directly placed in position on the walls, using a loam mortar. Stress tests were carried out by driving heavy vehicles over some of the cured bricks. A tractor with a trailer-load of stones failed to cause any damage to them. It was only when a steamroller was driven over them that cracks began to appear.

In all, some 64,500 bricks were used in the reconstructed section of the wall. (Between 328 and 720 bricks were made each day.) The fact that this represents only 0.6 per cent of the total fortification system at Hattusa gives some idea of the magnitude of the task undertaken by the Hittites, without any aids such as the trucks and water vehicles used in the modern reconstruction (which required over 1,000 tonnes of water) to transport the materials to the places where the bricks were made, and then to the site where they were laid. The bricks for the modern reconstruction were made on the spot. In Hittite times, they had to be made some 10 or more kilometres distant from the city. Can you suggest why?

Once the bricks were in place they had to be coated in plaster, probably a loam containing a certain quantity of lime. This was essential, for the biggest threat to a mudbrick structure is erosion through wind and rain. Once protected by a plaster coating, mudbrick structures can last a long time – provided the plaster itself is constantly renewed. Ongoing maintenance of the fortifications of Hittite cities, and indeed of all the kingdom's mudbrick buildings, both sacred and secular, must have imposed a heavy drain on the available human resources, especially at a time of the year when lots of able-bodied men were required for military service on distant campaigns as well as for producing the kingdom's food supplies.

The reconstruction project is proving an extremely valuable one in many respects. Of course, one incentive for it was to attract visitors to a site which is pretty bare of the ancient remains that many other ancient sites have in abundance. But more importantly, the project has provided valuable insights into how the Hittites went about protecting their cities, and the actual techniques they used in constructing their fortifications and other buildings. Above all, it has given us a far greater appreciation than ever before of the substantial challenges the Hittite people faced in elevating their capital into one of the great showplaces of the Near Eastern world.

CHAPTER 22

AN ELITE FRATERNITY: THE CLUB OF ROYAL BROTHERS

A ROYAL DIPLOMATIC MISSION

As the first rays of dawn light the eastern sky, the gathering outside the main gate prepares to enter the city. The officials don their robes of state, their attendants pack their tents and other travelling equipment, the military escort forms its ranks, and the consignment of gifts is checked for the last time, to ensure it is still intact. After many weeks of travel from the deep south, the travellers' journey is at an end. They now wait patiently at the bottom of the steep ramp leading up to the main city-gate. Flanked by two sculpted lions, whose mouths are open in a silent roar of challenge, their tongues protruding, the gate is still locked. But soon an official from inside comes and inspects the seal affixed the previous evening when the gate was bolted. Satisfied that it has not been tampered with, he unbars the gate. The visitors are admitted, along with the armed escort that has accompanied them, to guard both their persons on the long, hazardous route from Egypt, and the crates of valuable gifts that form part of their entourage. They are emissaries from Ramesses II, pharaoh of Egypt. They have come to Hattusa bearing letters, along with their gifts, for Ramesses' Royal Brother and other members of his family. His Majesty Hattusili III has sent his own palace guard to escort the emissaries to his palace on the city's acropolis. Here their leader, Ramesses' diplomat-in-chief, will hold audience with him.

Inside the gate, numerous mudbrick buildings spread across the terrain that slopes downwards to the lower section of the city, which is enclosed by another set of walls. The royal palace is located on a plateau just inside them. Recently replastered, the walls glisten in the early morning light. The king's guard clears a path for the pharaoh's men, escorting them through the crowds of bystanders across a causeway to the royal citadel. Once within the royal precinct, the emissaries are led through a succession of courtyards and up a flight of steps to a large pillared hall, with a throne at one end. Here they will pay their respects, on behalf of the pharaoh, to the Great King of Hatti, and deliver to him letters and gifts from his Royal Brother in Egypt.

For some time, they are kept waiting. The king has yet to emerge from his private apartments. And the delay gives his own people time to inspect the crates of gifts, delivered to another part of the palace. The crates are opened, the gifts checked against a clay tablet inventory to make sure that everything tallies up, and some of the gold is taken and melted down to confirm that it is pure. All the gifts are assessed to ensure they are worthy of their recipient. To judge from the itemised lists that accompanied other diplomatic missions from one Royal Brother to another, the gifts might include pieces of furniture made of ebony, silver cosmetic flasks, ceremonial weapons, delicately wrought combs of ivory, oil flasks shaped like oxen, special novelty pieces like a silver monkey with a baby in her lap, an abundance of linen cloth and linen garments of the finest quality, and large bars of gold. Word is passed to one of the officials that everything is in order. All the items will be laid out for public display, or at least for viewing by the privileged members of the king's court.

It is now time for the king to make his grand entrance. He's accompanied by his queen. Both are decked out in full ceremonial garb, suitable for receiving envoys from a royal peer. The pharaoh's chief emissary is summoned before the king and queen and given permission to speak. He does so in Akkadian, and one of the king's translators is at hand to render his speech in Hittite. The emissary recites a letter from the pharaoh to the Hittite king, having committed every detail of it to memory.[1] His words are carefully checked by one of the king's scribal staff against the tablet on which the actual letter is written, also in Akkadian. This is to ensure that the recited version of the letter corresponds with the written version, down to the last word. If there are discrepancies, the emissary might not only lose his job, but also his head. In important diplomatic correspondence between two Great Kings, there must be absolutely no possibility of misunderstanding or errors in translation. Good relations between the kingdoms very largely depended on getting everything right in the transmission of communications between their overlords.

The pharaoh's letter begins with all the usual formalities – greetings and blessings upon the king and all his family and all his children and all his livestock and all his subjects etc. etc. This is a necessary diplomatic preliminary before the envoy gets to the nitty-gritty of the letter. With the exception of one small fragment found in Egypt, all the surviving communications between the Hittite and Egyptian courts during the reigns of Hattusili III and Ramesses II have been found in the archives of the Hittite capital. Often in fragmentary form, these include the letters sent by Ramesses and other members of his family to Hattusili and other members of *his* family, particularly his wife Puduhepa. Indeed, Puduhepa and Ramesses wrote directly to each other, and·Ramesses often sent her copies of letters whose originals were addressed to her husband. The letters were written in the years before and after 1259 BC. This was the year of the famous peace treaty between the two kings. Among other things, the letters discussed arrangements for a marriage between Ramesses and one of Hattusili's daughters. There was also talk of a possible visit by Hattusili to Egypt, though this never eventuated.

Despite the formal peace between the two kings, the letters they exchanged were not always cordial. Let's sit in on one of the royal audiences. After the initial pleasantries have been dealt with and the real business begins, the Great King of Hatti listens carefully as his Royal Brother's words are translated and read out to him. Some of them are clearly not to his liking, and he scowls as he glances at

Puduhepa who shares his displeasure. Has his Royal Brother really said this? He looks across inquiringly at the scribe who is checking the clay tablet copy of the speech. The scribe verifies with a nod that the emissary's words are exactly those of the letter's written version. Already in his mind the king is framing a suitable response to his Royal Brother. And so is his queen! I have discussed elsewhere in the book the important matters of state with which the letters deal, and the sorts of things written in them that pleased or displeased their recipients. See how many you can identify.

When all is done, the pharaoh's envoys await the king's approval for their return home. Letters of response will be written to the pharaoh, by both the king and the queen, and these along with appropriate gifts will be conveyed by the king's own envoys to the pharaoh in his royal capital Pi-Ramesse in the Egyptian Delta.

THE ROYAL CLUB

Hattusili and Ramesses were members of what we might call a Club of Royal Brothers. Well, a club in a sense. It basically had only four members, and these never actually met. But their regular diplomatic missions to one another's courts kept them in relatively close contact – despite the vast distances between them and the weeks, even months, it must have taken for travel between their courts.

The qualification for membership was that you had to be one of the Great Kings of the age. In Hittite texts, the term 'Great King' is represented by a combination of the Sumerian logograms GAL (meaning 'great') and LUGAL (meaning 'king' – literally 'great man'). There were plenty of LUGALs – 'kings' – in the Bronze Age Near East, for the term was used of a range of smaller-scale rulers, like those who held immediate sway over the kingdoms subject to one or other of the great powers. But if you're able to attach GAL to LUGAL in your title, you'll find yourself in very elite company. In Hattusili's and Ramesses' time, the four Great Kings were the rulers of Hatti, Egypt, Assyria and Babylon. The home territory of Assyria and Babylon lay in northern and southern Mesopotamia respectively. Admission to membership was dependent on acceptance as a Great King by your peers, and once they accepted you, they addressed you as their Royal Brother.

But let's be clear that what I've referred to as a club was in no sense a formal organisation, with written rules and regulations. Your 'membership' was defined purely in terms of the recognition accorded to you by other 'members', by the diplomatic missions they sent to your kingdom, and you to theirs, by the value of the gifts included in a number of these missions, by their references to you as a Great King and Royal Brother, by treaties they drew up with you, and sometimes by marriage-alliances contracted with your family. And of course recognition by foreign peers did much to enhance your status among your own subjects. This was certainly the case with Hattusili, who sought from Ramesses – and was granted – acknowledgement as the legitimate Great King of Hatti. This we learn from their correspondence. Such acknowledgement was particularly important for a man who had usurped his kingdom's throne and at least initially received snubs from the other two Great Kings, the rulers of Assyria and Babylon.

The Amarna letters

We learn more about the diplomatic interactions between the Royal Brothers by going back almost a century before the reigns of Hattusili and Ramesses – to the time when one of the most controversial of all pharaohs, Akhenaten (formerly called Amenhotep IV), was overlord of Egypt and its subject-territories. Akhenaten built himself a new royal capital on the east bank of the Nile in middle Egypt, and called it Akhetaten, 'Horizon Aten', on the site now called el-Amarna. Aten was the Sun God, and Akhenaten devoted himself exclusively to his worship, at the expense of Egypt's traditional gods. This allegedly led him to neglect the affairs of his kingdom, including his responsibilities to maintain Egypt's status as an international power. But many scholars now believe that this negative image of the so-called 'heretic pharaoh' is considerably overstated, due largely to the hostility towards him of the conservative elements among his subjects, especially the traditional priesthood of the land.

Indeed, the claim that Akhenaten neglected his kingdom's international interests seems to be negated by one of our most important sources of information about international relations in the Near East during the fourteenth century. This is the cache of 382 clay tablets accidentally discovered at el-Amarna in 1887, in the remains of Akhenaten's short-lived city Akhetaten. Three hundred and fifty of these documents are letters, or copies of letters, exchanged by Akhenaten or his father and predecessor Amenhotep III (whose letters had been preserved and brought to the new city after his death), with foreign rulers and the pharaoh's vassal subjects in Syria-Palestine.[2] As these letters clearly demonstrate, the pharaoh who was allegedly indifferent to his kingdom's affairs, and to maintaining Egypt's influence on the international scene, kept in close communication with his vassal rulers in the Syro-Palestinian region and with his foreign peers, just as his father had done.

The pharaoh exchanged both letters and diplomatic missions with his Royal Brothers in Hatti, Mittani, Babylon and finally Assyria. That's a total of four other Great Kingdoms with which the pharaoh had dealings. But Mittani was at this time on the way out. Its empire was finally destroyed by another of the pharaoh's correspondents, the Hittite king Suppiluliuma, and the upstart Assyria quickly moved to fill the power vacuum which Mittani's fall left in its wake. Indeed we can already see the beginning of its rise in a letter of bitter complaint to the pharaoh from the Babylonian king Burnaburiash.[3] Representatives of the Assyrian king had presented themselves at the pharaoh's court. 'How dare they!' Burnaburiash protested. 'The Assyrians are my vassals! They have no authority to send delegations to you on their own behalf.' But the Assyrians had been hospitably received by the pharaoh, who no doubt foresaw that Assyria was on the verge of becoming the next Great Kingdom, successor of the soon-to-be-extinguished Mittanian empire. The Babylonian king had good reason to be concerned. For most of the rest of the Bronze Age, Assyria and Babylon became bitter rivals and were often locked in conflict.

Yet with few exceptions, and despite the bickering and complaints with which a lot of the high-level diplomatic exchanges between the royal courts are laced, the letters and diplomatic missions from one Royal Brother to another played an important role in maintaining a reasonably high level of political stability in the Near Eastern world. Apart from frequent clashes between the Hittite and Mittanian Great Kings, Hatti appears to have had only three all-out conflicts with another Great Kingdom – two with Egypt at Qadesh in Syria, and one with Assyria (the battle of Nihriya) in northern Mesopotamia. (We'll say more about the last of these in the next chapter.)

On the other hand, military campaigns of one kind or another were an almost yearly event in which Hatti like the other Great Kingdoms independently engaged. For the most part, these campaigns were directed against rebellious subject-states and insurrectionists, or hostile independent cities and countries, and mountain tribes like the Kaska people. Indeed, Hatti's struggles to maintain its authority over its subject-states and to ward off attacks by hostile independent forces made ever greater demands on its increasingly limited military resources, and imposed ever greater hardships on its homeland population and loyal subjects elsewhere as the empire moved irrevocably towards its end.

CHAPTER 23

THE EMPIRE'S
STRUGGLE FOR
SURVIVAL

T here could have been fresh problems in the royal family over the succession when Hattusili died and kingship was passed on to his son, another Tudhaliya (commonly designated as the fourth of that name). Not just because Urhi-Teshub's branch of the family might have made a new bid to put one of its own members on the throne, but also because another of Hattusili's sons, Nerikkaili, had already been designated as the crown prince and was now passed over in favour of Tudhaliya. Our texts provide no explanation for this. It may be that important considerations of state were involved.

But it has also been proposed that Tudhaliya's appointment as heir was due to Hattusili's wife Puduhepa, on the (unproven) grounds that Tudhaliya was her own son by Hattusili, and she was seeking to promote his interests above those of her stepson(?) Nerikkaili. That could be right, and would give a nice air of intrigue to the matter, with the whiff of the shenanigans of Rome's Julio-Claudian dynasty about it. In any case, Nerikkaili seems to have accepted his displacement with good grace and continued to play an important role in the affairs of the kingdom. Before his death, perhaps for some years before it, Hattusili appears to have been preparing Tudhaliya for the highest office of the land by appointing him at a very early age to the highly prestigious post of Chief of the Bodyguards, and giving him extensive battle experience by sending him on campaigns in the Kaska region. He may even have made Tudhaliya his co-regent for a time, as he became increasingly debilitated by the illnesses which may have affected him for much of his life.

But Tudhaliya's crown never rested easily on his head. Throughout his reign, he was beset with grave fears for his safety, not only from members of his extended family, but also from those of his immediate family. One of his own brothers hatched a plot to assassinate him while he was on one of his regional tours. The plot was discovered in time and the brother and his co-conspirators arrested. But the whole nasty affair left Tudhaliya feeling more vulnerable than ever. This is evident from a set of instructions he issued to his high officials and the dignitaries of the land, demanding their unconditional loyalty. He made clear in these instructions that the greatest threats to his safety were likely to come from members of his own family:

> My Sun has many brothers and there are many sons of his father. The Land of Hatti is full of the royal line: in Hatti the descendants of Suppiluliuma, the descendants of Mursili, the descendants of Muwattalli, the descendants of Hattusili are numerous. With regard to kingship, you must acknowledge no other person (but me, Tudhaliya), and protect only the grandson and great grandson and descendants of Tudhaliya. And if at any time (?) evil is done to My Sun – (for) My Sun has many brothers – and someone approaches another person and speaks thus: 'Whomever we select for ourselves need not even be a son of our lord!' – these words must not be (permitted)! With regard to kingship, you must protect only My Sun and the descendants of My Sun. You must approach no other person.[1]

A LOYAL SUBJECT OR AN AMBITIOUS PRETENDER?

Initially at least, there was one close family member Tudhaliya felt he could trust. Ironically this was Kurunta, son of King Muwattalli and brother or half-brother of Muwattalli's successor Urhi-Teshub, whom Tudhaliya's father Hattusili had overthrown. Tudhaliya and Kurunta were cousins, and had become particularly close friends during Hattusili's reign – despite Hattusili's seizure of the throne from Kurunta's brother. This we learn from the text of a bronze tablet, found in 1986 quite by accident under a pavement just outside the Sphinx Gate of the royal capital.[2]

The text is that of a treaty which Tudhaliya as king drew up with Kurunta. The treaty tells us that Muwattalli had assigned this second son of his, while still a child, to the care of his brother Hattusili in Hakpis, where Hattusili had been appointed as local king. Muwattalli may have acted in this way to keep Kurunta safe from intra-family disputes in the royal court. A close relationship developed between Kurunta and Hattusili's family, and Kurunta apparently remained loyal to his uncle during the latter's war with Urhi-Teshub. Hattusili subsequently rewarded his loyalty by appointing him ruler of Tarhuntassa, formerly Muwattalli's royal seat and still enjoying a prestigious status after Hattusa once again became the royal capital.

And now Kurunta's allegiance to Hattusili's successor was confirmed in the bronze tablet treaty – which contained a number of special concessions granted to Kurunta additional to those granted by Hattusili in an earlier treaty with him. These concessions were intended as a further acknowledgement of his loyalty, and/or to ensure that it continued. Here was one family member on whom Tudhaliya could safely rely. Or could he?

That brings us to a mystery. During excavations conducted late last century in Hattusa, three seal impressions came to light bearing the inscription 'Kurunta, Great King'. What were they doing there? What makes the mystery all the greater is that no Hittite ruler, no matter how exalted his status, would use the title 'Great King' unless he were the ruler of the entire Hittite world. That at least is the standard view, and even though the name Kurunta was previously known from other texts, there is no indication in any of these that he was ever supreme overlord of the Hittite world. So how do we explain these seals?

One explanation suggested in the past was that for a time Kurunta did become the Great King in Hattusa, breaking his allegiance to Tudhaliya and seizing his throne briefly before Tudhaliya won it back. What were thought to be indications of a destruction of parts of Hattusa in Tudhaliya's reign were seen to support this view; it was concluded that there had been a violent takeover of the city by Kurunta. Evidence for a partial destruction of Hattusa at this time is now discounted. But can we rule out the possibility that Kurunta at least aspired to supreme sovereignty, and that these seals were made in advance, in anticipation of a successful coup? The mystery has deepened with the discovery of a relief monument on a site called Hatip near modern Konya in southern Anatolia. The relief, depicting a god kitted out for battle, is accompanied by an inscription which reads 'Kurunta, Great King, son of Muwattalli, Great King, Hero'.[3]

How do we fit together this information with the Kurunta seals? Several possibilities have been proposed. The first I've already mentioned: that Kurunta rebelled against his cousin, and either succeeded for a time in becoming Great King, or had seals struck and inscriptions carved in anticipation of this but failed in his attempt. A second possibility is that Kurunta did in fact become Great King for a short time, but only after his cousin's death. There's a further possibility we'll discuss later. And you may have thoughts of your own.

RISING UNREST THROUGHOUT THE KINGDOM

Beyond difficulties Tudhaliya may have faced in securing and maintaining his position within his own extended family, the king was confronted with ever-mounting problems in many parts of his kingdom at large. Unrest was on the increase throughout the subject-states, particularly in the west. Inscriptions from Tudhaliya's reign refer to one or more campaigns conducted by the king in the west against the chronically troublesome Lukka Lands, and against one of the Arzawa states, Seha River Land; its throne had been seized by an upstart after the death of its previous ruler Masturi, an uncle-in-law of Tudhaliya and loyal Hittite subject. As we've noted, Masturi's marriage with Tudhaliya's aunt (his father Hattusili's sister) had failed to produce offspring, leaving the vassal throne up for grabs when he died. Its new occupant immediately repudiated all links with Hatti, and led his kingdom in rebellion against it, apparently with some sort of support, or promise of support, from the king of Ahhiyawa.[4]

This was another major crisis in the making, and Tudhaliya responded to it at the earliest possible opportunity. It was perhaps in the same context as his Lukka campaign(s) that the king marched deep into Arzawan territory, inflicted a crushing defeat on the rebel forces, capturing the upstart king and his family and deporting them to Hattusa, along with many prisoners and 500 teams of horse. He rounded off his operations in the region by installing on the kingdom's throne a member of the legitimate ruling family, and no doubt resecuring his allegiance to the Hittite crown.

But how sure could the king be that there would be no further outbreaks of rebellion in his western states as soon he led his troops back home? Especially while Ahhiyawa remained an active and menacing presence in the region. Any attempts Hattusili, Tudhaliya's father, may have made to win Ahhiyawan cooperation in maintaining stability in the region had obviously failed. So Ahhiyawa remained one of Hatti's chief problems. And would continue to be so at least as long as it had a base, Milawata, on the Anatolian mainland.

It's time now for some more speculation. I start with the very fragmentary text of a letter commonly referred to by scholars as 'the Milawata letter'.[5] In the surviving pieces of the letter, neither the name of the sender nor of the recipient is preserved. But we can work out that the author was almost certainly Tudhaliya and its recipient an important and loyal Hittite vassal ruler in western Anatolia. The letter is so named because it records a successful attack by the Hittite king and the letter's recipient on the land of Milawata. In the wake of this attack, Milawata's boundaries were redefined and the letter's recipient given immediate authority over the land. Indeed, he seems to have exercised this authority as a kind of regional overlord whose sway extended as far north as the kingdom of Wilusa in the region of the Classical Troad in northwestern Anatolia.

This raises several questions. Firstly, who was this regional overlord? The best answer, I believe, is provided by David Hawkins. I earlier mentioned (in Chapter 6) the relief sculpture located in a mountain pass near Izmir, the so-called Karabel monument. The inscription indicates that the figure depicted in the relief was a man called Tarkasnawa, ruler of the Arzawan kingdom Mira, at that time the largest and most powerful of the western Anatolian states. Hawkins has proposed, convincingly, that Tarkasnawa was Tudhaliya's partner in the attack on Milawata. In an attempt to provide a lasting solution to the constantly recurring problems in his western territories, Tudhaliya may now have given the king of Mira extensive authority over much of the western Anatolian region, from as far south as Milawata to Wilusa in the north. In effect, the local king may have been granted powers as substantial as those exercised by the king's viceroys in Syria.

All this obviously begs an important question. Where, if anywhere, does Ahhiyawa fit into this scenario? We have noted that Milawata had been subject to Ahhiyawan overlordship since at least the reign of Muwattalli some decades earlier. But there is no reference at all to Ahhiyawa in the Milawata letter, or at least in what survives of it, so we cannot be sure that Ahhiyawa was still in control of Milawatan territory at the time of the Hittite attack on it.

But we *may* have indirect evidence that at some time during Tudhaliya's reign, if not already before, the Ahhiyawan king had lost control over his Anatolian base and had therefore ceased to be an influential player in the region. This is perhaps to be inferred from a passage in the draft of a treaty which Tudhaliya drew up with one of his Syrian vassals, Shaushgamuwa, king of the land of Amurru. In one of the treaty's clauses, Tudhaliya provides a list of all the Great Kings who are his peers, and potential enemies:

And the kings who (are) of equal rank with me, the king of Egypt, the king of Karadunia (= Kassite Babylonia), the king of Assyria, ~~the king of Ahhiyawa~~, if the king of Egypt is a friend of My Sun, let him also be a friend to you, if he is an enemy of My Sun, let him be your enemy also [...][6]

The most interesting feature of this clause is its *initial* inclusion of the Ahhiyawan king amongst Tudhaliya's peers, and then the *erasure* of his name, by having a line drawn through it while the treaty was still in draft form and the clay on which it was written still damp and soft. This suggests to me that the scribe who had drafted the treaty had simply copied the list of Great Kings from an earlier, perhaps quite recent document, but that the Ahhiyawan had suddenly lost this status; he therefore no longer warranted the designation 'Great King', at least in a Near Eastern context. If he had lost control over Milawata, or withdrawn his sovereignty from it, for whatever reason, that might explain his elimination from the list. Perhaps Tudhaliya himself pointed out to the scribe when the draft was read to him that the Ahhiyawan should no longer be included among the Great Kings, and the reference to him was crossed out. It would have been omitted entirely from the final version.

THE ASSYRIAN MENACE

Fear of Assyrian aggression against his eastern subject-territories remained one of Tudhaliya's chief concerns throughout his reign. When a new king Tukulti-Ninurta occupied the Assyrian throne *c.*1233, there were some prospects of a lasting peace being established between the two kingdoms. Initially, the kings wrote to each other in cordial terms. But Tudhaliya became increasingly concerned about repeated Assyrian raids on Hittite border territory, despite his Royal Brother's denial of these, and about Tukulti-Ninurta's aggressive, overtly expansionist campaigns in northern Mesopotamia against a number of Hurrian states in the region. If these states fell to him, Tudhaliya reasoned, the Assyrian might well turn his attention westwards to the lands across the Euphrates, to Hittite subject-territory. Better to forestall this by attacking the Assyrian first.

No longer accepting Tukulti-Ninurta's assurance of peaceful intentions towards Hatti, Tudhaliya launched a pre-emptive strike against him in what is commonly called the battle of Nihriya, probably in the region north or northeast of modern Diyarbakır.

We have only the Assyrian version of this battle and its outcome. This is preserved in a letter which Tukulti-Ninurta wrote to Tudhaliya's vassal, the king of Ugarit, probably with the intention of winning the king away from his Hittite allegiance.[7] But as far as we can judge from it, the Hittite forces were routed, the survivors, including Tudhaliya, returned home, and the triumphant Assyrian completed his conquest of the Hurrian lands. Tukulti-Ninurta might well have set his sights now on what Tudhaliya had tried to prevent, a full-scale invasion across the Euphrates leading to the conquest of a large swathe of Hittite subject-territory in Syria. But fortunately for the Hittites, Tukulti-Ninurta turned his attention south – to the kingdom of Babylon and created havoc in the land before he finally fell victim to an assassination plot.

TUDHALIYA'S CYPRUS CAMPAIGN

With all the problems confronting him throughout his Anatolian and Syrian territories, one would have thought that Tudhaliya had enough problems on his plate without taking his operations further afield – especially given his apparent defeat by the Assyrians in northern Mesopotamia. But we then find him embarking, perhaps towards the end of his reign, on a fresh new enterprise – against the land of Alasiya, the eastern Mediterranean island we know as Cyprus.

How did he get there? Since Hatti's core region had no sea outlets, its kings would have needed ships supplied by vassal or allied states with coastal territory and seaports for any Hittite ventures involving naval operations. The Syrian states Ugarit and Amurru were so endowed. Very likely one or both of these provided Tudhaliya with sufficient naval resources to launch an attack on Alasiya.[8] He succeeded in conquering the island, or at least parts of it, taking prisoner its king and his family, deporting them to his homeland, and declaring Alasiya henceforth a Hittite tributary. We do not know what Alasiya had done to provoke the Hittite attack. Quite possibly Hatti's increasing dependence on grain supplies from abroad prompted disruption of these supplies by a hostile regime on the island, or by pirates who used its ports as bases for attacking ships with lucrative cargoes passing through or across the eastern Mediterranean.

Despite the mounting pressures from almost every part of his empire, and despite a devastating defeat by his Assyrian counterpart, Tudhaliya proved an able leader of his kingdom and achieved some considerable successes in the course of his long reign. Not least of these was his consolidation of Hittite authority in the west, including the apparent elimination of Ahhiyawan influence in the region, the crushing of rebellions in other parts of his kingdom, the stabilisation of his Syrian territories, and the conquest of Alasiya. Yet on his death his kingdom had almost run its course. Within a few years, the Hittite empire and its royal capital would be no more – despite all that Hatti's multiplicity of gods, its warriors and its last Great Kings could do to save them.

CHAPTER 24

HATTI'S DIVINE
OVERLORDS

THE THOUSAND GODS

'**L**and of a Thousand Gods!' Though this proud Hittite boast was a somewhat exaggerated one, the Hittite pantheon could certainly claim hundreds of members. Statues of gods taken from the temples of the enemy lands seized by Hittite armies were laden into wagons as spoils of battle and trundled back to the homeland where they joined the ranks of their fellow-deities. They too were worshipped and had offerings made to them by their conquerors. They too were included in the long list of gods to whom oaths were sworn when Hittite treaties were drawn up. In Hittite religion, as in all polytheistic religions, the word 'infidel' had no meaning. The capture of an enemy's gods provided the clearest token of the enemy's defeat and submission. But his gods were gods nevertheless, even if of inferior status, and were so treated in the land of their conqueror.

The Thousand Gods claim also reflects the rich eclecticism of Hittite civilisation, and the ways in which this civilisation was shaped by the adoption into it of many elements of its Near Eastern contemporaries and predecessors. For the foreign gods brought with them important aspects of the traditions and cultures of their native regions, which became part of the fabric of Hittite civilisation. Of course, many of the lesser gods were simply local versions of the chief gods of the land. We find, for example a myriad of storm gods, sun gods and Ishtars (or Ishtar-equivalents) in the texts, often located in obscure parts of the Hittite realm. Tolerance in recognising the individuality of each of these was sometimes outweighed by the inconvenience of doing so. Particularly when it came to identifying a deity to whom offence had been given and who needed to be appeased by appropriate rituals.

As we noted in Chapter 13, the causes of a wide range of afflictions, whether suffered by an individual or by the whole land, were attributed to divine wrath. And before the afflictions could be cured, the offended deity or deities had first to be identified. Which could mean a lengthy period of oracular consultation. Thus King Mursili II probably had to go through a protracted trial-and-error process to find out *which* god had caused his speech affliction before he got his answer. In this case, the Storm God of an obscure region called Manuzziya was finally identified as the cause of his ailment. Once that was established, the next step could be taken – appeasing the offended deity with a prescribed ritual, which hopefully resulted in a cure. (We never find out whether in Mursili's case it did.)

So we can see here one of the big advantages that monotheistic religions, like Judaism, Christianity and Islam have over polytheistic ones. They are much more economical. The monotheistic god is omnipresent. He can be prayed to everywhere and anywhere without having to be summoned to a particular synagogue, church or mosque to hear what you want to say to him or ask him. And there's no chance of your prayer going astray and reaching the wrong god – because there isn't any other god. Later in the empire, Queen Puduhepa, of Hurrian origin and Hattusili III's chief wife, realised that 'extreme polytheism' was getting rather out of hand, and she began a process of syncretising at least the chief deities – that is, identifying Hittite gods with their foreign counterparts. Thus the Hittites' chief goddess, the Sun Goddess of Arinna, was identified with her Hurrian counterpart Hepat. Her husband, the Storm God of Hatti, was identified with his Hurrian equivalent Teshub, and a son of the pair, called Sharrumma in Hurrian, was identified with the Storm God of Nerik. The rationalisation of the Hittite pantheon never really proceeded beyond this point. But it does reflect the progressive Hurrianisation of many aspects of Hittite civilisation, particularly religious aspects, during the thirteenth century. Queen Puduhepa was largely responsible for this, with the clear support of her husband and son Tudhaliya. The rock sanctuary at Yazılıkaya provides our most striking visual example of the Hurrianisation of Hittite religion.

YAZILIKAYA[1]

When Charles Texier visited Yazılıkaya in 1834, he was completely mystified by what he saw. Even now, when we know so much more than he did (which was virtually nothing) about the site and the civilisation to which it belonged, we can still sense much of the awe and mystery which he felt as he made his way through the open-air chambers, with their sombre array of carved figures and accompanying hieroglyphic symbols. The large rocky outcrop which contains these chambers was once the holiest sanctuary in the Hittite world. Lying just a kilometre northeast of the royal capital, it must have played a major role in the Hittites' calendar of religious festivals, especially in the empire's last century, from the time when King Hattusili III built a gatehouse and temple-complex across the front of the site. Almost certainly this was the place where the Hittite New Year festival was celebrated and the rites of spring were performed. And all the gods were assembled for the occasion. We know this from the images of the gods commissioned by Hattusili's son Tudhaliya on the walls of the sanctuary's two chambers.

The most impressive of Yazılıkaya's sculptures is the procession of deities in 'Chamber A' – 66 of them in total – divided into two files approaching each other, males on the left (with two exceptions), females on the right (with one exception), in descending order of importance. The males, armed for battle, wear conical caps, often with horns attached (the more horns, the greater the gods' importance) and short kilts. The females wear tall cylindrical hats, crenellated like castle battlements, and ankle-length pleated skirts. Both sexes wear shoes with upturned toes. We know the identity of a number of these deities from the names in Luwian hieroglyphs which accompany them (though in many cases the names are too worn to read). The deities have Hurrian names. Thus the two parades of figures are led by the Hittites' chief deities, the Storm/Weather God and the Sun Goddess of Arinna – but are here given their Hurrian names, Teshub and Hepat.

Behind Chamber A, a narrow passage flanked by a pair of winged, lion-headed demons, leads to the smaller, narrower 'Chamber B'. On the right of the chamber is a frieze of 12 male gods armed with sickle-shaped swords. Their legs astride, they appear to be running, walking briskly, or marching, towards something to their right. A similar group of gods also appears at the tail end of the male gods in Chamber A, though in this case they are unarmed. What do these gods signify?

Before answering this question, let's say something about the other main reliefs at Yazılıkaya. Tudhaliya's close association with the sanctuary is illustrated by two of its most striking reliefs. The first appears on the wall of Chamber A opposite the parade of deities (see Figure 11.3). It depicts the king in priestly garb bearing a long staff ending in a circle. We have suggested that it is a stylised crook, symbolising the king's role as 'shepherd' or protector of his people.

Figure 24.1   Teshub and Hepat lead the parade of deities, Yazılıkaya.

Figure 24.2   The 12 gods, Yazılıkaya.

He is identified by a royal cartouche, a panel carved on the wall to the left of his head bearing his name in hieroglyphs, surmounted by a winged sun-disk. In Chamber B Tudhaliya is again depicted (Figure 24.3), this time as the protégé of his patron deity Sharrumma, son of Teshub and Hepat. In a suitable display of humility the king is towered over by his god. But Sharrumma's endorsement of Tudhaliya's authority is made clear by the god's protective embrace. He extends his arm around the king's shoulder and clasps his right wrist.

To the left of this scene is another powerful image. It is a carving of a figure whose top half consists of a human head (or rather a divine head to judge from its horned, conical hat), underneath which are the foreparts of two lions (or lion-pelts) with their heads hanging down. This part of the carving represents the hilt of a sword. Its bottom half consists of a sword-blade which appears to be plunged into the ground. The figure is almost certainly a representation of the underworld god Nergal. And very likely the 12 figures on the opposite wall are underworld deities. They recall a Hittite ritual text which mentions 12 underworld deities in the same context as Nergal, and another ritual text which describes an

Figure 24.3 Tudhaliya and Sharrumma, Yazılıkaya.

incantation priest making clay images of deities banished to the Underworld in the shape of swords plunged into the ground.

So how do we put all this information together? At present, the most convincing interpretation proposed for Chamber B is that it provided the burial place for King Tudhaliya. The chief figures in Chamber B face towards the chamber's north end, directing attention to what *may* have been a monumental statue erected

Figure 24.4 The Sword God, Yazılıkaya.

there. The statue could have been that of a god. But could it alternatively have been a statue of the king, set up in the place where he was buried? We have already noted other strong associations between the sanctuary and Tudhaliya. And we know that Hittite kings were buried in stone houses, called *hekur*-houses. No stone structure, either natural or built, has yet been identified as a royal tomb. But it is quite possible that Yazılıkaya did provide such a tomb – a tomb on a grand scale for one of the last Hittite kings, who sought in other ways as well to impress his subjects with the monuments he had built to mark his reign.

So Yazılıkaya would have been a place of both death (the niches and crevices in rocks on the path between Hattusa and Yazılıkaya contained the remains of a number of burials, both inhumations and cremations) and new life. A close nexus between death and renewed life is common to many religious beliefs, as illustrated by Egyptian and Christian notions of death and resurrection. In the cyclic pattern of things, death and decay are followed by new beginnings, new life. Yazılıkaya may have been the Hittite world's most prominent expression of this notion.

A final word on the sanctuary. Mountains and outcrops of rock were closely associated with gods in the Hittite world. They had special mystical powers and were indeed considered the dwelling places of gods. This gave them great significance in Hittite religion. Mountain gods, depicted with human upper torsoes whose lower torsoes were represented by mountains, figure prominently among the deities of the Hittite pantheon, though often fairly low down in the divine pecking order. But rocks and mountains were places from which gods could be summoned to participate in the festivals held in their honour. And Yazılıkaya was a prime place for summoning forth the gods.

If you visit the site today, you may need a lot of time and patience to see clearly everything there. Many of the sanctuary's reliefs were shallow when first carved, and are now very worn. Depending on the hour of the day and the season of the year, some of them, including the great parade of deities in Chamber A and the demons at the entrance to Chamber B, can be difficult to see. At other times, they stand out clearly. Figure 24.1 illustrates a midway stage. As the light changes with the change of the angle of the sun, the deities appear to emerge slowly from their rock dwellings, at first faintly, but then with ever-increasing clarity, as they respond to calls for their presence at the festivals held in their honour.

THE FESTIVAL YEAR

The New Year festival was but one of a multiplicity of festivals that dominated the Hittite religious year. That's reflected in the enormous number of festival texts that have come to light, particularly in the archives of Hattusa, far exceeding the total number of documents belonging to all other genres. 'Not another festival text,' you can almost hear the excavators groan when a new tablet is unearthed – and proves to be just that. One hundred and sixty-five festivals or more were included in the religious calendar, and there may well have been many others of a purely local-community nature that were never preserved in written form.

The major festivals were closely linked with the year's major seasons, understandable in a society whose survival depended so much on its agricultural productivity. Of the four most important festivals, two were held in spring and at least one in autumn. And some went on for many days like the spring AN.TAH.SUM festival, held in honour of 'the Sun Goddess of Arinna and the gods of the Hatti Land'. This lasted 38 days, and was celebrated partly in the capital and subsequently in other religious centres of the homeland. Pilgrimages to these centres was an important part of being king, and at least some of them contained royal residences to accommodate His Majesty while he was there for festival celebrations (as well as for other reasons). For the king was expected to participate personally in all major festivals, as the gods' chief representative on earth, and was likely to offend his divine lords if he did not, sometimes with dire consequences for the kingdom. Sometimes he put off a military campaign to fulfil his obligation to attend certain festivals, though as with other responsiblities there were times when he delegated his religious duties to other members of his family.

Much as we might feel that we have more than enough festival texts, they do give us a very good idea of what a festival programme included. Indeed these texts served as instruction manuals for the conduct of the festivals, with detailed accounts of all the procedures to be followed, the rituals to be enacted, the equipment to be used, the robes to be worn and the foods to be consumed by both the gods and their worshippers. Instructions had to be followed to the last detail, for to get something wrong was likely to invalidate the whole process and incur the fury of the god or gods in whose honour the festival was being held.

Indeed the gods themselves directly participated in the ceremonies and celebrations, for they literally inhabited their statues when they were taken from the innermost recesses of their temples and carried in procession to the various festival venues. Parts of the celebrations may have taken place within the courtyards of their temples, parts in other sacred places, in open areas and in rock sanctuaries. Let us imagine the gods, resplendent in their gleaming statues, sheeted with gold or other polished metals and bedecked with jewels being conveyed along the processional route. They are followed by the king and the queen mounted in their chariots, and the priests and other dignitaries of the land, and the armed escort, and all other participants in the festival including the musicians and other entertainers – acrobats, singers and dancers. Crowds must have assembled at every available vantage spot to enjoy the splendour and pageantry of the occasion.

To be honest, the festival texts don't make rivetting reading, for they are full of tedious repetitious minutiae, which don't vary much from one text to another. But they do provide us with detailed descriptions of the rites, the liturgies, the ritual paraphernalia used in the ceremonies, the menus of the banquets enjoyed by both their human and their divine participants, and the entertainments provided by the singers and dancers and contenders in the sports contests which were part of the festival programme. They give us a taste of Hittite religion in practice, in its most tangible form.

You might well ask how the gods actually joined in the banquets. Perhaps as in other religions they were discreetly screened off from the rest of the participants as they consumed the food set before them. Certain privileged members of the priesthood were allowed to finish off what they left on their plates.

THE HUMAN FACE OF THE GODS

The Hittites didn't know what their gods actually looked like because they could take whatever form they wanted when they appeared to their mortal worshippers. They might sometimes appear in an abstract form, for example as gold and silver disks, or in animal form. The best known instance of the latter is the representation of the Storm God as a bull in a scene which forms part of a series of sculptured panels on the walls of the site now called Alaca Höyük; this was very likely the most important cult centre of the Sun Goddess of Arinna. The bull, symbolising male strength and fertility, epitomises basic qualities of the Storm God. At Alaca, he appears on a base behind an altar before which the king and queen pay homage to him.

But most commonly the gods take human form, or at least inhabit the human statues set up in their honour when they are summoned by their worshippers. The sacrifical food and drink offerings made to them and their participation in festival banquets indicate a belief that they have the same need for sustenance as their mortal worshippers. Indeed King Mursili II warns them that if they don't end the great plague ravaging the Hittite land, all the land's food-producers and food-preparers will die and there'll be no-one left to feed their divine overlords, let alone having anything to feed them with.

Like the gods of many civilisations, these divine overlords were prone to the full range of emotions experienced by their mortal worshippers. They could lose their temper, be jealous, seek revenge for perceived or real slights, they could be rebuked, argued with and reasoned with in the prayers offered to them, and they could sometimes neglect their responsibilities.

HITTITE MYTH

The clearest example of this last is provided by one of a small body of native Anatolian myths that have been passed down to us from the Hittite world. The subject of the myth is a 'Vanishing God', who simply abandons his people and goes walkabout to some unknown location (obviously an impossibility in a monotheistic belief system). Sometimes the great Storm God himself is the offending deity, but more commonly the culprit is the vegetation god Telipinu, an old Hattian deity and son of the Storm God.[2]

Of the several fragmentary versions we have of his story, the common elements seem to be these: For some reason or other, Telipinu has flown into a rage, puts on his shoes and abandons his lands. Crops wither and die, sheep and cattle reject their young, humans and gods starve. The Storm God becomes very worried and despatches an eagle to find his son. But in vain. The Storm God himself tries to find him. But he too fails. Finally a bee is sent to look for the absentee, and discovers him in a meadow, apparently asleep. The bee stings his hands and feet, which wakes him up and makes him even more angry. He vents his fury by unleashing devastating thunder and lightning and great floods, destroying houses, livestock, crops and wreaking havoc on humankind. Finally, the goddess of magic Kamrusepa is sent to make peace with him and bring him back. A ritual which she conducts for this purpose dispels the god's anger, and his way back to his people is made smooth for him by spreading oil and honey along his route.

This is no mere story, narrated by a story-teller for the entertainment of a local audience. I believe that it was an important ritual performed within a sacred complex – a temple courtyard or an open-air sanctuary – each year at the beginning of spring, to ensure that after the dead winter season, the crops and flocks and herds would flourish in the season of growth. This is, in fact, the Hittite way of accounting for the cycle of seasons. In Greek mythological tradition, the cycle is explained by the grief of the earth goddess Demeter when her daughter Persephone is abducted to the Underworld and the earth becomes barren. But life returns when Persephone is restored to her mother at the beginning of spring. In Hittite tradition, it is the disappearance and return of the vegetation god that explains the cycle of seasons. In his case at least, the use of sympathetic or mimetic magic is used to ensure his return, involving quite literally the spreading of oil and honey along at least the last part of the god's homeward route to make smooth his return, with appropriate liturgies and ritualistic activity to welcome him home.

Other Hittite myths too have to do with renewal of life at the beginning of spring. One of the major spring events on the religious calendar was known as the Purulli Festival, which lasted just under a month. Presided over by the king and queen, its ceremonies began in Hattusa, but then the festival procession travelled through a number of Hittite cities, stopping in them to repeat or carry out further sacred rites, before reaching its destination in the northern homeland city of Nerik, a major cult centre of the Storm God.

The myth of the dragon Illuyanka, representing the forces of evil and destruction, plays an important part in this festival. The opening of one of two versions of the myth reads thus:

> This is the text of the Purulli Festival [...]. When they speak thus: 'Let the land prosper and thrive, and let the land be protected' – and when it prospers and thrives, they perform the Purulli Festival.[3]

The myth tells of Illuyanka's emergence from the bowels of the earth to do mortal battle with the Storm God. It's a fierce battle, and far from one-sided. The god has to call on both divine and human assistance before he finally triumphs and kills the dragon. Once more the land is safe. But Illuyanka will rise from the dead again the next year, and the battle will have to be fought all over again. Mortal participation reflects the cooperation needed between gods and humans to ensure that the land is kept safe from evil forces.

I believe that the story of Illuyanka and his conflict with the Storm God was actually acted out, in a dramatic performance before the festival participants, probably repeatedly at various venues along the festival route. Actors would have taken the roles of Illuyanka, the Storm God and other participants in the drama. No doubt they were decked out in appropriate costumes, and equipped with weapons and other accoutrements normally kept with other ritual paraphernalia in the temple storerooms.[4]

'VENGEANCE IS MINE'

One last word about the gods. While they had plenty of shortcomings of their own, they were the ultimate arbiters of their mortal worshippers' behaviour. And as the ultimate beneficiaries of human endeavour and productivity, they knew that it was in their own interests to ensure the exercise of justice, morality, and right conduct on earth. Those of their worshippers who lived a righteous life in obedience to them and the laws of the land could expect the benefit of divine protection and blessings. But those who offended them, either through neglecting their ceremonies or through sinful conduct – like the violation of an oath, the murder of a father or brother, or the illegal seizure of another's rightful authority – would incur the full weight of divine vengeance. All mortal beings, including the king himself, were answerable to the gods for their conduct. Hatti's divine overlords could be bountiful in the blessings they bestowed, but utterly ruthless in punishing those who incurred their wrath.

CHAPTER 25

DEATH OF AN EMPIRE[1]

ON THE VERGE OF DISINTEGRATION

The longest of all hieroglyphic inscriptions is carved on a cliff-face on the rocky outcrop now called Nişantaş (Nişantepe) in the Hittite capital. Unfortunately, it has weathered to the point where it's almost unintelligible. But a few words here and there can be read – enough to indicate that the inscription contains a triumphant catalogue of the victories of the last Hittite king, Suppiluliuma II, over his enemies and rebellious subjects. No doubt this included an account of his western campaign, recorded in the better preserved 'Südburg inscription' in the cult complex near the city's acropolis.[2] 'Don't worry, everything's under control' is the message Suppiluliuma seems to be conveying to his subjects. If so, the message was a totally delusional one.

Within a short time of Tudhaliya's death *c*.1209, it was clear that the empire he had tried to restore to its former glory was in serious trouble. Things began badly when Tudhaliya's son and first successor Arnuwanda (III) died within a few months of his accession, leaving no son and heir of his own. His younger brother Suppiluliuma now quickly assumed kingship and bound his officials in oaths of allegiance to him. Implying that Arnuwanda was the victim of foul play by his own subjects, this second Suppiluliuma declared that he had taken royal office only because there was no other rightful heir to the throne. That of course was not strictly true. There were still the descendants of

Urhi-Teshub, the legimitately installed king overthrown by Suppiluliuma's grandfather Hattusili. Were they still intent on putting one of their own members on the throne? If so, did they plot such action from the southern Anatolian kingdom of Tarhuntassa where Urhi-Teshub's brother Kurunta had been installed as local ruler?

The last thing Suppiluliuma needed at this time was increasing instability within the extended royal household, for the empire's subject-states were growing restive, and increasingly defiant of Hittite authority. Uprisings in the southwest forced the king to undertake at least one major campaign to the region, as referred to in the 'Südburg inscription', where he conquered and subjected a number of lands lying in or near Lukka territory. Suppiluliuma then may have marched back eastwards, completing his campaign by entering the land and city of Tarhuntassa.

OR *DID* HE ENTER TARHUNTASSA?

There's a bit of a problem here. Scholars are now saying we can't be sure that Tarhuntassa *is* referred to in this inscription. The problem lies in the fact that in the hieroglyphic text the place in question is called '(the city of) the Storm God', whose name in Luwian is Tarhunta. Hence the conclusion that the city so called in the Südburg inscription is Tarhuntassa. But many cities where the Storm God was the chief deity might be called '(the city of) the Storm God', like Nerik in northern Anatolia. Even so, I still think it most likely that the city referred to twice in this inscription as the Storm God's city is Tarhuntassa.

But that doesn't completely solve our problem, since Suppiluliuma's relationship with Tarhuntassa at the time, and his purpose in entering it, are not clear from the inscription. Was the regime his father had established there now openly rebellious? Had he entered Tarhuntassa to reassert his authority over the local kingdom, and perhaps depose its current ruler? Reconstructing this part of our story is again like trying to solve a puzzle when most of the clues are missing. Let's see what we can deduce from the few that have survived. Here are some of them:

1. Urhi-Teshub's (step-?)brother Kurunta had remained loyal to Hattusili and his son and successor Tudhaliya, and had been given rule over the important appanage kingdom Tarhuntassa. Previously, during the reign of Urhi-Teshub's father Muwattalli, the city of Tarhuntassa had become the Hittite capital. Urhi-Teshub shifted the capital back to Hattusa.

2. A hieroglyphic inscription found at Hatip near modern Konya identifies Kurunta, son of Muwattalli, as a 'Great King'. Hatip probably lay near Tarhuntassa's northern border.

3. Three seal impressions found at Hattusa bear the name Kurunta and call him a 'Great King'.

4. Hieroglyphic inscriptions found at three sites in south-central Anatolia, and probably to be dated to this period, were commissioned by a ruler called Hartapu. The inscriptions identify this man as a 'Great King' and the 'son of Mursili' who is also called a 'Great King'.[3]

5. Mursili (III) was the official throne-name of Urhi-Teshub. Hartapu's father and Urhi-Teshub may thus be identical. If so, Hartapu would have been a nephew of Kurunta.

6. We would therefore have a family-line of three rulers, Mursili (Urhi-Teshub?), Kurunta (his son) and Hartapu (Kurunta's nephew) who all bore, or assumed, the title 'Great King'.

7. But Hattusili and his direct descendants Tudhaliya, Arnuwanda (III) and Suppiluliuma (II) also bore this title.

8. Conventional wisdom is that only the supreme ruler of Hatti, whose royal seat was in Hattusa, could call himself 'Great King'. That applied to Hattusili and his heirs.

9. But at least two members of the collateral branch of the royal family, based in Tarhuntassa, also claimed the status of 'Great King'.

10. In the Südburg inscription, Suppiluliuma claims a successful military campaign against a number of countries in southern Anatolia, as far west as the Lukka lands. He also refers (we have concluded) to the land and city of Tarhuntassa. But the passages in which he does so are unclear. He certainly entered the land and city, but we cannot be sure why. Was his intention to conquer it, or did he enter it for some other reason?

May I invite you to play the part of detective and try to reconstruct from these snippets a plausible scenario for what was going on in the royal family at this time? While you're thinking about it, let me suggest two possibilities.

The first is that the Urhi-Teshub branch of the royal family never abandoned its hopes of regaining the main prize, the throne of Hattusa. Though initially loyal to the usurper and his descendants, at least outwardly, Kurunta used Tarhuntassa as a base for building resistance against the Hattusa regime, eventually declaring his position by proclaiming himself 'Great King'. Suppiluliuma's campaign through southern Anatolia may have been in response to uprisings prompted by the Tarhuntassa regime, and may have ended with the kingdom's conquest.

In several of his inscriptions, Hartapu states his credentials as a great military conqueror, with the support and blessing of the Storm God. The belligerent nature of these inscriptions and the spread of the monuments on which they are carved in the north of the land of Tarhuntassa and beyond (there may well have been many more that have not survived) may represent early stages in a rebellion against Hattusa and attempts to win support from the local populations. Suppiluliuma's campaign through southern Anatolia may have been in response to uprisings prompted by the Tarhuntassa regime, and may have ended with the kingdom's conquest.

The perception of an empire on the verge of disintegration when Suppiluliuma mounted the throne could have prompted the Tarhuntassa-based regime to make its bid for the main prize – the Great Kingship of the entire Hittite realm. To counter such a move, it was essential that Suppiluliuma give clear proof, at the earliest possible opportunity, that despite his sudden and unexpected elevation to the Hittite throne, the reins of imperial power were firmly in his hands. This he sought to demonstrate by his military progress through southern Anatolia, bringing to heel a number of rebellious states. He completed his campaign with a comprehensive conquest of Tarhuntassa and the elimination of the regime there. The long and now almost illegible hieroglyphic inscription on the cliff-face called Nişantaş in Hattusa was a public record of his achievements, one in which his victorious southern campaign no doubt figured prominently.

That's scenario 1. A second, and quite different scenario is that far from rebelling against the Hattusa regime, Kurunta and Hartapu collaborated with it. In an attempt to arrest the disintegration of the empire, Suppiluliuma, and perhaps already his father Tudhaliya, had assigned virtual sovereignty of Tarhuntassa, and perhaps large swathes of neighbouring lands in southern Anatolia, to Kurunta and his successors, just as Muwattalli had earlier assigned sovereignty over a large part of northern Anatolia to his brother Hattusili. The viceroys in Syria at Carchemish and Aleppo, had exercised a similar sway since Suppiluliuma I appointed his sons as the first of these viceroys. So is what we have *not* a conflict between two branches of the royal family, but an apportionment among them of rule over different parts of the empire?

My main reservation about scenario 2 is the use of the title 'Great King' by Kurunta and Hartapu. The title LUGAL 'King' is OK. The Syrian viceroys were so called, as was Hattusili when Muwattalli appointed him ruler of the northern part of the kingdom. But even in a power-sharing arrangement, would the last occupants of the throne in Hattusa have ever allowed anyone else, no matter how exalted their status, to assume the title 'Great King' (LUGAL.GAL), which would indicate equality of status with the Hattusa regime?

KEEPING ALIVE THE LAND OF HATTI

Suppiluliuma's reasons for entering Tarhuntassa can perhaps be linked with another major event in his career. Following several successful sea battles which his forces fought against enemy ships off the coast of Alasiya (Cyprus) (these are the only recorded sea battles in Hittite history), Suppiluliuma invaded the island, as his father Tudhaliya had done, and presumably reclaimed it as Hittite subject-territory. Tudhaliya had apparently failed to establish any more than temporary control over the island, or even a part of it.

Remember that since the core land of Hatti had no sea outlets, the ships in Suppiluliuma's fleet must have come from allied coastal states like Ugarit and Amurru.

That raises another intriguing question. Why suddenly did the empire's tail-end rulers, with all the problems they faced in their mainland territories, turn their attention to an island in the eastern Mediterranean? I believe this question can be largely answered by looking at another problem the last Hittite kings faced. There is good reason to believe that the Hittite land, especially its core region, was suffering increasingly from food-shortages at this time. Periods of prolonged drought and famine have been suggested to explain this. Indeed, harsh natural conditions may have played their part in severely reducing food production. But man-made conditions, I suggest, played at least as great a part.

Once more we return to one of Hatti's most serious problems, its chronic shortage of manpower. This affected its ability not only to keep its army operational, but just as importantly to maintain an adequate level of food production for the land, as well as servicing Hatti's other important needs. Years of military campaigning, which drew many of the able-bodied workers from their fields, inevitably took their toll on the kingdom's population, for even successful campaigns must have resulted in significant casualties, and thus a constant drain on the kingdom's human resources. In the past, losses due to war and other factors like plague could be replenished from the large numbers of deportees brought back to the homeland, in the wake of military conquests, to restock its labour force and to swell the ranks of the kingdom's armies. But in the kingdom's final century, the supply of new workers and fighters from conquered areas had dropped off considerably – at a time when instability in the subject-territories made ever greater demands on the kingdom's military resources for restoring control over rebellious subjects.

Redeployment of the kingdom's able-bodied men from the fields to the defence forces almost certainly occurred now on a greater scale than ever before, forcing the Hittites to rely increasingly on grain imports from abroad. Following the 'Eternal Peace', representatives from the Hittite king had arranged transportation of large quantities of grain from Egypt to the homeland via Hittite-controlled ports on the southern Anatolian coast. The Hittites' Syrian vassal states, notably Ugarit and Amurru, were also called upon to send grain to the homeland, via ships to Anatolian ports like Ura, on the southeast coast, for overland transport. Serious problems would arise if the supply-routes, from Egypt or Syria, were cut off or seriously disrupted.

Attacks by land and sea

At this point we should introduce another element into our story – the so-called Sea Peoples. Records from the reign of the Egyptian pharaoh Ramesses III (1184 – 1153) tell us that in the early twelfth century, large groups of peoples coming from across the sea swept through many parts of the Near Eastern world, from Anatolia to Cyprus and across much of Syria and Palestine, leaving a trail of devastation in their wake before they were finally repulsed in Canaan and on the Egyptian coast by the pharaoh's forces. Though commonly known as 'the Sea Peoples', their movements involved extensive operations on land as well as by sea. Some of them had already attacked the Egyptian Delta in the reign of one of Ramesses'

Figure 25.1   Sherden warriors (a Sea Peoples group), Luxor.

predecessors Merneptah (1213–1203). On the walls of his temple at Medinet Habu, Ramesses tells us of the trail of destruction left by these marauders, and his victory over them.[4]

But even if we accept the basic truth of Ramesses' account, it's clear that the movements of these so-called Sea Peoples were not merely military operations. They involved large masses of people, including families and their portable possessions, who were seeking new lands to settle. Very likely many of them had been displaced from their original homelands, perhaps in western Anatolia as well as elsewhere, in the widespread upheavals associated with the end of the Late Bronze Age. Many were probably as much the victims as the perpetrators of these upheavals, being forced to take on a marauding aspect in their search for new homelands. Besides, it's possible that Ramesses has condensed into a single episode events that may have taken place over many years, perhaps going back to attacks on the coasts of Cyprus and Egypt during the pharaoh Akhenaten's reign 150 years earlier.[5]

In any case, it's very likely that as the Hittite kingdom became increasingly unstable from the late thirteenth century on, ships manned by enemy forces and pirates threatened severe disruption to sea traffic in the eastern Mediterranean, as well as to seaports along the Anatolian and Syrian coasts. Ugarit seems to have been a highly vulnerable target, particularly when Suppiluliuma allegedly stripped the vassal state of its defence forces by ordering their reassignment to other areas under threat. This is what we're told in a letter despatched by Ugarit's last king Ammurapi to the king of Alasiya: 'The enemy ships have been coming and burning my cities and doing terrible things in my country. All my troops and chariots are in the land of Hatti, and all my ships are in Lukka. My land has been left defenceless!' Other letters too warn of the imminent danger faced by Ugarit as large numbers of sea raiders approached its shores.[6]

Whether or not Ammurapi was exaggerating his plight, the disruptions caused by enemy forces in the eastern Mediterranean and its seaports were very likely prompts for the attacks on Alasiya (which may well have provided bases, voluntarily or involuntarily, for enemy ships) by both Tudhaliya and Suppiluliuma, and for

Figure 25.2   Ugarit.

Suppiluliuma's naval operations off Alasiya's coast. One of the chief objects of these operations must have been to ensure safe passage for the food shipments which were of vital importance for sustaining the Hittite homeland's population. We get some idea of the seriousness of the crisis from an inscription of the pharaoh Merneptah, who states that he has despatched a cargo of grain 'to keep alive the land of Hatti'. And in a letter sent from the Hittite court to one of the last kings of Ugarit an urgent demand is made for a ship and crew to transport 450 tonnes of grain to Ura, whence it will be transported to the Hittite homeland. 'It is a matter of life or death!' the letter states.[7] Some scholars think that this claim may be exaggerated. But even so, the text does point to Hatti's increasing dependence, in its final years, on imports of grain from Egypt and its vassal states.

This brings us back to Tarhuntassa and Suppiluliuma's claim to have entered it. In the context of what we've just been talking about, we can see a specific, compelling reason why the king could not afford to allow hostile forces to occupy this land and its capital. For Tarhuntassa covered a large part of the southern Anatolian coast.

And Ura, probably the most important seaport from where goods brought by sea were transported to the homeland, very likely lay within its boundaries. Hostile occupation of the land could deprive Hatti of at least one of its important supply-routes. This *may* have provided the reason for Suppiluliuma's entry into Tarhuntassa, whether to eliminate a rebellious regime there, or to ensure that it did not fall into, or remain, in enemy hands.

A ROYAL CITY ABANDONED

What was the outcome of all this? Let me suggest one possible answer – but with the warning that what I'm going to say is again based almost entirely on speculation. My suggestion is linked to another question. What happened to the royal capital at the end of the empire? A long-held assumption was that it eventually fell to besieging enemy forces who captured, sacked and burned it, and that the king himself perished along with his city. Rather like the fate suffered by Constantinople and its last ruler nearly 2,700 years later. That assumption has now been discarded.

When I was in Hattusa a few years ago to participate in Tolga Örnek's documentary about the Hittites, the film crew was invited by Jürgen Seeher to have dinner with him one evening. Jürgen was then Hattusa's Director of Excavations. He told us of some interesting results he was obtaining from his most recent excavations on the acropolis and other parts of the city. These showed that Hattusa did not go up in flames in a final single conflagration. On the contrary, there was clear evidence that the last Hittite king Suppiluliuma systematically removed everything of value from the palace quarters and other major buildings, including important documents preserved on clay tablets (and perhaps metal tablets as well?), and simply abandoned what was still an intact city, even if already in decline. No doubt he took with him a large retinue, including his family and advisers, his chief bureaucrats, others who were an essential part of the city's infrastructure, and the royal militia. We have no idea of the size of the group leaving the city, or how many of the sub-elite population were included – or simply left to their fate.

Of course, this new scenario raises two big questions. Suppiluliuma could not have simply walked out into the wilds of Anatolia with no idea of where he was going. So where *did* he and his entourage go? The other main question is *why* did they leave the city in the first place – when it was still intact with no indication that it was under imminent threat of enemy attack? Indeed it seems that after their departure, the city continued to exist for some time, perhaps just a matter of weeks or months, perhaps longer, before it finally fell into ruin and was plundered by marauders or enemy forces of anything still worth taking. Then what was left of it was put to the torch. Later, there was an Iron Age settlement on the site. But the royal city of the Hittites was lost to human memory, along with the empire it ruled, until its rediscovery in the modern era.

So why did Suppiluliuma evacuate Hattusa? Let's recall that this was the third known time in Hittite history that a Hittite king abandoned his capital. The first was during the reign of Tudhaliya III, in the first half of the fourteenth century, when the land of Hatti fell prey to comprehensive attacks by its enemies. The king was forced to leave the city and take up temporary residence somewhere to the east where he organised the reconquest and restoration of his kingdom. The second occasion was when Muwattalli II shifted his royal capital to Tarhuntassa early in the thirteenth century. This was partly perhaps to provide himself with a more convenient base for his looming showdown with Egypt. On the first occasion, Hattusa was destroyed by its enemies. On the second, it was left under the command of a local administrator. But Muwattalli had no intention of moving the royal seat back there, and it was only under his son Urhi-Teshub that Hattusa was restored as the imperial capital.

So what about this third occasion? Let me continue with my speculations. It's possible that once more a Hittite king decided to shift his royal seat southwards to Tarhuntassa, just as Muwattalli had done. The entry into Tarhuntassa recorded by Suppiluliuma in his Südburg inscription may have paved the way for its restoration as the new centre of the Great Kingdom of Hatti. It was perhaps here that Suppiluliuma was heading when he left Hattusa. And as far as we know, he may have installed an administrator to govern

Hattusa after its reduction in status, just as Muwattalli had done. But we have no proof of any of this, for the kingdom's written records now come to an end. Perhaps one day the remains of the chief city of Tarhuntassa will come to light. And if so, perhaps an archive will be found which may confirm my hypothesis – or completely invalidate it.

If, however, my hypothesis is right, then there may have been a number of reasons why Tarhuntassa once more became the administrative centre of the empire. Not the least of these was that as the empire crumbled, Tarhuntassa could provide a more secure base than Hattusa for the royal administration, located as Hattusa was near the periphery of an increasingly unmanageable empire. And at a time when food shortages appear to have become ever more critical, a royal capital which lay on or near the southern Anatolian coast was far more accessible to grain imports from Egypt and Syria. And far better located to organise and mount naval operations against enemy forces which threatened its supply-routes by sea.

Let me suggest another possibility for the shift. Amongst all the other crises that threatened to engulf it, was Hattusa and the core land of Hatti again subject to an outbreak of plague? If so, could this have been linked to urgent attempts to meet the food shortages in the region by the conveyance there of grain consignments which, because of the exigencies of time, had not been carefully checked for disease-carrying vermin? Examination of the grain silos in Hattusa indicate that food-storage areas like these were kept remarkably free of such vermin. But in the desperate times at the end of the empire, unchecked cargoes which attracted disease-bearing rodents and fleas might have precipitated a further outbreak of plague of the kind that had so devastated the land of Hatti in the reign of Mursili II. The evacuation of Hattusa, at least by its elite elements and 'essential others', as the first signs of plague appeared might provide part of the explanation for the king's decision to relocate his capital elsewhere. So too in the seventeenth century AD a major outbreak of bubonic plague in England during the reign of Charles II led the king and his entourage to abandon

London and relocate the royal court first in Salisbury, until the plague struck there as well, and then in Oxford.

The early decades of the twelfth century witnessed the collapse of the Hittite empire, and of many smaller centres of power throughout the Near Eastern world. In the following period, the so-called Iron Age, some of the former Bronze Age cities and states disappeared altogether, like the wealthy Hittite vassal kingdom

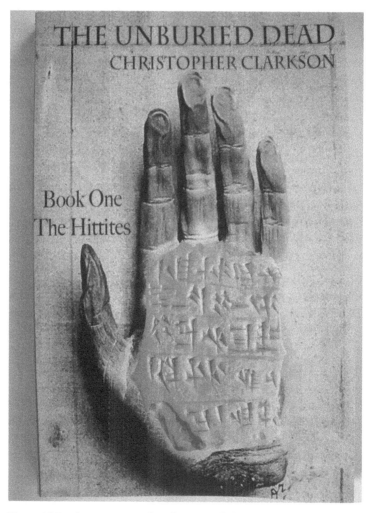

Figure 25.3 A gruesome sci-fi explanation of what ended the Hittite world.

Ugarit. But others survived and gained a new lease of life, like Byblos and Tyre in the Levant. In southeastern Anatolia and northern Syria there also emerged a number of kingdoms whose rulers preserved distinctive features of the old Hittite empire. For example, the ruling class of these kingdoms used the hieroglyphic Luwian script for recording on public monuments their military and building achievements, and their devotion to the gods. (The cuneiform script used for official Hittite documents now disappeared entirely.)

Some of the rulers of these kingdoms assumed the names of former illustrious Hittite kings – like Labarna, Suppiluliuma, Muwattalli, Hattusili and Tudhaliya. Elements of imperial Hittite art and religion were often embedded in the culture and material civilisation of the lands over which they held sway. For all these reasons, we commonly refer to these Iron Age states as the Neo-Hittite kingdoms.[8] Apart from Carchemish on the Euphrates, where a collateral branch of the Hittite royal family ruled for at least several generations in the Iron Age, we know very little about how these states emerged, and how close their connections really were to the Bronze Age Hittite world. But we cannot rule out the possibility that one of these states originated as the final place of refuge of the last Great King of Hatti.

Maybe one day we will find key information including written records, about what actually dealt the final blow to the Hittite empire, why the capital was abandoned by its last king, and where he set up his new capital. Archaeological and written records with answers to these questions may still exist. All we need to do is to find out where.

RULERS OF HATTI

(All dates are approximate.)

(The names between the brackets {...} indicate kings who should be grouped together, datewise. Thus the dates 1560–1525 cover the reigns of the three kings Zidanta, Ammuna, and Huzziya, because we don't know their individual dates.)

Predecessor(s) of Labarna?
Labarna ?–1650
*Hattusili I 1650–1620
Mursili I 1620–1590
Hantili I 1590–1560
{Zidanta I
Ammuna 1560–1525
Huzziya I}
Telipinu 1525–1500
{Alluwamna
Tahurwaili
Hantili II 1500–1400
Zidanta II
Huzziya II
Muwattalli I}
{**Tudhaliya I/II *(start of New Kingdom)*
Arnuwanda I 1400–1350
Hattusili II?
Tudhaliya III}

Suppiluliuma I 1350 – 1322
Arnuwanda II 1322 – 1321
Mursili II 1321 – 1295
Muwattalli II 1295 – 1272
Urhi-Teshub (Mursili III) 1272 – 1267
Hattusili III 1267 – 1237
Tudhaliya IV 1237 – 1209
Arnuwanda III 1209 – 1207
Suppiluliuma II 1207 – ?

* I have suggested that Hattusili *may have been* preceded as sole ruler by his aunt whose personal name was Tawannana.
** It is uncertain whether there were one or two early New Kingdom rulers of this name.

OUTLINE OF MAIN EVENTS IN HITTITE HISTORY

(All dates are approximate.)

THE OLD KINGDOM

Labarna (?–1650), founder(?) of the Hittite dynasty, extends by military conquest the kingdom of Hatti through much of the eastern half of the Anatolian peninsula.

Hattusili I (1650–1620) establishes Hattusa as the Hittite capital and conducts extensive military campaigns in Syria and western Anatolia.

After rebellion and faction strife within the royal family, Hattusili appoints his grandson Mursili as his successor.

The reign of Mursili I (1620–1590) is noteworthy for successful military campaigns across the Taurus, including the conquests of Aleppo and Babylon.

The assassination of Mursili by his brother-in-law and successor Hantili begins a period of weakness and instability in the kingdom (1590–1525). This is characterised by disputes over the royal succession, and invasions by the Hurrians who emerge as a major power in northern Mesopotamia, northern Syria, and eastern Anatolia.

The throne is seized by Telipinu (1525–1500), who restores authority over some of Hatti's lost territories and lays down fixed principles for the royal succession. He concludes the first attested peace treaty in Hittite history, with the ruler of the southeastern Anatolian state Kizzuwatna.

Further periods of weakness are evident in the poorly attested reigns of Telipinu's successors (1500–1400).

THE NEW KINGDOM

Tudhaliya I/II claims the throne (c.1400 or a bit earlier) and begins re-establishing Hatti as a major power by conducting successful campaigns in Syria and western Anatolia. But both he and his successor Anuwanda I are confronted with further widespread unrest in their subject-territories and increasing threats to their core-territory from hostile independent lands.

Anti-Hittite activities culminate, in the first half of the fourteenth century, in the so-called 'Concentric Invasions'. The Hittite homeland is subject to onslaughts by enemy forces attacking it from many directions. These attacks take place particularly during the reign of Tudhaliya III. Hattusa is sacked after Tudhaliya's apparent evacuation of the capital and the shift of his base of operations to a temporary new location in the east.

Tudhaliya and his comrade-in-arms Suppiluliuma restore Hittite authority over Hatti's invaded territories and Suppiluliuma completes the process of driving the enemy forces back to their own lands.

Suppiluliuma seizes the throne after Tudhaliya's death (1350), destroys Hatti's arch-rival the Hurrian kingdom of Mittani after a protracted series of military campaigns, and raises Hatti to the status of the most powerful kingdom in the Near Eastern world.

On his death probably from plague (1322), he is succeeded briefly by his son Arnuwanda II whose death leads to the accession of another son Mursili II (1321–1295). Mursili completes the restoration of Hatti's authority over its subject-territories in Anatolia and northern Syria.

He is succeeded by his son Muwattalli II (1295–1272), during whose reign worsening relations between Hatti and Egypt culminate in a major battle between Mursili's forces and those of the pharaoh Ramesses II at Qadesh on the Orontes river in Syria (1274). The battle itself ends in a stalemate, but Muwattalli subsequently wins control of the disputed territories which had been a primary cause of the conflict.

Muwattalli is succeeded by his son Urhi-Teshub (1272–1267), from whom power is seized by his uncle Hattusili (III) after a brief civil war.

During Hattusili's reign (1267–1237), a peace treaty is signed with Ramesses II (1259), marking the end of all hostilities with Egypt. Hattusili conducts further campaigns in western Anatolia, with limited success.

Hattusili's son and successor Tudhaliya IV (1237–1209) is confronted with increasing unrest among his subject-states, and is defeated by the king of Assyria in a battle fought in northern Mesopotamia. Assyria had emerged as a major power in the region following the fall of the kingdom of Mittani.

The Hittite kingdom ends during the reign of Tudhaliya's second successor Suppiluliuma II (1207–?), within the context of a general collapse of many Late Bronze Age centres in the early twelfth century. Egyptian records associate this collapse with groups of invaders we call the Sea Peoples. These groups allegedly sweep through much of the western half of the Near Eastern world both by land and sea, leaving a path of destruction in their wake, though much doubt has been cast on the historical validity of the Egyptian records.

NOTES

(Asterisks indicate English translations of Hittite and other texts.)

CHAPTER 3   THE DAWN OF THE HITTITE ERA

1. Billie Jean Collins' book, *The Hittites and their World* (Atlanta, 2007), also discusses many aspects of Hittite history and civilisation covered in the following pages.
2. Though we cannot be sure whether or to what extent all inhabitants of the kingdom referred to themselves in this way.
3. For possible connections between Bronze Age and biblical Hittites, see Trevor Bryce, *The World of the Neo-Hittite Kingdoms* (Oxford, 2012), pp. 64–75, and Billie Jean Collins, *The Hittites and their World*, pp. 197–218.
4. *Mark Chavalas, *The Ancient Near East* (Oxford, 2006), pp. 228–35 (transl. P. Goedegebuure).
5. There is much uncertainty about the family links between the earliest Hittite rulers. In the following pages, and later in the book, I make Hattusili I the grandson and successor of the first Labarna, though I also allow the possibility that he succeeded his aunt Tawananna. But there are other possibilities; see e.g. Richard Beal, 'The Predecessors of Hattusili I', in G. Beckman, R. Beal, and G. McMahon (eds), *Hittites Studies in Honor of Harry A. Hoffner Jr* (Winona Lake, 2003), pp. 13–35.
6. On this episode, see *William Hallo and K. Lawson Younger (eds), *The Context of Scripture* (3 vols.) (Leiden, Boston, 2002) 2/3, p. 81, §20 (transl. G. Beckman).
7. *Chavalas, *Ancient Near East*, pp. 219–22 (transl. G. Beckman).

CHAPTER 4   THE LEGACY OF AN AILING KING

1. *Ibid., 222–8 (transl. P. Goedegebuure), *Hallo and Younger, *Context of Scripture* 2/3, pp. 79–81 (transl. G. Beckman).

CHAPTER 6   THE SETTING FOR AN EMPIRE

1. For a series of maps depicting the lands of the Hittite kingdom and its contemporaries during the Middle and Late Bronze Ages, see Trevor Bryce and Jessie Birkett-Rees, *Atlas of the Ancient Near East* (London and New York, 2016), pp. 106–54.
2. See J. David Hawkins, 'Tarkasnawa, King of Mira "Tarkondemos" Boğazköy Sealings and Karabel', *Anatolian Studies* 48 (1998), pp. 1–10.
3. *Gary Beckman, Trevor Bryce and Eric Cline, *The Ahhiyawa Texts* (Atlanta, 2011), pp. 134–9.

CHAPTER 7   BUILDING AN EMPIRE

1. *Gary Beckman, *Hittite Diplomatic Texts* (Atlanta, 1999), pp. 93–5.
2. See Bryce, *The Kingdom of the Hittites* (Oxford, 2005), pp. 124–7, with references and quoted passages.
3. *William Moran, *The Amarna Letters* (Baltimore and London, 1992), p. 101, no. 31.

CHAPTER 8   LION OR PUSSYCAT?

1. *Beckman, Bryce, Cline, *The Ahhiyawa Texts*, pp. 69–100.
2. It seems that Arnuwanda was the recipient of the letter, perhaps while still co-regent.
3. After *Itamar Singer, *Hittite Prayers* (Atlanta, 2002), p. 42.
4. *Beckman, *Hittite Diplomatic Texts*, pp. 13–17.

CHAPTER 9   FROM NEAR EXTINCTION TO THE THRESHOLD OF SUPREMACY

1. For a discussion of these, with a selection of translated texts, see Trevor Bryce, *Letters of the Great Kings of the Ancient Near East* (London and New York, 2003/14), pp. 170–86.
2. After *Albrecht Goetze, *Kizzuwatna and the Problems of Hittite Geography* (New Haven, 1940), pp. 21–2.
3. See *Hans Güterbock, 'The Deeds of Suppiluliuma as told by his son, Mursili II', *Journal of Cuneiform Studies* 10 (1956), pp. 41–68, 75–98, 101–30, for translations of the surviving fragments.

CHAPTER 10   THE GREATEST KINGDOM OF THEM ALL

1. *After Moran, *The Amarna Letters*, p. 114, no. 41, lines 7–13. I have concluded that the letter's addressee was either Smenkhkare (Akhenaten's co-regent and short-lived successor), or Smenkhkare's successor

Tutankhamun, on the assumption that Akhetaten and the Amarna archive continued several years after Akhenaten's death. In diplomatic parlance, Akhenaten might be termed the 'father' of either of them, though his precise relationship with them is uncertain.

2. *Ibid., pp. 41–2, no. 17, lines 30–8.
3. A record of the letter and the consequences that followed from it are contained in Suppiluliuma's biography. See Bryce, *Letters of the Great Kings*, pp. 187–98 with translated passages.
4. *Beckman, *Hittite Diplomatic Texts*, pp. 41–58.
5. Ibid., p. 41.

CHAPTER 11　INTERMEDIARIES OF THE GODS: THE GREAT KINGS OF HATTI

1. Thus Bryce, *Life and Society in the Hittite World* (Oxford, 2002), p. 176, with references.
2. See *J. David Hawkins, *The Hieroglyphic Inscription of the Sacred Pool Complex at Hattusa (Südburg)* (Wiesbaden, 1995), p. 89 (Emirgazi inscription) §34, with note, p. 101.

CHAPTER 12　KING BY DEFAULT

1. *Hallo and Younger, *Context of Scripture* 2/3, pp. 82–90 (transl. R. Beal).
2. After *Singer, *Hittite Prayers*, pp. 52–3.
3. Siro Trevisanato 'The Hittite Plague, an Epidemic of Tularemia and the First Record of Biological Warfare', *Medical Hypotheses* 69 (2007), pp. 1371–4.

CHAPTER 13　HEALTH, HYGIENE AND HEALING

1. Extract from 'Instructions to Temple Officials', in *James Pritchard (ed.) *Ancient Near Eastern Texts relating to the Old Testament* (3rd edn), (Princeton, 1969), p. 207 (transl. after A. Goetze).
2. *Ibid. for full text.
3. See Bryce, *Life and Society*, p. 206.
4. *Gary Beckman in Jack Sasson (ed.), *Civilizations of the Ancient Near East* (New York, 1995) 3/4, p. 2010.
5. Extract from *Gabriella Frantz-Szabó in Sasson, ibid. 3/4, p. 2014.
6. See Jared Miller, 'Paskuwatti's Ritual: Remedy for Impotence or Antidote to Homosexuality?', *Journal of Ancient Near Eastern Religions* 10 (2010), pp. 83–9.
7. On Egyptian doctors on loan to Hatti, see Kenneth Kitchen, *Pharaoh Triumphant* (Warminster, 1982), pp. 91–2.

8. For a more detailed treatment of this topic, see Gary Beckman, 'Birth and Motherhood among the Hittites', in S. Budin and J. Turfa (eds), *Women in Antiquity* (London and New York, 2016), pp. 319–28.

CHAPTER 14   JUSTICE AND THE COMMONER

1. *Harry A. Hoffner, *The Laws of the Hittites: A Critical Edition* (Leiden, New York, Köln, 1997a) and 'Hittite Laws' in M. Roth (ed.), *Law Collections from Mesopotamia and Asia Minor* (Atlanta, 1997b), pp. 213–47. All translations from these Laws in the following pages are by Hoffner, or adapted from his translations.
2. *Oliver Gurney, *The Hittites* (London, 1990), p. 76.
3. *Pritchard, *Ancient Near Eastern Texts*, p. 211 (transl. A. Goetze).
4. *Laws of Hammurabi §229, transl. Martha Roth, *Law Collections*, p. 125.
5. * Hittite Laws §10.
6. *Ibid., §106.
7. Talents, minas, and shekels were basically units of weight. The ratio of one to the others varied in the different civilisations in which they were used. But broadly speaking, a talent was equivalent to about 60 minas, and a mina to about 60 shekels. Since on average a mina weighed about half a kilogram, a talent weighed about 30 kgs. The value of each of these measures depended on the nature of the metal of which they consisted. Thus a talent of gold was much more valuable than a talent of silver, or a talent of bronze.
8. Bryce, *Life and Society*, p. 38.

CHAPTER 15   NO SEX PLEASE, WE'RE HITTITE

1. After *Beckman, *Hittite Diplomatic Texts*, pp. 31–2, §§25–6 (treaty between Suppiluliuma I and Huqqana of Hayasa).
2. *Hittite Laws §193.
3. See reference, Chapter 13, n. 4.
4. See Harry Hoffner, 'The *Arzana* House', in K. Bittel, Ph. Houwink ten Cate, and E. Reiner (eds), *Anatolian Studies Presented to Hans Gustav Güterbock* (Istanbul, 1974), pp. 113–22.
5. See Billie Jean Collins, 'Women in Hittite Religion', in S. Budin and J. Turfa (eds), *Women in Antiquity* (London and New York, 2016), p. 332, with references.

CHAPTER 16   WOMEN, MARRIAGE AND SLAVERY

1. *Pritchard, *Ancient Near Eastern Texts*, p. 354 (transl. A. Goetze).
2. *Gurney, *The Hittites*, p. 148.
3. Following Hoffner's interpretation of §171 of The Laws; see Hoffner, 'Legal and Social Institutions of Hittite Anatolia', in Sasson (ed.), *Civilizations* 1/4, p. 567, and *The Laws of the Hittites*, p. 171.

4. *Hittite Laws §28a.
5. *See Hammurabi's Laws §§175, 176a and b, transl. Roth, *Law Collections*, pp. 115–16.
6. *Beckman, *Hittite Diplomatic Texts*, pp. 131–5.
7. *Kitchen, *Pharaoh Triumphant*, p. 88.
8. For a more detailed account of this episode, with text references, see Bryce, *Kingdom of the Hittites*, pp. 310–12.
9. See Bryce, *Life and Society*, p. 163.

CHAPTER 17   WAR WITH EGYPT

1. For a more detailed account of the Amurrite terrorists, with references to and translations from the relevant Amarna letters, see Bryce, *Ancient Syria* (Oxford, 2014), pp. 46–61.
2. As attested, for example, in the *Apology of Hattusili III*, *Hallo and Younger, *Context of Scripture* 1/3, pp. 200, 201, §§6, 8 (transl. Th. van den Hout).
3. *Ibid.*, §8.
4. *Beckman, *Hittite Diplomatic Texts*, pp. 87–93.
5. *Hallo and Younger, *Context of Scripture* 2/3, pp. 32–40 (transl. K. Kitchen).
6. E.g. Kitchen, *Pharaoh Triumphant*, pp. 53–62, Healy, *Qadesh 1300 BC* (Oxford, 1993), Spalinger, *War in Ancient Egypt* (Oxford, 2005), pp. 209–34.
7. On the size of the Hittite army based on Ramesses' figures, see Beal, *The Organisation of the Hittite Military* (Heidelberg, 1992), pp. 291–2.

CHAPTER 18   ALL THE KING'S HORSES AND ALL THE KING'S MEN: THE HITTITE MILITARY MACHINE

1. For more detailed accounts of this topic, see Beal, *Organisation of the Hittite Military*, and 'Hittite Military Organization', in J. Sasson (ed.), *Civilizations* 1/4, pp. 545–54, Bryce, *Hittite Warrior* (Oxford, 2007).
2. *Annelies Kammenhuber, *Hippologia Hethitica* (Wiesbaden, 1961).
3. See Beal, *Organisation of the Hittite Military*, pp. 32–3, 197–8.
4. For a selection of Hittite king's treaties with vassal and international rulers, see *Beckman, *Hittite Diplomatic Texts*, pp. 11–124.
5. *Transl. ibid., p. 88.
6. *After ibid., p. 70.
7. Extract from Mursili's 'Ten-Year Annals' for Year 4, transl. R. Beal in *Hallo and Younger, *Context of Scripture* 2/3, p. 86.

CHAPTER 19   THE MAN WHO WOULD BE KING

1. *Ibid. 1/3, pp. 199–204 (transl. Th. van den Hout).
2. After *Beckman, *Hittite Diplomatic Texts*, p. 149.

3. *Beckman, *Hittite Diplomatic Texts*, pp. 96–100 (the version found in Hattusa).
4. *Beckman, Bryce, Cline, *Ahhiyawa Texts*, pp. 101–22.

CHAPTER 20   PARTNERS IN POWER:
THE GREAT QUEENS OF HATTI

1. See Bryce, *Kingdom of the Hittites*, p. 389, with refs and discussion in nn. 33–4.
2. *Hallo and Younger, *Context of Scripture* 1/3, pp. 181–2 (transl. H. Hoffner).
3. For references and further discussion, see Bryce, *Kingdom of the Hittites*, pp. 93–4.
4. For references and further discussion, ibid., pp. 207–10.
5. For references and further discussion, ibid., pp. 298–9.

CHAPTER 21   CITY OF TEMPLES AND BUREAUCRATS:
THE ROYAL CAPITAL

1. For references and further discussion, see Bryce, *Life and Society*, pp. 230–56, Seeher, *Hattusha Guide. A Day in the Hittite Capital* (Istanbul, 2011).
2. The gradual decline of the city possibly dates back to the time when Muwattalli relocated the capital at Tarhuntassa.
3. For a detailed, first-hand account of this topic, see Seeher, *A Mudbrick City Wall at Hattusha. Diary of a Reconstruction* (Istanbul, 2007).

CHAPTER 22   AN ELITE FRATERNITY: THE CLUB OF
ROYAL BROTHERS

1. For a detailed discussion of the letters exchanged between the Great Kings of the Near East, with translated excerpts, see Bryce, *Letters of the Great Kings*.
2. *Moran, *Amarna Letters*. The Amarna archive *may* have extended to the first years after Akhenaten's death. See Chapter 10, n. 1.
3. *Ibid., pp. 18–19, no. 9.

CHAPTER 23   THE EMPIRE'S STRUGGLE FOR SURVIVAL

1. For references to the full text of this document and other documents in similar vein, see Bryce, *Kingdom of the Hittites*, pp. 299–301.
2. *Beckman, *Hittite Diplomatic Texts*, pp. 114–24; *Hallo and Younger, *Context of Scripture* 2/3, pp. 100–106 (transl. H. A. Hoffner).

3. For references and further details, see Bryce, *The World of the Neo-Hittite Kingdoms* (Oxford, 2012), p. 21.
4. *Beckman, Bryce, Cline, *Ahhiyawa Texts*, pp. 154–7.
5. *Ibid., pp. 123–33.
6. *Ibid., pp. 50–67.
7. *For references and translated excerpts, see Bryce, *Kingdom of the Hittites*, pp. 316–18.
8. For references and further details, ibid., pp. 321–3.

CHAPTER 24   HATTI'S DIVINE OVERLORDS

1. For a detailed account, see Seeher, *Gods Carved in Stone. The Hittite Rock Sanctuary of Yazılıkaya* (Istanbul, 2011).
2. *Hoffner, *Hittite Myths* (Atlanta, 1998), pp. 14–20.
3. After Hoffner. For translations of both versions, see *Hoffner, ibid., pp. 10–14.
4. For further discussion of the myth, see Bryce, *Life and Society*, pp. 215–19.

CHAPTER 25   DEATH OF AN EMPIRE

1. For a detailed account of the collapse of the Bronze Age civilisations, see Cline, *1177 BC. The Year Civilization Collapsed* (Princeton, 2014).
2. *Hawkins, *The Hieroglyphic Inscription of the Sacred Pool Complex at Hattusa (Südburg)* (Wiesbaden, 1995), pp. 21–2.
3. Further on these inscriptions, with references, see Bryce, *Neo-Hittite Kingdoms*, pp. 21–2.
4. *Pritchard, *Ancient Near Eastern Texts*, pp. 262–3 (transl. J. A. Wilson).
5. See most recently Marc Van De Mieroop, *A History of the Ancient Near East* (3rd edn) (Oxford, 2016), pp. 207–8. On the Sea Peoples in general, see Elezier Oren, *The Sea Peoples and Their World: A Reassessment* (Philadelphia, 2000), Cline, *1177 BC*.
6. *For further discussion, text references, and translations from the relevant texts, see Bryce, *Ancient Syria*, pp. 90–3.
7. For the text and other relevant material, see Bryce, *Kingdom of the Hittites*, pp. 331–2.
8. See Bryce, *Neo-Hittite Kingdoms*.

BIBLIOGRAPHY

(*Asterisks indicate English translations of Hittite and other texts.*)

Beal, Richard H., *The Organisation of the Hittite Military* (Heidelberg, 1992).
—— 'Hittite Military Organization', in Jack M. Sasson (ed.), *Civilizations of the Ancient Near East* (New York, 1995) 1/4, pp. 545–54.
—— 'The Predecessors of Hattusili I', in G. Beckman, R. Beal, and G. McMahon (eds), *Hittite Studies in Honor of Harry A. Hoffner Jr* (Winona Lake, 2003), pp. 13–35.
*Beckman, Gary M., *Hittite Diplomatic Texts* (Atlanta, 1999).
—— 'Birth and Motherhood among the Hittites', in S. L. Budin and J. M. Turfa (eds), *Women in Antiquity* (London and New York, 2016), pp. 319–28.
*Beckman, Gary M., Bryce, Trevor R., and Cline, Eric H., *The Ahhiyawa Texts* (Atlanta, 2011).
*Bible (New International Version).
Bittel, Kurt, Houwink ten Cate, Philo, and Reiner, Erica (eds), *Anatolian Studies Presented to Hans Gustav Güterbock* (Istanbul, 1974).
Bryce, Trevor R., *Life and Society in the Hittite World* (Oxford, 2002).
—— *Letters of the Great Kings of the Ancient Near East* (London and New York, 2003/14).
—— *The Kingdom of the Hittites* (new edn) (Oxford, 2005).
—— *Hittite Warrior* (Oxford, 2007).
—— *The World of the Neo-Hittite Kingdoms* (Oxford, 2012).
—— *Ancient Syria* (Oxford, 2014).
Bryce, Trevor R. and Birkett-Rees, Jessie, *Atlas of the Ancient Near East* (London and New York, 2016).
Budin, Stephanie. L. and Turfa, Jean. M. (eds), *Women in Antiquity* (London and New York, 2016).
*Chavalas, Mark W. (ed.), *The Ancient Near East* (Oxford, 2006).
Cline, Eric H., *1177 BC. The Year Civilization Collapsed* (Princeton, 2014).
Collins, Billie Jean, *The Hittites and their World* (Atlanta, 2007).
—— (2016), 'Women in Hittite Religion', in S.L. Budin and J.M. Turfa (eds), *Women in Antiquity* (London and New York, 2016), pp. 329–41.
Frantz-Szabó, Gabriella, 'Hittite Witchcraft, Magic, and Divination', in Jack M. Sasson (ed.), *Civilizations of the Ancient Near East* (New York, 1995) 3/4, pp. 2007–19.

Goedegebuure, Petra; van den Hout, Theo; Osborne, James; Massa, Michele; Bachhuber, Christoph; Sahin, Fatma: 'TÜRKMEN-KARAHÖYÜK 1: A new Hieroglyphic Luwian inscription from Great King Hartapu, son of Mursili, conqueror of Phrygia', *Anatolian Studies* 70 (2020), pp. 29–43.

Goetze, Albrecht, *Kizzuwatna and the Problems of Hittite Geography* (New Haven, 1940).

Gurney, Oliver R., *The Hittites* (rev edn) (London, 1990).

*Güterbock, Hans G., 'The Deeds of Suppiluliuma as told by his son, Mursili II', *Journal of Cuneiform Studies* 10 (1956), pp. 41–68, 75–98, 101–30.

*Hallo, William W. and Younger, K. Lawson (eds), *The Context of Scripture* (3 vols) (Leiden, Boston, 2002).

*Hawkins, J. David, *The Hieroglyphic Inscription of the Sacred Pool Complex at Hattusa (Südburg)* (Wiesbaden, 1995).

——— 'Tarkasnawa, King of Mira "Tarkondemos" Boğazköy Sealings and Karabel', *Anatolian Studies* 48 (1998), pp. 1–31.

Healy, M. (1993), *Qadesh 1300 BC* (Oxford, 1993).

Hoffner, Harry A., 'The Arzana House', in K. Bittel, Ph. Houwink ten Cate, and E. Reiner (eds), *Anatolian Studies Presented to Hans Gustav Güterbock* (Istanbul, 1974), pp. 113–22.

——— 'Legal and Social Institutions of Hittite Anatolia', in J.M. Sasson (ed.), *Civilizations of the Ancient Near East* (New York, 1995) 1/4, pp. 555–69.

——— *The Laws of the Hittites: A Critical Edition* (Leiden, New York, Köln, 1997a).

——— *'Hittite Laws' in M.T. Roth (ed.), *Law Collections from the Ancient World* (Atlanta, 1997b), pp. 213–47.

——— *Hittite Myths* (Atlanta, 1998).

*Kammenhuber, Annelies, *Hippologia Hethitica* (Wiesbaden, 1961) (in German).

Kitchen, Kenneth A., *Pharaoh Triumphant* (Warminster, 1982).

Mieroop, Marc Van De, *A History of the Ancient Near East* (3rd edn) (Oxford, 2016).

Miller, Jared. L., 'Paskuwatti's Ritual: Remedy for Impotence or Antidote to Homosexuality?', *Journal of Ancient Near Eastern Religions* 10 (2010), pp. 83–9.

*Moran, William L., *The Amarna Letters* (Baltimore and London, 1992).

Oren, Eliezer (ed.), *The Sea Peoples and Their World: A Reassessment* (Philadelphia, 2000).

*Pritchard, James B., *Ancient Near Eastern Texts relating to the Old Testament* (3rd edn) (Princeton, 1969).

*Roth, Martha T. (ed.), *Law Collections from Mesopotamia and Asia Minor* (2nd edn) (Atlanta, 1997).

Sasson, Jack M. (ed.), *Civilizations of the Ancient Near East* (4 vols) (New York, 1995).

Seeher, Jürgen, *A Mudbrick City Wall at Hattuša. Diary of a Reconstruction* (Istanbul, 2007).

——— *Hattusha Guide. A Day in the Hittite Capital* (rev. edn) (Istanbul, 2011).

——— *Gods Carved in Stone. The Hittite Rock Sanctuary of Yazılıkaya* (Istanbul, 2011).

*Singer, Itamar, *Hittite Prayers* (Atlanta, 2002).

Spalinger, Anthony J., *War in Ancient Egypt* (Oxford, 2005).

Stavi, Boaz, *The Reign of Tudhaliya II and Suppiluliuma I* (Heidelberg, 2015).

Trevisanato, Siro I., 'The Hittite Plague, an Epidemic of Tularemia and the First Record of Biological Warfare', *Medical Hypotheses* 69 (2007), pp. 1371–4.

INDEX

Page nos in **bold** indicate main refs.